T0348988

PRAISE FOR MAVERICKS

"Engaging and witty, this is a rip-roaring ride through the lives of 24 eccentrics. Jenny is a master-storyteller and has a knack for digging out the weird and wonderful."
Jack Chesher, author of *London: A Guide for Curious Wanderers*

"These are stories you won't learn about in history class. Draper's research and storytelling skills are on full display as she shines a spotlight on a cast of impressive historic characters who deserve to be remembered."
Max Miller, founder of the YouTube account Tasting History

"*Mavericks* is a lively and a laugh-out-loud funny journey through time. It [...] shines a deserved light on fascinating people you've never heard about until now. Jenny has a wonderful knack of fleshing out historic characters into real people. You feel like you're right there in the room with them. Thoroughly researched and delivered in a chatty, engaging style, the book really draws you into these mavericks' lives."
Katie Wignall, Founder of Look Up London

"Had me hooked from the introduction."
Tom Scott, founder of the YouTube account TomScottGo

MAVERICKS

MAVERICKS

LIFE STORIES AND LESSONS OF HISTORY'S MOST EXTRAORDINARY MISFITS

JENNY DRAPER

WATKINS
Sharing Wisdom
Since 1893

Mavericks
Jenny Draper

First published in the UK and USA in 2025 by
Watkins, an imprint of Watkins Media Limited
Unit 11, Shepperton House, 83–89 Shepperton Road
London N1 3DF

enquiries@watkinspublishing.com

Commissioning Editor: Lucy Carroll
Managing Editor: Sophie Blackman
Project Editor: Brittany Willis
Head of Design: Karen Smith
Production: Uzma Taj

A CIP record for this book is available from the British Library

ISBN: 978-1-78678-898-6 (Paperback)
ISBN: 978-1-78678-899-3 (eBook)

10 9 8 7 6 5 4 3 2 1

Typeset by Lapiz
Printed and bound by CPI Group (UK) Ltd, Croydon, CR0 4YY

www.watkinspublishing.com

MIX
Paper | Supporting
responsible forestry
FSC® C171272
www.fsc.org

To James Knowles – the best person I know

CONTENTS

Introduction   **xiii**

1. **Thomas Blood**
   Notorious rogue who steals the Crown Jewels and gets
   away with it   1

2. **Lady Mary Wortley Montagu**
   Ingenious woman who becomes Britain's first female travel
   writer and popularizes smallpox inoculation   9

3. **Ellen and William Craft**
   Married couple who make a daring escape from slavery
   in the American South by disguising Ellen as a white man   17

4. **Noor Inayat Khan**
   Courageous secret agent dropped behind enemy lines to
   do one of the most dangerous jobs of World War II   25

5. **Mary Frith**
   Ladette who shocks the 16th century with her trousers and
   her thieving ways   33

6. **Lady Hester Stanhope**
   Cutting-edge archaeologist who dresses as an Arab man
   and lives as a recluse in Lebanon   41

7. **William Buckland**
   Eccentric geologist who discovers a dinosaur and eats his
   way through the animal kingdom   49

8. **Eleanor Rykener**
   *Gender-bending medieval English sex worker who spills
   juicy gossip about her clients in the clergy*   57

9. **James Chuma and Abdullah David Susi**
   *Intrepid travellers who make a transcontinental journey on
   foot to return David Livingstone's notes and body to Britain*   63

10. **Black Agnes**
    *Scottish countess who heroically defends her castle from
    a siege while keeping her cool*   69

11. **Margery Kempe**
    Normal medieval housewife who gets married to God Almighty   75

12. **La Chevalière d'Éon**
    *Fencing master, spy and diplomat who comes out as a
    woman in 18th-century London*   81

13. **Ira Aldridge**
    The first professional black Shakespearean actor   89

14. **The Rebecca Rioters**
    *Roving crowds of Welshmen who destroy tollbooths, dressed
    in bonnets and skirts*   97

15. **Julius Soubise**
    *Distinguished horseman and fencer whose relations with
    women bring him first wealth and later notoriety*   103

16. **Ethel MacDonald**
    *Anarchist whose radio reporting on the Spanish Civil War
    makes her famous around the world*   109

17. **The Chartists**
    *Britain's first suffrage movement, demanding the vote
    for working-class men*   117

18. **Gerrard Winstanley**
    *17th-century activist who tries inventing communism
    on a hill in Surrey*   125

19. **Mary Anning**
   Working-class girl who discovers the bones of gigantic long-dead monsters — 131

20. **Caroline Herschel**
   The first British woman to be paid for scientific work and a discoverer of comets — 137

21. **Peter the Wild Boy**
   Feral child found living in the woods in Germany and brought to the royal court in England — 145

22. **Sabrina Sidney**
   Girl stolen from an orphanage and subjected to a very strange series of tests where the prize for passing would be to marry her guardian — 153

23. **Radclyffe "John" Hall**
   Lesbian author who fights to keep her queer novel from being banned — 161

24. **Paul Robeson**
   Athlete, singer, actor, polyglot, activist, and handsome to boot: is there anything he can't do? — 167

References — 175
Further Resources — 189
Acknowledgements — 197
About the Author — 199
Index — 201

INTRODUCTION

Juliana Popjoy is the toast of 18th-century Bath society, riding through the countryside with her horsewhip frayed at the end like a broom, earning her the nickname "Lady Betty Besom". For a few years, she goes out with the hottest thing in the city: Richard "Beau" Nash, who basically runs the fashionable party scene in town. He's so important that everyone calls him "the Master of Ceremonies" (a totally made-up role) and even though he doesn't have any official position at all, he still, somehow, gets to tell the posh folk of Bath where they're allowed to gamble, who they're allowed to dance with, and when they have to go to bed. Juliana must be completely smitten with him, because when they split up, she supposedly vows "never more to lie in a bed", gives up her comfortable life and spends the next 30 years living in a tree. I swear this is what the newspapers at the time say: "For thirty or forty years she lived in a hollow tree, and never lay in a bed."[1] But I'm afraid I can't give you any more detail, because at the time they are completely incurious about the *how* of living in a tree: does she carve a set of drawers into the trunk? Do squirrels bring her food? Does she get rained on all the time? We get no explanation whatsoever. It is an utterly unhinged line to just casually drop into the historical record.

When geologist Leslie Bairstow is hired at the Natural History Museum in the 1930s, he's a genius straight out of university. There's so much hype about him that when he takes the job, his head of department supposedly runs through the corridors yelping, "We've got Bairstow! We've got Bairstow!" Bairstow takes this plum job at one of the top research facilities in the country, only to sit in his office publishing absolutely nothing for his entire career. But he's not totally idle: when he retires, his successors tentatively open the door to his office. There, weaving through the stacked boxes and cabinets, they find Bairstow's byzantine organization system, understood only by its creator and held together with filing cards and knitting needles. According to the palaeontologist Richard Fortey, Bairstow saved everything anyone had ever sent him and meticulously squirrelled it all away in boxes. And we're not talking about just fossils and geological samples here – when they are clearing out his room, they find one box labelled "pieces of string: 2–3 feet" and another marked "pieces of string too small to be of use".[2] What a way to spend your one wild and precious life.

If you have a thousand monkeys at a thousand typewriters and you get them to write people's life stories, most of them are going to end up pretty similar, right? "Mr X grew up, worked on a farm all his life, and died aged 59"; "Mrs Y had three kids and died in childbirth"; "Miss Z, beloved daughter". But every now and then, they'll throw up something completely wild, like a palaeontologist who collects useless string or a lady who lives in a hollow tree. These are the stories of those weird ones, the ones written by a monkey who's eaten a particularly mouldy banana and gone on a three-day typewriting rampage, who the other monkeys learn not to get into conversation with around the Um Bongo fountain because he's just a bit *odd*. These are the stories of people whose lives have taken an unusual turn, and who have ended up very different to us ordinary folk, either because they've done something truly unusual in life, or because life has done something truly unusual to them. They are the mavericks.

In this book, I'm going to introduce you to some of these strange folks. We're going to meet the Rebecca Rioters, who smash up tollbooths while wearing women's clothing; Ellen and William Craft, who escape from slavery by dressing Ellen up as a white man; and Peter the Wild Boy, who lives in the woods and is taken in by the British royal family. These are all people to whom life has thrown a complete curveball and have found themselves on the weird side of history. We're also going to think about what we might be able to learn from these lives lived on the outskirts of probability, and see if they have anything we can use in our own, more statistically normal, lives.

I've borne in mind the limits of my knowledge and kept myself to subjects with connections to the UK, my home country, and the place whose history I know the best. That doesn't mean they're all British – we have Americans like Ira Aldridge and Paul Robeson; Africans like James Chuma and Abdullah David Susi; and even someone from the distant, exotic land of France, La Chevalière d'Éon – but knowing that I won't be able to do justice to a whole globe's worth of mavericks, I've stuck to ones who at least visited Britain at some point.

Something else to bear in mind about our *dramatis personae* is that just because someone has an interesting life that we can learn from does *not* mean I'm suggesting we emulate them in everything. These were not all good people! Radclyffe Hall cheated on her partners; Margery Kempe believed some awful things about Jewish people; Paul Robeson once hit his lover, Uta Hagen, while she was pregnant. They're all cancelled, okay? But it doesn't mean we can't be fascinated by their stories.

Throughout the book, you'll occasionally see speech written in italics, *like this.* These are lines I've written for our characters when we don't know exactly what was said, or when I'm translating their words into modern-speak. When you see speech in speech marks, that's something that was said word for word. When I've quoted someone exactly, you'll find the source at the back of the book.

I also realize that this book has a certain amount in common with those "eccentrics" compendia that people used to write. If you've never seen one, they're sort of *Ripley's Believe It or Not!* books for grown-ups – lists of oddballs throughout history and the strange things they get up to. They're generally called things like "Sports Eccentrics" or "Essex Eccentrics" or "American Eccentrics". You might have seen one in a charity shop, or being used as bathroom reading: they were really popular in the 20th century and have fallen out of fashion a bit lately. They rarely cite any sources, and repeat any and all wacky stories totally uncritically. They tend to be a bit weird about who gets to be "eccentric" – I challenge you to find one of these books with a single non-white person in it. Generally you need to be pretty rich to be classed as an "eccentric" as well, partly because the sorts of things eccentrics do in these books mean any employer would immediately bin their CV (you can't dress funny if you have to put on a Tesco uniform every day) and partly because being eccentric is often very expensive (a lot of people in these books get there by building tunnels under their mansions or owning a pet cheetah). Muttering to yourself or refusing to wash are bonkers eccentricities when rich people do them, but mundane and frightening when homeless people do them. So, I'm using the term "mavericks" rather than "eccentrics" to talk about people who did things outside the norm in a broader sense than we're used to with these other books. We have some traditional eccentrics like the omniphage (no, I'm not going to explain what that word means; you're just going to have to wait and see) William Buckland here, but also some people who broke the mould in ways that we wouldn't generally consider eccentric, like the master sword fighter Julius Soubise.

Finally, a weird theme that arose throughout the book as I wrote it was "side characters with truly incredible names". Did you know that there was really a person called Clotworthy Skeffington? St George Lane Fox Pitt? James James? Fanny Burney? If you're not certain that you're going to make it into the annals of history, it might not be a bad shout to change your name to something truly breathtaking, just so that historians of the future can't help but mention you. Every time I found one of these in the historical record, I simply *had* to include it, even if it meant going off on a bit of a tangent to introduce them. So, I hope you enjoy those as you're reading – that's a little bonus gift from me to you.

Jenny Draper

CHAPTER 1

THOMAS BLOOD

teaches us that you can get away with anything
if you do it with enough confidence.

Imagine the amount of money it would take to remake the British Crown Jewels from scratch: all the diamonds, emeralds, sapphires and rubies, all the gold and silver and platinum, and all the gem-cutting, silversmithing, embossing and engraving it takes to put them all together. Now imagine shelling out all that money to have an entire set made new, and then having someone steal your jewels and squish them to bits. And now, imagine that person being so cool and likeable and funny that instead of, I don't know, stringing him up by the goolies outside the city gates and driving screws under his fingernails, you tell him, *Ah, run along, you little scamp. Don't do it again!* That's what happens when King Charles II (reigned 1660–85) has his jewels stolen by the notorious Thomas Blood. (I told you there'd be some good names.)

The Crown Jewels of the United Kingdom aren't just pieces of jewellery that the monarch happens to own. We're not talking here about the tiaras or necklaces or brooches that you might wear to a party. These are particular ceremonial pieces that get used in coronations. These great events involve presenting the new king or queen with all these jewels that have different symbolic meanings: golden spurs for chivalry, a diamond-topped sceptre for justice and bracelets for wisdom. The monarch touches these items, or holds them, or puts them on, as part of the ritual. Finally, an orb is placed in one hand, a sceptre in the other and the crown is placed on the head. If you've never seen these artefacts up close, you might not have clocked how utterly *dripping* with gems they are. They are not meant to be minimalist. Imagine a normal crown, and then put a frankly silly number of stones on it. So the natural question is, how much are the Crown Jewels worth? If you wanted to, you could probably look up what the value of gold is at the moment, and calculate how much you'd get if you melted down all the crowns. You could add up the carats of all the diamonds and rubies and sapphires, and you could come up with a figure that way. But there is no accounting for the fact that they have been worn by British monarchs for centuries. There is nothing else like them in the world. They are not insured. They are priceless.

In the 1660s, Charles II is lucky to have any Crown Jewels at all. When he's young, his father, Charles I, goes to war against his own Parliament, and loses. Parliament imprisons him, finds him guilty of treason and cuts off his head. Young Charles flees to the Continent for the next ten years, and Britain is kingless! Instead, the country is governed by Parliament, and, in particular, the head of their army, Oliver Cromwell, who takes the title of Lord Protector. The new rulers absolutely don't want any king coming back, so to make extra sure he can't, Parliament takes the Crown Jewels and melts them down. All the gems are prised off their settings; all the gold is made into coins. To this day, there are only four pieces in the Crown Jewels that managed to survive the purge: three swords and a golden spoon.

But young Charles does come back. After Cromwell dies in 1658, he arrives in London to take the throne as King Charles II, and Britain has remained a monarchy ever since. Yet things aren't all smooth sailing for him. As well as rooting out his old enemies who beheaded his father, he needs to find the cash to make an entire set of Crown Jewels from scratch. In the end, he scrapes together over £12,000 – enough to get him three brand-new warships – to make 11 new pieces, including two crowns, an orb and a sceptre, and even a fancy gold walking stick.[1] He is crowned in Westminster Abbey in a ceremony that pulls out all the stops, and then he puts the Crown Jewels in his formidable fortress, the Tower of London.

However, even top-notch security in the 1670s isn't quite what it is today – there are no CCTV cameras or laser tripwires yet. Instead, the jewels are kept in a poky little tower on the corner of the castle in a locked cupboard behind a wooden grate. The Tower is a big visitor attraction, so they employ a Keeper to look after the Crown Jewels – an elderly gentleman named Talbot Edwards, who lives on site with his wife, daughter and daughter-in-law, with his son Wythe serving as a soldier on the Continent. Slip Talbot Edwards a few coins, and he'll take you into the room and show you the jewels behind the grate. Slip him a couple more, and he might even let you try them on! Imagine what good Instagram fodder that'd be these days. But in 1671, security is lax enough that the Crown Jewels are ripe for the plucking by the notorious rogue Thomas Blood (1618–80).

Thomas is born in Ireland. We don't know much about his parents or his early life, but his family are relatively well-off – in 1640, they're given land in Dunboyne, County Meath. If Thomas keeps his head down and plays his cards right, he could have a comfortable life as a member of the petty gentry. But the safety of being a small landowner doesn't last. Partway through Charles I's war against Parliament (1642–51), Thomas leaves the king's forces and switches sides, joining up with Oliver Cromwell, and so when Charles II takes the throne back, the new king is none too happy with this turncoat. Thomas is stripped of his land, and swears vengeance. He tries to kidnap Charles' representative in Ireland, the Duke of Ormond, several times, nearly lynching him on Piccadilly, of all places, before the duke manages to escape. You'd think after a botched job like that, Thomas would lie low for a while, or perhaps flee the country. But being in trouble only makes him bolder. His next plan is to steal the Crown Jewels right out of His Majesty's fortress at the Tower of London.

Early in the spring of 1671, he arrives at the Tower in disguise as the humble Dr Ayliffe, a sweet-mannered clergyman, with an actress called Jenny Blaine pretending to be his wife. Talbot Edwards shows the good parson and his wife the Crown Jewels, but during the visit Mrs Ayliffe takes ill and has to be rushed to the Edwards' flat for a reviving sip of brandy and a nice lie-down. The care that the Edwardses take over her gives the Aycliffes a great excuse to come back later, once she's recovered, to thank them for their kindness, and it's then that Thomas gets chatting with Talbot Edwards himself. Thomas must be a brilliant conversationalist, because in less than a month the pair have become such good friends that they even hatch a plan to marry the Edwards daughter to Dr Ayliffe's wealthy nephew, a totally made-up person. On 9 May, Dr Ayliffe returns to the Tower, this time with a four-man back-up: three guys to go into the Tower, and another waiting outside with the getaway horses. Dr Ayliffe apologizes profusely – his wife isn't here yet! *But while we wait for her, how about you show my friends here the Crown Jewels?* Talbot Edwards is only too happy to oblige his new friend.

Once they're in the Jewel House, the men throw a cloak over Talbot Edwards' head and tie him up. Even though they tell him that they'll kill him, he tries his best to yell and raise the alarm. They club him over the head nine or ten times, stab him in the gut and leave him for dead. Then they grab the jewels. But there's a problem, which you might have guessed already. A crown does not fit into your pocket. So they have to smash it flat. Thomas takes out a wooden mallet and hammers the top of the crown, gemstones popping out and spilling over the floor. The gang then stuff the loot under their cloaks and into sacks, and head out, clinking with gold, trying to look nonchalant. Once they've left, Talbot Edwards raises his head. He's alive! Holding his side, he manages to yell once more. This time, his daughter Elizabeth (the one who was going to be married off) hears him, rushes in and finds her father covered in blood. Thinking quickly, she raises the alarm.

The thieves are not away yet. Thomas still has to pass through two checkpoints to get out of the Tower: the Bloody Tower gate and the Water Gate. But something you realize reading through the history of the Tower is that any castle is only as strong as your guards are loyal. Once Thomas fires his pistol, the guards at both these gates decide that they are absolutely not paid enough to deal with this, and the gang pass through pretty much unimpeded. They make a dash for St Katharine Dock to the east of the Tower, where their horses are waiting. As they head toward the dock, they pull another utterly audacious manoeuvre, pretending that they are the ones giving chase. They start yelling, "Stop the rogues!", and so people let them pass. But still, before they get to the horses, one of the soldiers from the Tower manages to catch up with Thomas, and the gang are apprehended.

With Thomas and his accomplices safely behind bars, the residents of the Tower start to slowly gather up the gemstones that tumbled from the crown. A barber's apprentice hands in a diamond, and a sweeping woman turns over a great pearl. Thomas is thrown into a cell to await interrogation by the Lieutenant of the Tower, and what will happen to him next is pretty clear: a traitor's execution.

In the 17th century, high treason incurred the worst kind of execution the English legal system had to offer. First, you'd be taken to your execution site tied to a hurdle behind a horse. Then you'd be stood up on a cart and a noose tightened around your neck before the cart was pulled away, leaving you to twist desperately in mid-air. They'd cut you down just before you asphyxiated. Next, they'd cut off your genitals,[2] tear your stomach open and take your insides out. Now, you might think that would kill you, but executioners who knew what they were doing could occasionally make sure you were alive just long enough to watch your insides being burned in a fire. When Major General Harrison was hanged, drawn and quartered at Charing Cross just 11 years before Thomas's stunt, he somehow managed to punch the executioner mid-disembowelment. After being gutted, you'd get beheaded (probably not going to punch anyone after that) and your decapitated body would be cut into four pieces. The head would be put on a spike at London Bridge, and your body parts sent to places around the country where you had friends, to warn them not to mess with the king again. This was called being "hanged, drawn and quartered", and such was the fate of hundreds of men in England for centuries. But our Thomas has one final masterstroke to play.

Under arrest, Thomas insists he will not speak to anyone except the king. Magistrates, guards and the Lieutenant of the Tower all try to get him to talk, but to no avail. In the end, they tell King Charles II that Thomas wants to see him. Charles thinks this is hilarious, and just three days after being thrown in prison, Thomas is conveyed across London to the king's palace at Whitehall. There Charles asks him if he's the guy who tried to kidnap the Duke of Ormond, and Thomas is like, *Oh yeah, that was me. He deserved it.* And then he starts confessing to stuff that Charles doesn't even ask him about: *Also, one time, you were swimming in the Thames at Battersea, and I was going to shoot you from the riverbank, but you were so kingly and sublime that I changed my mind.* He says he was overcome with an "awe of majesty."[3] (Flattery will get you everywhere.)

And then Thomas gets really brazen. He tells Charles, *Look, there are loads of people who would totally try to avenge me if I get executed. You want all of them to come after you? It's your funeral.* Then he suggests that, if the king lets him go, the royal mercy will "oblige the hearts of many who [would] perform eminent services for the Crown."[4] Here it is, then: spare me, and I'll spy for you among people who would otherwise be plotting against you.

Charles asks him outright, "What if I should give you your life?" and Thomas replies, "I would endeavour to deserve it."[5] This is the exact opposite of what you'd normally think might work. You'd expect some sort of grovelling apology, and the names of any other co-conspirators – but Thomas gives neither. The courtier Thomas Henshaw reports that Thomas "answered so frankly and undauntedly that everyone stood amazed."[6] Finally, Thomas is sent back to the Tower while Charles decides what to do with him.

Why did Thomas do it? Surely if he was in need of money, there were easier and less risky ways of getting it. How could you ever sell the British Crown Jewels? Was he part of a massive conspiracy that was eventually planning to assassinate Charles and take the throne, and having the Crown Jewels ready to go would bulk up the legitimacy of the usurper? There is a single strand of evidence to support this – around the same time, someone breaks into the Lord Chancellor's house and steals almost nothing, leaving behind his expensive clothes and jewels and taking only one thing: the Great Seal of England, which is needed to approve government documents. If you're going to say you're the real king, then this would be a powerful bit of supporting evidence. This sounds like a terrible plan, though – if the jewels get stolen in a big flashy heist, and then six months later the king ends up dead and a new guy turns up wearing the jewels, everyone's just going to say, *Oh, you're the guys that stole them, then.*

So, was it some other kind of conspiracy? Maybe Charles was in on it from the beginning, as part of a ploy to sell off the jewels and make some sorely needed cash? Maybe Thomas was working under cover for the king to test the effectiveness of the Tower's defences? They're both cool ideas and would make great thriller movies, but there's no evidence to support either of them. Even people at the time can't figure it out – General Edmund Ludlow writes that he can't think "what advantage there would have been to the public cause, should they have succeeded in their enterprise."[7] We don't know what drove Thomas to commit his wild and foolhardy heist. What we do know is what the king decides to do about it – and it's somehow even more shocking.

Thomas gets a full pardon, with a condition – that he apologize to the Duke of Ormond. Thomas is like, *I'll let him kick me in the arse if it'll get me out of prison*, and writes the most cowering, grovelling, desperately apologetic letter you've ever read, calling himself an "unworthy monster" and his actions "a most heinous crime".[8] The duke accepts his apology (he can hardly not, if the king's going to forgive him for stealing his crown). On 14 July 1671, Thomas becomes a free man again, pardoned not just for the jewel heist, but for every crime he's ever committed up to that point. Not only that, but he's given a pension of £500 per year and gets his land in Ireland back.

Why would the king do such a thing? Does Thomas have some dirt on him? Was the king in on it to begin with? Both are exciting theories, but neither has ever been proven. Instead, Thomas has something else he can offer Charles in exchange for his life. You see, war with the Netherlands is on the horizon, and it's going to sorely test the loyalty of Thomas's friends, many of whom are deeply committed Nonconformists – Protestants who belong to sects other than the Church of England, such as Baptists and Presbyterians. At the moment, these people don't have many rights to worship as they please in England, so they stand to gain if the Netherlands wins the war. Thomas could be a really good spy on these people, telling them how great the king is and keeping tabs on anyone who gets too treasonous. One of Charles's ministers later says that Thomas's help as an informer is worth "ten times" the crown.[9]

Within a few weeks, Thomas is strutting around the king's palace at Whitehall with a new suit and wig, being invited to dinner at the homes of noblemen, and even buying himself a fancy new house near Westminster Abbey. Poor old Talbot Edwards, the man tasked to keep the Crown Jewels safe, is nowhere near as lucky: Charles writes a royal warrant granting him £200 for his efforts, but he never actually gets it, and has to struggle to raise the money for his medical treatment himself.

Thomas, though, goes on to have a grand old life, hobnobbing with the Archbishop of Canterbury and mooching around the king's palace. When he's arrested for debt, he's bailed out by a mysterious benefactor, and when he finally dies of illness in 1680, he's so notorious for scheming and treachery that people think he's faked it to get out of paying his debts. People swear they've seen him walking around Westminster, bold as you please. So, six days after he's buried, an inquest digs up his grave to check he's really down there. Horrifyingly, they find the corpse so bloated from the August heat that even his friends can't identify him, and they have to rebury him without a verdict. Maybe Thomas really does cheat both death and his creditors!

Thomas Blood committed one of the most audacious, outlandish crimes in British history, and he didn't even have a good explanation as to why. To this day, the question of exactly what he was thinking remains a mystery – one where there aren't even enough titbits of documentary evidence for historians to have a proper argument about. Even more mysterious is the question of why Charles decided to give him a pardon when it seems like Thomas didn't have any leverage at all. Maybe Charles really did just think Thomas was funny. Only one thing seems to come clearly out of Thomas's story, and it's that you can get away with anything if you do it with enough confidence.

CHAPTER 2
LADY MARY WORTLEY MONTAGU

teaches us that men have no idea what women get
up to when they're naked and alone together.

As an aristocratic woman in the 17th century, Mary Wortley Montagu (1689–1762) is not expected to do much – just make an advantageous political marriage and bang out a couple of kids – but her mind burns so brightly with ingenuity and determination that she is able to bend the world's expectations around her. She ventures into the farthest reaches of Europe, becoming Britain's first female travel writer, and starts a fashion for life-saving smallpox inoculations. French philosopher Voltaire (1694–1778) calls her "a woman of as fine a genius, and endued with as great a strength of mind, as any of her sex in the British Kingdoms."[1]

She is born into the high-class Pierrepont family. When I say high class, I mean it – her father, Evelyn Pierrepont, becomes the Duke of Kingston; her mother is the Earl of Denbigh's daughter. You'd think this means that Mary has every advantage in life, but there's something she's missing: an education.

At this time in Britain, wealthy boys get a broad education. In their early years, they might have a tutor at home, before being packed off to a public school like Winchester or Harrow, where they learn Latin, Greek, maths, literature, oratory and sports – all subjects they'll need for getting into Oxford or Cambridge. At university, they might study divinity, Hebrew, Greek, Arabic, law, medicine, history, botany, astronomy, geometry, science, philosophy, music and poetry. Once they finish university, many aristocratic boys round off their education with a Grand Tour, taking a friend and a tutor round Europe, especially Italy, for at least a year, to see classical art and architecture up close.

But for Mary – pff! What would be the point? She's a girl, and hence her education is seen as much less important. Because girls can't go to university anyway, they won't be needing Latin or Greek. When girls get any education at all, it's generally more about preparing them to be good housewives and hostesses rather than intellectual rigour. So Mary teaches herself Latin from her dad's library, pretending to be reading novels when really she's interested in the classics of ancient Greece and Rome. As a young woman, she says she wants to become an abbess so that she can read quietly all day. In 1710, she writes a translation of *Enchiridion* by Greek philosopher Epictetus and sends it to a bishop, saying, "My Sex is usually forbid studys of this Nature."[2]

The one subject on which she does get a thorough education is, of all things, meat carving, for which she has a tutor a whopping three times a week. Her grandfather is the king's official meat cutter, the ludicrously titled Grand Carver of England, so her family considers it a particularly important skill (yeah, reading can only get you so far, but a lady must know how to carve a chicken). In some aristocratic families of this period, the carving of meat for the dinner table is elevated to practically an art. When stately homes (the ones that don't have a Grand Carver of England, at any rate) host large dinner parties, the man of the house is expected to keep the wine flowing, while the job of the lady of the house is to personally carve the joint at the table for each guest. Since Mary's mother died when she was young, she has to fill this role at her father's dinner parties from a young age. Carving the meat for all the guests is such an arduous job that often she doesn't have time to eat her own meal: she dines alone an hour before everyone turns up, so she can spend her whole evening carving meat for them.

When Mary grows up, she starts a relationship with a pen pal of hers, Edward Wortley Montagu (1678–1761), a politician. He goes to her father and asks permission to marry Mary, but the two men can't agree on a deal. For people of Mary's class, marriage is much more about power and money than love. For Mary to go to work and earn her own money as an aristocratic woman is utterly unthinkable, so she needs a husband who will be able to provide for her. Any suitor of hers is carefully vetted for his prospects, and the family haggles over the size of her "portion": money to be paid by her father to her new husband to sweeten the deal and make her a more attractive marriage prospect. It's important to choose carefully. Once you marry, you legally become the same entity as your husband. A married woman has no possessions; everything she has belongs to her husband, including their children, whom she has no rights to see. Seeing her father and her prospective husband haggling over her, Mary says that women in her position are "sold as slaves, and I cannot tell what price my master will put on me."[3] Pierrepont wants Wortley to promise to leave his estate to his first-born son right now, but Wortley objects. He hasn't even had a son yet! What if his first son is a dissolute layabout? (As it turns out, Wortley is prescient on this point.)

Mary's dad then tries to marry her off to the fantastically named Clotworthy Skeffington. We don't know much about this man, but Mary is adamant. She says she'd rather "give [her] hand to the Flames" than marry him.[4] Her father tries to get her away from Wortley by taking her out of London into the country, and Wortley and Mary hatch a desperate plan for him to rescue her from an inn along the road. Wortley gallops after her, snatching her away from her overbearing father, and the couple elope together. Mary has a son almost exactly nine months later. But after all the letter-writing and heartache and jealousy over rival suitors, it turns out to be a pretty loveless marriage. Mary feels constantly guilty that Wortley missed out on the "portion" from her father; Wortley leaves Mary at home alone for long periods at a time and often doesn't bother replying to her letters.

Luckily, she doesn't have to rely on him alone. In 1714, George I becomes King of England and Mary goes to pay her respects, entering the glittering world of the Georgian court. She mixes with literary types like Alexander Pope and John Gay, and powerful courtiers like Sarah, Duchess of Marlborough and John Hervey. Mary becomes known among her new friends for her literary talent. Although it certainly won't do for a lady of her station to *publish* her writing, Mary's poems and essays are passed around among her friends, and often written *about*. She gains a reputation for cleverness and wit, and her work is highly regarded. But her successful career among the royal favourites is brought sharply to an end the following year when she catches smallpox.

Smallpox has been around in Europe since the medieval period, but in the 17th century it kicks up a gear. London basically has constant endemic smallpox from 1650, with particularly bad episodes every two to four years. The disease starts as a kind of flu, with headaches and a fever, followed by the beginnings of a red rash. This very rapidly blossoms into pustules covering your face, neck, chest, and spreading down your limbs. These pustules can get so big that they might not only make you unrecognizable, but they can even suffocate you. After about a week, they mature, turning into hard round lumps. When they start to burst, they smell terrible, but if you can survive them bursting, you have a good chance of survival. They'll start to scab up and flake away, leaving behind white scars. In Mary's day, it is common to see people from all walks of life with smallpox scars all over. Unlike some diseases, smallpox affects rich and poor more or less equally: among famous sufferers were Queen Mary II, who died from it in 1694, and Emperor Joseph I of Austria, who succumbed in 1711. Mary has some of the best doctors of her day, and it still almost kills her.

Although Mary is accounted a beauty before catching the disease, she totally loses her looks to scarring, and even her eyebrows and eyelashes fall out (although you'd never know this from any of her portraits, which unfailingly show her with perfect skin – Photoshopping yourself to get rid of your flaws is nothing new). Her so-called "friends" at court are really cruel about it, and her husband says he's happy that she will now have fewer admirers. It's little wonder that for the rest of her life Mary is less than enthusiastic about going back to court.

But luckily, she doesn't have to quite yet, since in the same year, 1715, her husband is made ambassador to the Ottoman Empire. Once she's recovered, Mary goes with him to Constantinople (modern Istanbul), setting off in July 1716. Although today we're used to thinking of Britain as a powerful country on the world stage, in Mary's day it is a small fish dwarfed by the mighty Ottoman Empire, which is based in modern-day Turkey and controls Greece, Bulgaria, the north coast of Africa, and the western coast of the Arabian peninsula.

When she arrives, her curiosity and intellectual openness are able to really shine for the first time. Here she can finally be something other than a housewife who reads Latin, or a courtier who makes good jokes. She writes letters to her friends and family back home, describing the country, the people and local practices. This is Britain's earliest travel writing by a woman. English men have already visited the Ottomans and written about the country, but Mary is often quite contemptuous of these predecessors, saying that their accounts don't match what she sees at all. She learns Turkish and talks to the people around her as much as she can to get information straight from the source.

One of her most famous exploits takes place in Sofia, where she visits a women's Turkish bath. Plenty of male English writers see that there are many female-only spaces in the Ottoman Empire, and they write about what goes on there, even though they've never set foot inside them and have no first-hand experience. In their imaginations, these harems are salacious places full of sexual intrigue and conniving courtiers. But Lady Mary thoroughly skewers those writers. When she enters the baths, all the other women are naked, while she stays fully clothed, but she is very impressed by how they treat an oddly dressed stranger compared to how she'd been treated by her so-called friends back home. She writes, "There were two hundred women, and yet none of those disdainful smiles, and satirical whispers, that never fail in our assemblies, when anybody appears that is not dressed exactly in the fashion."[5] The women encourage her to sit with them, at which point they start trying to undress her so that she can use the baths. They are so insistent that, in the end, she undoes her shirt and shows them her corset. They're like, *Oh wow, you* really *can't get out of that thing by yourself. Your husband must be a full-on freak,* and they leave her be.

She also calls out previous British writers for spreading the myth that Muslim women are all hugely oppressed, an idea which she calls "certainly false, though commonly believed in our parts of the world."[6] As a woman whose father basically bargained with her suitors to sell her off, she notices that women in the Ottoman Empire can inherit and control their own property and manage their own finances. She writes that the Prophet Muhammed "promises a very fine paradise to the Turkish women. He says, indeed, that this paradise will be a separate place from that of their husbands: but I fancy the most part of them won't like it the worse for that."[7] She even states that the practice of wearing headscarves and veils that cover everything except the eyes affords Turkish women freedoms that she doesn't have. When a woman goes out in a veil, she notes longingly, she is effectively in disguise, and can go anywhere she pleases without a jealous husband following her.

Mary also looks at how the Ottomans deal with smallpox. She notices that they don't seem to have any fear of the disease at all. She learns of a procedure she calls "ingrafting", always performed by elderly women (sadly, Mary doesn't record any of their names). They take a nutshell full of pus from the smallpox blisters, give you a scratch somewhere inconspicuous, dab the wound with the pus, and then bandage it up. In total, you get four or five scratches on different parts of your body. Mary describes how, afterward, you get sick for two or three days, but you rarely get marks on your face and thereafter you will have just the same immunity as if you'd caught the full-blown disease like she did. It sounds really dangerous, but the death rate for the procedure is only two per cent compared to the 60 per cent chance of death you have if you catch smallpox without the inoculation. Mary is so certain about its success that she tries the practice on her own five-year-old son, getting a Greek woman to instruct her doctor friend, Charles Maitland, on how to perform a proper ingrafting.

Now, Mary wasn't the first English person to hear about "ingrafting". In 1714, the Royal Society received a report by Dr Emmanuel Timoni (1669–1718/20) on the practice in Constantinople, and in 1716, the previous Ottoman ambassador, Sir Robert Sutton, had his son inoculated in this way against smallpox. But it hadn't caught on.

In 1718, the Montagus return to England; in 1721, another smallpox outbreak rampages through London and Mary finds herself in a position to use her knowledge and society connections to do something about it.

She's not going to quietly write a scientific paper to be read and summarily shelved – this needs to be big. Mary asks Dr Maitland to perform another inoculation, this time on her three-year-old daughter, in front of witnesses from the College of Physicians. It must be an utterly astonishing thing, in the middle of an epidemic of a deadly disease, to hear about a lady who is deliberately going to expose her young child to it. But the girl survives, and Mary subsequently tours her around aristocratic houses, even taking her into the bedrooms of people sick with the smallpox, to prove that she is safe, healthy, and can't catch it again.

Once the news gets out, ingrafting becomes all the rage at court, and the Princess of Wales, Caroline of Ansbach, wife of the future King George II, herself a previous victim of the disease, decides to get her own children inoculated. However, before they carry out the procedure on the royal heirs, they decide to do a couple more experiments, just to be sure it's safe. The first subjects are six prisoners from the notorious Newgate gaol. We don't know if the test was voluntary or not, but all six do survive, and are given full pardons. And then, to be extra-double-certain, they ingraft a group of orphans from the local area around the palace, and then put a notice in the paper saying that the children are on display for the public to inspect. But happily, all this possibly involuntary medical experimentation on vulnerable people is successful, and demonstrates to the public that it really works. The royal children are ingrafted, and by 1723 Mary and her daughter are thoroughly in demand.

Not everyone is convinced. Even as far back as the 1720s, there is what we'd now call an "antivax" movement in the press. One writer calls inoculation "an experiment practised only by a few Ignorant Women, amongst an illiterate and unthinking People."[8] Part of the opposition

14

comes from the fact that it *does* seem counterintuitive and scary to, well, deliberately rub pus in your open wounds. But part of it is also from the fact that it is performed by elderly Turkish and Greek women, so it is seen by some as a superstitious folk remedy. Although Mary is responsible for a flurry of inoculations among the upper classes in the 1720s, the practice doesn't catch on in Britain until years later, when Edward Jenner (1749–1823) develops vaccination, which turns out to be a safer method.

Her whole life, Mary was told by men that she didn't know what she was talking about. Her father told her she couldn't pick a husband; she had to push back against inaccurate depictions of Turkey by previous male writers; and the inoculation procedure she popularized was ridiculed. But she never meekly accepted these perspectives. She chose her own husband, corrected inaccuracies and false assumptions in the writings of others, and although the inoculation procedure she advocated was criticized at the time, modern science has backed her up on that too. Mary proved them wrong every time.

CHAPTER 3

ELLEN AND WILLIAM CRAFT

teach us that if you're going to tell a lie, make it an audacious one.

This remarkable couple are born into slavery in the Southern United States. They fall in love and get married, and together make one of the most daring and audacious escapes from slavery in the history of the country. Is their plan to run from home to home and hope they don't get spotted? Hide in safehouses and pretend they're on an errand? Nope – they dress Ellen as a white man, act as if she is William's master and ride to freedom in style, travelling by boat and train right under the noses of slave catchers. In this disguise, they cross more than a thousand miles of dangerous territory from Macon, Georgia, to find their freedom in Boston, Massachusetts.

In the US in the 1840s, black people who are enslaved are legally considered property, and can be treated in any way their owners see fit: they can be assaulted, tortured and even murdered with impunity. Their marriages are not legally valid, and they can be sold away from their families at any time. William (1824–1900) says that this was the worst part of being enslaved for him – the constant fear that a slave owner might take his child at any moment. William himself had his parents and siblings sold away from him, and Ellen (1826–91) is so afraid of losing a child in the same way that she refuses to sleep with William before they escape. However, compared to some enslaved people, William and Ellen are in a relatively lucky position. She is working as a lady's maid, and he is contracted out to work for a furniture maker – both professions with a far higher life expectancy than, say, sugar farming or mining, and both jobs that allow them a little more leeway than other enslaved people might get. Finally, they're able to leverage Ellen's appearance to their advantage – Ellen can pass for white.

William describes Ellen as a "quadroon":[1] someone with only one black grandparent. She is the daughter of an enslaved woman and a white slave owner. This might sound like Ellen must have been an unusual anomaly, but William notes that "almost white" enslaved people are so common that there is a practice at the time of kidnapping white children into slavery;[2] if they try to get justice, their kidnapper can just say they are mixed race, like Ellen. But, crucially, if these white children manage to prove their race by reuniting with their free families, the law *will* side with them, a protection which Ellen, an actual mixed-race woman, won't get. William recounts the story of Dorothea and Salome Müller, white German children aged eight and four respectively, who emigrate to New Orleans in 1818 with their father and work on the Miller plantation as free labourers. When their father dies, they continue working on the plantation, imperceptibly sliding into a state of slavery for decades until 1843, when Salome is discovered enslaved in a wine store by a friend of the family (Dorothea disappears from the historical record). The case goes to court, where Salome's owner, Louis Belmonte, argues that he bought her legally, although he knew she was white. The court decides that she is "free and white, and therefore unlawfully held in bondage."[3] Obviously the court thinks that Salome's race has something to do with whether or not she can be enslaved, or they wouldn't have mentioned it.

In fact, during their escape, William and Ellen meet a lady who, thinking Ellen is white like herself, tells them about an enslaved woman that she sold away from her husband. The enslaved woman must have been white-passing like Ellen, because the lady describes her as "much whiter than I am" – but that doesn't stop her calling her the n-word.[4] Basically, the modern idea of race was invented by racists to help them be racist, so it doesn't have to make sense. It doesn't even have to be internally consistent – the important thing is only that it helps slave owners keep as much power as possible. What they don't count on is William and Ellen using this illogic against them as a tool to help in their escape.

If there's one thing that slave owners are afraid of, it's rebelliousness. Runaways and rebels are clamped down on with frightening ferocity. William and Ellen know that if they are caught trying to escape, they will be separated and possibly tortured to death. There are no second chances; they have to get it right first time. They come up with the plan in December 1848. Ellen will pretend to be white, and they'll use the money that William has been able to save to travel 1,600km (1,000 miles) to a Northern state. William and Ellen are aiming to cross the

Mason-Dixon line, a border separating slaveholding Southern states from Northern states, where slavery is abolished.

Now, Ellen can't simply pretend to be a white woman; no white woman would travel alone with a black man. She not only has to pretend to be white, but also pretend to be a man. William uses money saved from his carpentry job to head into town and buy her disguise one piece at a time, so as not to arouse suspicion, and they hide it in a locked chest of drawers in Ellen's room. Their next task is to get a few days' leave as a head start. They decide their best chance will be at Christmas, since it won't look unusual to request a few days off to see friends and relatives around the holiday. They go to their respective bosses and are granted permission. William writes the incredible power line that his boss "wished me to return as soon as the time granted was up. I thanked him kindly; but somehow I have not been able to make it convenient to return yet."[5]

The last big hurdle to surmount before they leave is their illiteracy: neither William nor Ellen can read. Teaching enslaved people to read in Georgia is illegal under penalty of a heavy fine or even imprisonment. So Ellen has the idea to wear her arm in a sling so she has a good excuse if someone asks her to write her name, and they also get a bandage for her chin and a pair of dark glasses to cover her face, so she has a good excuse not to talk to people. William cuts her hair, and they sneak out to the train station.

This is the most dangerous part of the whole journey – the beginning, where they're most likely to run into someone who recognizes them. They take their seats in separate carriages on the same train and hold their breath, waiting to feel the engine pull away. Before it sets off, Ellen is horrified to discover a familiar face peering in the window at her: William's boss! She looks away and thankfully, her disguise holds. The boss moves away from the window. But her relief is turned to terror when she realizes that he's moving down the train, peering in all the windows, heading toward William's carriage. If he sees William, all will be lost. William will be pulled off the train and punished, possibly killed. Just as he's about to get to William's carriage, Ellen feels movement under her feet, and the train pulls away, leaving William's boss on the platform, scratching his head.

There is no direct route from Macon to Boston, so they board a series of trains, steamboats and omnibuses, stopping in hotels and local houses overnight where they have to. Although they try to keep themselves to themselves, their fellow travellers often engage Ellen in conversation, thus providing the couple with fascinating insights into how slave owners talk when they think they are among friends. In Charleston, South Carolina, a steamboat captain warns Ellen not to take William north, saying "I have known several gentlemen who have lost their valuable n****** among them damned cut-throat abolitionists."[6] On the train to Richmond, Virginia, a woman tells them how her husband freed all their enslaved people in his will, "but I and all our friends knew very well that he was too good a man to have ever thought of doing such an unkind and foolish thing, had he been in his right mind, and, therefore we had the will altered as it should have been in the first place."[7] The slave owners consistently see themselves as put-upon and hard done-by, and cannot conceive of a black person who's smarter than they are.

The journey gets difficult again when they arrive in Baltimore, Maryland, just south of the Mason-Dixon line. Here, train officers and ticket sellers are particularly on the lookout for escapees trying to make it north. When they board the train, an officer stops William, saying that "it is against my rules to let any man take a slave past here, unless he can satisfy them in the office that he has a right to take him along."[8] Ellen has no papers proving that Willian "belongs" to her. They think they are done for. Luckily, this is when Ellen's disguise really pays off. The other passengers actually stick up for them! Seeing an officer harass what they think is a disabled man, they start tutting and giving him disapproving looks, and at the last moment, as the bell rings for the train to leave, he gives in, saying, "As he is not well, it is a pity to stop him here."[9] They rush across the platform and collapse safely into their seats.

As they're approaching the line, they notice a change in the air. William is woken by the train conductor, who advises him to run away from his "master" when they reach Philadelphia: "Leave that cripple, and have your liberty."[10] William is put in the awkward position of having to pretend he would *never* run away from his good, kind master, no sir! Another traveller recommends an abolitionist boarding house where he can safely hide. Finally, they cross the line, and the train pulls into Philadelphia. They head for their boarding house, Ellen in tears. It's Christmas Day.

In Philadelphia, Ellen is finally able to shed her disguise, and they ask the boarding house master for advice on what to do next. He tells them that they aren't completely safe yet: slave owners have the right to come into Northern states and kidnap people back into slavery.

They would be safer further north, in Boston. He puts them in contact with an abolitionist network, and they are taught to write their names for the first time by the daughters of Barkley Ivens, a Quaker abolitionist.

Once they make it to Boston, they are able to settle down. William sets up as a furniture maker, Ellen as a seamstress. They become part of the local black community, which is small but well organized. About 2,000 black people live in Boston in 1848, with 400 of them being escapees. They run social clubs and charity organizations, and even raise money to buy each other's freedom. This is where Ellen and William get their first try at being part of a small abolitionist movement – something they will get much more practice at later.

However, their quiet life in Boston does not last long. In 1850, the US passes the Fugitive Slave Act, forbidding people in the North from giving an escapee food or shelter, and mandating that they comply with authorities to kidnap escapees back into slavery. William and Ellen's former masters send slavecatchers to Boston, and recruit the force of the office of the President himself against them. President Millard Fillmore declares that the Crafts should be returned to Georgia immediately, and sends soldiers into Boston to recapture them. Ellen and William realize that they are no longer safe anywhere in the US, and they decide to flee to Britain. Britain abolished slavery a few years earlier, in 1833, and has already played host to quite a few famous black American abolitionists such as Frederick Douglass (1818–95) and Henry Highland Garnet (1815–82). With the full might of the country seeking them out, you'd think two ordinary people like the Crafts wouldn't stand a chance but, with the help of their abolitionist network, the pair successfully sneak out of Boston, dodging their army pursuers, and board a ship to England. They won't be back until slavery is abolished in the US.

In England they join up with the British abolitionist movement and get onto the public speaking tour circuit with author William Wells Brown (1814–84), another fugitive from slavery. The events open with Brown explaining the Fugitive Slave Act to the audience, and telling them to cut off any American friends and colleagues who support slavery. Then William Craft tells the thrilling story of his escape, and as the grand finale, Ellen is invited up onto the stage. Tears are shed; the audience leaps up to applaud, and the abolitionist movement gets more money for the cause.

After their speaking tour, the Crafts teach in an agricultural school in Ockham, Surrey, for three years. William teaches furniture-making, and Ellen teaches needlework. It's an unusual school, and considered one of the best working-class schools of its day. Students spend half their time in the classroom, learning reading, writing, maths, history, geography, drawing, music and the Bible, and half in gardens and workshops, learning practical skills like agriculture, printing, carpentry and basket-making. It turns out that William and Ellen are really good at this, and William even travels to west Africa for three years to establish his own school there, in the kingdom of Dahomey (modern Benin), along the same principles.

Speaking tours are all well and good, but there are only so many people who will be able to make it to the church halls and meeting rooms where you're telling your story. You can reach a much wider audience by publishing a book. *Running a Thousand Miles for Freedom* is a gripping and powerful story, and a book that is still totally readable today, 150 years on. Despite not being able to read at the time of their escape, the Crafts have picked up an education since their flight, and not just the ABCs. In their book, William name-drops other works of literature like *The Pilgrim's Progress* by John Bunyan, *Uncle Tom's Cabin* by Harriet Beecher Stowe, the biblical books of Deuteronomy and Isaiah, and even a bit of history: Princess Elizabeth being locked up in the Tower by Queen Mary I. This is part of the image they want to project as abolitionists: *we are not the dumb brutes you've heard about from slave owners. We are intelligent, we are well-read, and we've been through tribulations, like the characters from these stories.*

After 19 long years in exile, the Crafts finally hear the news: the American Civil War is over, and slavery has been abolished throughout the US. You might think that they don't want anything to do with that country ever again, but they are excited to go back to the place where they were born. They raise the money to buy a farm back in Georgia, which they run as a cooperative with 16 other freed families. There is no boss, no master, and no one scraping off the profits of someone else's work. Instead, the families all decide how to run the farm between themselves and split the proceeds. The Woodville Cooperative Farm also has a school attached for the families' children, where 75 formerly enslaved children can learn to read and write for free.

Ellen and William Craft went from being illiterate and enslaved to freeing themselves and getting an education so thorough that they were able to pass it on to dozens of others. They snuck away from slave owners and slave catchers who underestimated them at every turn. Their pursuers were looking for someone telling a small lie: that their papers were real, that they were on their way home, that they were allowed to be where they were. They were not looking for someone who looked them in the eye and told them a massive whopper like *This mixed-race woman is a white man.* If you've got to do something big, it's worth attempting a really audacious manoeuvre rather than a small, timid one.

CHAPTER 4
NOOR INAYAT KHAN

teaches us that a cuddly exterior can hide a core of steel.

As a wealthy children's writer related to royalty, Noor Inayat Khan (1914–44) isn't required to do anything demanding or difficult during World War II. She could easily have spent the conflict doing some light work for the local branch of Air Raid Precautions or the Ministry of Information, say, from the comfort of her London flat. Instead, she becomes a secret agent, the first woman to work as a covert wireless operator behind enemy lines in one of the most dangerous jobs of the war. The life expectancy of a wireless operator in France in 1943 is just six weeks. Noor makes it through four months before she's caught, and lives for another year in Gestapo custody before being killed. During her time in France, she helps 30 Allied airmen safely pass through occupied France and back to safety, narrowly avoiding the Gestapo numerous times. Even when she is captured and tortured, she gives the Nazis no information. Behind her kind, unassuming exterior she hides an unbending resolve.

Noor has a truly international upbringing. She is born in Russia and lives in London and Paris. Her father, a descendant of Tipu Sultan ("the Tiger of Mysore", 1751–99), is credited with popularizing Sufism, an Islamic tradition of mysticism, in Europe. Her mother is American, the half-sister of Pierre Bernard (1875–1955), a famous yogi also known as Oom the Magnificent (incredible name).

Noor is brought up as a Sufi Muslim, and she is educated in some of the most prestigious centres in France: she learns child psychology at the Sorbonne and music at the Paris Conservatoire. She composes for harp and piano, and writes Buddhist-inspired children's stories, some of which are broadcast on Radio Paris. She doesn't need to do any of this – she's wealthy enough that she could just sit back and move in fancy social circles if she wanted to. But her curiosity and intelligence drive her to try new things and learn about totally disparate fields. She's having a fantastic time, playing the harp and writing books about monkeys and pigs getting up to adventures, but her whole life is smashed sideways in 1940 when Germany invades France.

Even though she has a deep commitment to pacifism, Noor decides to join the fight. Her brother Vilayat agrees, saying, "If an armed Nazi comes to your house and takes 20 hostages and wants to exterminate them, would you not be an accomplice in these deaths if you had the opportunity to kill him but did not do so because of your belief in non-violence?"[1] One thing is clear, though – she can't stay in France. As the Nazis advance, a tide of French refugees runs ahead of them, and Noor and her family join the stream of people heading to the northern coast. She makes it with only minutes to spare, and they board one of the last boats to England. As Noor crosses the gangplank onto British soil, she knows immediately that she wants to help the war effort.

She applies to the Women's Auxiliary Air Force, but is astonished to receive a rejection letter! Apparently her Moscow birthplace is a red flag for the recruiting officer (the Soviet Union hasn't joined the Allies yet). Noor isn't having any of that rubbish – she gives them a good telling-off, writing that there's no reason to block her from serving, and they sheepishly let her in. She is chosen to train as a radio operator. Radio operators were vital in many arenas of the war, sending messages in Morse code and listening in on enemy frequencies. It turns out Noor is great at sending Morse code, maybe because of her harp skills, and she gets super fast at it. She gets recommended for an advanced signalling course, where she has to study a lot of geometry and trigonometry, and again she excels in her class. Soon enough, she's noticed by the Special Operations Executive (SOE).

The SOE are the part of British intelligence that helps out resistance movements and spies in occupied countries around the world, but especially in France. Their work is absolutely secret – not even government ministers are told about what they are up to – and highly dangerous. If you're living in enemy territory, you don't get weekends off, and worse, you don't get the protection of a uniform. An enemy combatant has to be treated according to rules of engagement, but a spy will most likely be executed. You don't even get extra pay. The SOE are looking for women who speak fluent French to work as radio operators in France, and Noor is exactly what they're after. They bring her in for an interview with their recruiting officer, Selwyn Jepson (1899–1989). Jepson has to be able to spot someone with guts at a hundred paces, and claims that he can judge someone's character within the first 15 seconds of an interview. Noor impresses him so much that he only does one interview with her instead of the usual three. He later says that he was struck by the "fine spirit glowing in her."[2]

In her SOE training, Noor gets a whole new raft of skills to go alongside her harp-playing and child psychology: throwing grenades, setting explosives, reading maps, understanding codes, engaging in unarmed combat, fixing radios, hiding aerials, noticing people following her, and getting out secret messages. The SOE make sure that she can order coffee like a French person would, put down her knife and fork at the end of a meal like a French person would, and do her hair like a French person would. Any tiny Anglicism in speech or manners can give you away. Once while in the field, she's making tea for some French Resistance members when they notice that she puts the milk in first – a sure sign of a foreigner! Her trainers drag her out of bed in the middle of the night to perform a mock Gestapo interrogation, mimicking the sort of treatment she can expect at the hands of the Nazi secret police. They shine lights in her face, question her cover story over and over, and make her stand for hours. They also drop her in the middle of strange cities with instructions to find a place to transmit over radio while being tailed by an "enemy" agent.

Noor's superiors are really unsure what to make of her. On one hand, she has good radio skills and excellent French, and they are sorely in need of both. On the other hand, she's very trusting, gentle, and a little absent-minded – qualities that aren't particularly suitable for spy work. Once, during a training mission, she's stopped by a police officer and asked to explain herself, and she tells him, *Oh, I'm training to be a secret agent! Here's my radio – see?* When undergoing her mock Gestapo questioning, she becomes "so overwhelmed she nearly lost her voice",[3] and she's utterly astounded to learn that she might have to – gasp – *lie* to the Germans! The head of the French section of SOE, Maurice Buckmaster (1902–92), blames her dad, saying, "Do you know what the bastard taught her? That the worst sin she could commit was to lie about anything."[4] When her officers are discussing her in their training report, one says that she is not "overburdened with brains", and a dissenting voice scribbles in the margins, "We don't *want* them overburdened with brains."[5] It's not unanimously agreed that she should go to France, but they are in desperate need, and although she's not finished her training, she is keen. She asks to be posted to Paris – the most Gestapo-ridden part of France.

On 17 June 1943, Noor becomes the first woman from Britain to be dropped behind enemy lines as a wireless operator. Women have been sent there before, but only as couriers. A wireless operator's job is even more dangerous. You have to carry around a big radio set in a suitcase, finding places to set it up with its 21m (70ft) aerial to broadcast to London. If you're caught, there's no good explanation you can give for carrying the radio around, and while you're broadcasting, the Gestapo can find your signal, which will lead them straight to you. They can track you down within 30 minutes – much faster than their British counterparts.

Noor lands in France on a plane in the middle of a field and is met by French Resistance member Henri Déricourt (1909–62), who gives her a bike on which she can ride to the nearest train station. Once in Paris, she is introduced to her contact, Émile Garry (1909–44), who puts her in touch with a circle of radio operators codenamed Prosper. By the time Noor meets them, Prosper has sabotaged Chaingy power station in the Loire valley, killed dozens of Germans, and even derailed trains, so she's going to be learning from people who know what they're doing. While she's waiting for her radio to be parachuted in, she uses one of Prosper's sets to let London know that she's arrived safely, making her the fastest agent to send a message back to London after being dropped behind enemy lines – less than 72 hours.

And then, a week after she arrives, the leaders of Prosper are all arrested in a huge bust. Noor manages to get out, but now she has no one to show her the ropes and the Resistance's safehouses start being taken over one by one. As more agents are captured and interrogated, more people crack and reveal yet further information about the Resistance. Arrests run into the hundreds. Someone even gives them Noor's codename – "Madeleine". By the middle of July 1943, she is the sole radio operator left working in Paris – the only one broadcasting information back to London. She knows it's just a matter of time before she's arrested, and London offers to send a plane to pick her up, but she declines. If she goes, then the whole of Paris will go dark. Instead, she stays and tries to build a new radio circuit. Rather than working for one major Resistance organizer, as most radio operators do, she finds herself in demand from people all over the city, and she even ends up broadcasting directly to the office of Charles de Gaulle, the leader of Free France, in London. She moves from place to place, trying to find safe locations from which to transmit, and at one point ends up in a block of flats where most of the tenants are SS officers. Astoundingly, she gets away with that, too. She's trying to put up her aerial outside one day when one of them pokes his head out and asks, *Do you need any help?* And cool as ice, Noor says, *Oh yes, I'm just trying to put up this aerial – would you mind?* And thinking that she's just an ordinary woman trying to listen to the wireless, he helps her do it.

She starts moving locations every few days, even dyeing her hair from brown to red to blonde and then back again. She drives out to the suburbs or into the country to snatch 20 minutes of transmitting time, and without a network to rely on she starts reaching out to people she knew in France before the war, like her old music teacher and the family doctor. By this time, she's really getting into her stride. Her transmissions are perfectly encoded, with no errors that would make them hard for London to decipher. And she's getting better at lying, too. Once, two Gestapo officers corner her on a train while she has her radio with her, and demand to see what she's got in her suitcase. She opens it up, saying, *Well, I don't have to tell you what it is. I'm sure that you recognize cinematographic apparatus when you see it!* And they don't want to admit that they don't recognize it, so they take her at her word, like, *Oh, yeah. Cinematographic apparatus. I see it now.* During this period, Noor is doing her best work, contacting London to arrange safe passage for dozens of airmen, Resistance members, agents and their families out of occupied territory, and getting deliveries of money, equipment, weapons and false papers into the country. But the Gestapo's net is closing around her.

In mid-September 1943, the Gestapo try to lure her into a trap. Luckily, she realizes something's not right and doesn't go to the meeting-point. But now she knows that they are on to her. Even so, she keeps transmitting, and keeps dyeing her hair, even though it's starting to break under the stress of so many dye washes. She finally agrees that it's time for her to get out, and arranges a pick-up with London. She's so close to getting out of France and surviving the war. But three days before her plane is due to arrive, she returns to her flat to find the Gestapo waiting for her.

We don't know exactly who betrayed her, but two of her close French contacts have been suspected of working as double agents – Henri Déricourt, who met her on her first night in occupied France as she got off the plane, and Renée Garry, Émile's sister. Both are investigated after the war, but neither is convicted. When Noor finds the Gestapo waiting for her, she puts up a fierce fight, biting the guy who tries to handcuff her, but they manage to bundle her into a car and take her to their notorious Paris headquarters on Avenue Foch.

They question her for hours, getting her to repeat her story over and over again. They show her aerial photos of the places where she did her training in Britain, and a copy of a letter she'd sent home to her mother on a plane. They want to convince her that they already know everything anyway, so she might as well talk. But she doesn't budge. Although she struggled with lying in Britain, she consistently lies to the Gestapo. She doesn't even tell them her real name, instead calling herself "Nora Baker". However, they do find something of just as much value as her information – her notebooks. They find papers recording her codes and her previous messages, which she failed to destroy. Using these, they're able to imitate her style and pretend to be her on the radio for months, convincing London that she's fine and doesn't need help. The Germans ask them for supplies and weapons, and at one point Britain even sends them a whopping half a million francs in cash. Worse, while posing as Noor, they're able to capture more British agents, leading to several arrests and executions. London doesn't realize that Noor has been captured until March 1944.

Noor makes two escape attempts while in Avenue Foch. During her first few hours there, she asks if she can have a bath, and the Gestapo agents, wanting to play good cop, agree. When they lead her to the bathroom and close the door, she climbs out of the window and along the roof, but the Germans spot her and pull her back in. Later, she manages to contact two other prisoners there, Léon Faye and John Starr, by tapping on the walls in Morse code and exchanging tiny notes with them. Together, they hatch a daring escape plan. One day, the cleaning lady's carpet sweeper breaks, and Starr offers to fix it. He's given a screwdriver to take it apart, and he manages to hide it. All three pass it back and forth, unscrewing the bars on their windows, and finally, on the same night, they climb out of their windows and across the roof. They manage to get onto the building next door when they run into some truly terrible luck – an air raid. The guards go to check on them in their cells, and discover that they're gone. All three are swiftly recaptured. The Gestapo want Noor to sign an agreement promising that she won't try to escape again, but she refuses. So on 27 November 1943 she is transferred to a prison in Pforzheim, and thus becomes the first female British agent to be sent to Germany.

At the prison, Noor is kept on the lowest possible rations of cabbage and potato soup. She is chained by her hands and feet in solitary confinement, and they don't even remove the shackles to allow her to eat or use the toilet, so an attendant has to feed and clean her.

As a secret agent, she is designated as a *"Nacht und Nebel"* prisoner – literally, "Night and Fog", meaning that she is to be "disappeared". She is beaten by the guards on several occasions. Even the attendant and the guards are forbidden from speaking to her, and she can only mark the passage of time with meals. After a few months, some of the other prisoners manage to get a message to her by scratching "There are French girls here" on one of the food bowls. The bowl is collected, washed, and reused, and eventually makes its way to Noor, who scratches back, "You are not alone, you have a friend in Cell 1."[6] She tells them her London address and the address of a friend. In return, they tell her what they know about the progress of the war. It's going well for the Allies – which is bad news for Noor.

By September 1944, Germany is in retreat, being beaten back by the Americans and British from the west and by the Soviet Union from the east. As a result, the Nazis start ramping up their executions of prisoners, particularly secret agents. Noor is put on a train along with three other women, who are all told they're going to work on an agricultural camp. For the first time in months she's able to have a conversation, and the women are given tiny luxuries like cigarettes. But rather than a farm, they arrive instead at the notorious concentration camp at Dachau. We don't know for certain what happens to Noor there, as there are conflicting accounts, all second-hand, but there are two that corroborate each other.[7] These two accounts say that she is stripped, kicked and beaten all night. Finally, an officer puts a pistol to her head, and just before the gun goes off, she is heard to say her last word: *"Liberté!"*[8]

Noor is one of 30,000 people killed at Dachau. Just seven months later, the camp is liberated. Her body is cremated, so she has no grave, and since she gave the Gestapo a false name, she doesn't appear correctly on their records. We wouldn't know her story at all except for the work of SOE member Vera Atkins (1908–2000), who spends years tracking down what happened to all the agents she sent into the field, and Jean Overton Fuller (1915–2009), Noor's friend and biographer.

After the war, Noor was posthumously awarded the Croix de Guerre and the George Cross, the highest civilian awards in France and Britain respectively. She never gave the Germans any information, even keeping her true identity a secret to the bitter end. Despite her gentle and kind exterior, in the end she displayed a strength and resolve that her trainers in Britain could never have expected: her cuddly exterior truly hid a core of steel.

CHAPTER 5

MARY FRITH

teaches us that wearing the trousers isn't just for the men.

Another woman famous for her attitude is Mary Frith (*c*1584–1659). She simply will not be constrained by the gender roles of 17th-century England. Rollicking about London in men's clothes, spending her time in alehouses and tobacco shops among the denizens of the criminal underworld, and not only that, being celebrated for it in multiple plays of the time, Mary Frith proves that wearing the trousers isn't just for the men.

She's born around 1589 at the north end of Aldersgate, a street in the City of London. By all accounts, her parents are quiet, respectable folk in the shoemaking business. Young Mary is expected to read the Bible; learn to sew, knit, weave, spin and darn; make a good marriage to an up-and-coming tradesman and produce maybe half a dozen kids. But even as a girl, she bucks this path that society has set down for her. Sources from the time describe her variously as a *hoyden,* a *tomrig* and a *rumpscuttle* – roughly what we'd now call a *tomboy*. According to a biography published a few years after her death, she "delighted and sported only in Boys' play and pastime, not minding or companying with the Girls". She particularly hates sewing, comparing sitting with her needle to being in the grave: "a Sampler was as grievous as a Winding-sheet" and "her Needle, Bodkin and Thimble, she could not think on quietly, wishing them changed into Sword and Dagger for a bout at Cudgels."[1]

Her parents think that this is a phase, and that once she grows up she'll settle down and make a good match. But Mary simply isn't interested in men, and men aren't interested in her: "She was troubled with none of those longings which poor Maidens are subject to."[2] Instead, she spends her time down on Bankside, London's skeevy underbelly on the south bank of the Thames. Traditionally, London's centre is on the north bank of the river: that's where the Romans founded the city more than 2,000 years ago; it's a lot easier to build there than on the marshy south bank, and to this day it's where most of London's big sights are: Big Ben, Buckingham Palace, St Paul's Cathedral, etc. The south bank is where London shoves everything it *needs,* but doesn't want to *think about:* cemeteries, tanneries and brothels. In Mary's day, most of the land on the south bank is controlled not by the Crown or the powerful Lord Mayor of London, but by the Bishop of Winchester, a much smaller fish who has much less authority over his nominal jurisdiction. That means laws are a lot looser there, and people who commit crimes on the north bank can easily evade the reach of the law by fleeing to the other side of the river. It ends up as a bit like the Las Vegas of London – a pleasure district, to be sure, but what happens on Bankside stays on Bankside. It's where Shakespeare sets up the Globe after theatres (considered subversive and dangerous) are banished from the city centre, so there you can catch the world premiere of *King Lear* or head on down to the Bear Gardens to watch an angry, chained-up bear take on a pack of dogs. It's your choice! In 1603, the bishop's Bankside palace, by now very run-down, is used basically as a detention centre for 800 homeless people who are being deported to the Low Countries as a measure against the plague. To sum up, what I'm saying is that the area isn't fully gentrified yet. Mary fits right in.

She quickly settles herself down among London's criminal underworld. Society in general is a lot less law-abiding in Mary's time than it is today. The population is, on average, younger, and most blokes carry some sort of sword or dagger around with them all the time. Hot-headed bar fights and even riots are commonplace. There's no police force yet; instead, the law is enforced by a system of local volunteers acting as watchmen and constables. Corruption is endemic at all levels of the law, and even considered normal – judges and sheriffs will *expect* you to bribe them. The criminal class is in some ways much better organized than the legal system. Criminals are sorted into dozens of highly specialized roles, each with their own utterly fantastic names: a "jarkman" is a forger; a "prigger of prancers" is a horse thief; and a "dummerer" is someone who pretends to be mute to get sympathy. One particular kind of thief that doesn't exist in the modern day is a *cutpurse* – the 17th-century version of a pickpocket. People in Mary's day don't keep their wallets in their pockets, but instead have them hanging off their belts. If you're quick and nimble, you can cut through the strings and walk off with the purse before your victim notices. Hanging around with these types, Mary soon picks up the nickname "Moll Cutpurse".

Mary's biography insists that she never steals purses herself, but she does work with a pickpocket gang as a receiver of stolen goods. The book describes her induction into the gang, where they do a kind of palm-reading to see what work she's suited to: "I had no great promising symptoms of a lucky mercurial in my fingers, for they had not been used to any slight and fine work; but I was judged by these palmisters from the hardness and largeness of the table of my hand to be very well qualified for a receiver and entertainer of their fortunate achievements."[3]

So Mary becomes the fence for the gang. She helps them out of prison and, when they're low on funds, lends them money out of her own pocket to stop them committing reckless or dangerous crimes that could get them hanged. In return, they protect her from the law and keep her informed of everything the gang is doing: they "made it the chiefest of their religion to conceal me, and to conceal nothing of their designs from me."[4] For example, one time she's charged with stealing a watch, but just before the trial, she gets one of her pickpockets to steal the watch in question from right under the constable's nose. The judge asks the constable to produce the watch so that the victim can say if it's his or not, and the constable's like, *Of course, your honour. Er . . . just – could have sworn I had it a minute ago . . .* The judge knows that Mary must have done some sort of trick, but without a key piece of evidence he's forced to throw her case out.

Mary also starts wearing men's clothes, or mix-and-matching men's and women's clothes at the same time. She can often be found hanging out in low-life taverns wearing breeches or a man's doublet with her petticoats. Mary is not unique in this – there's a bit of a trend of women wearing men's clothes in this period; Mary is just the most prominent tip of a surprisingly large iceberg. In 1569 Joanna Goodman is sent to Bridewell Prison for dressing as a man in order to follow her husband to war; in 1575 Dorothy Clayton is sent to the pillory for wearing men's clothes;[5] and ballads are written about Mary Ambree, who in 1584 dresses as a man and becomes a captain in the English forces fighting against the Spanish to liberate Ghent (a city in modern Belgium).[6] In 1592 a Mrs Cornwall is brought before the court for wearing "young men's garters and said she would so to do until they came for them."[7] In 1615 a Mrs Turner, sentenced to death for the murder of Sir Thomas Overbury, goes to the gallows in men's clothes.[8]

But it's still rare enough that Mary really sticks out. She becomes a famous local figure, and within ten years of her first arrest there are already three plays about her. In 1610, dramatist John Day writes *The Mad Pranks of Merry Moll of the Bankside, with her Walks in Man's Apparel, and to What Purpose* (catchy). In 1611 she appears as a character in Nathaniel Field's *Amends for Ladies*, and in the same year the biggest Mary-themed play comes out: *The Roaring Girl* by Thomas Middleton and Thomas Dekker. I'd translate "roaring girl" into modern-speak as "ladette" – a boisterous, rambunctious woman who drinks, swears and is generally very unladylike. In *The Roaring Girl*, there are two lovers, Mary Fitz-Allard and Sebastian Wengrave, who want to get married, but Sebastian's father won't let him. So Sebastian pretends to have dumped the virtuous Mary and be dating the fighting, drinking, breeches-wearing Moll Cutpurse instead, the plan being that *any woman* will seem preferable to having Moll as your daughter-in-law. His dad is horrified, and tries to get Moll out of the picture through trickery, seduction, and playing on her greed, but Moll sees through his traps every time and comes out on top. Sebastian's plan works, he is reunited with Mary, and Moll declares that Sebastian's dad should have known it was a trick – she would never marry anyone: she likes taking up the whole bed!

In Mary's day, women are not allowed on stage, meaning that the Moll Cutpurse of this play is being played by a man dressed as a woman dressed as a man. But for at least one performance in 1611, patrons at the Fortune Theatre can see Mary Frith on stage. We're not exactly sure what she does – whether she plays herself for the whole show (seems unlikely – I can't see Mary learning lines) or has a cameo, or simply turns up after the bows for a post-show song and jig. We don't know if her appearance is planned by the theatre, or whether she just gets up onstage unprompted. What we do know is that nine months after *The Roaring Girl* opens, Mary appears in court charged with misdemeanours, including appearing on stage and wearing men's clothes. At the trial, she confesses that she has "long frequented all or most of the disorderly & licentious places in the City as namely she hath, usually in the habit of a man, resorted to alehouses, taverns, tobacco shops & also to playhouses" and that at the Fortune Theatre she "sat there upon the stage in the public view of all the people there present in man's apparel & played upon her lute & sang a song."[9] Mary makes a big show of acting penitent, promising to do better from now on.

She's ordered to do penance in the churchyard of St Paul's Cathedral. Her punishment involves standing on a platform in public, dressed in nothing but a white sheet, while a priest tells a crowd about her crimes. These humiliation punishments are common in Mary's day, and designed to be an eye-catching way for the state to teach its citizens what behaviour is expected of them. There are no newspapers yet, but if something loud and unusual is happening at the end of your street, you will probably head along to see what all the fuss is about. Once you're there, the priest tells you who's wearing the Sheet of Shame and why, and you'll think to yourself, *Right, I'd better not do whatever that person did.* In a period where everyone knows their neighbours, and all shops and businesses run on credit and reputation, a humiliating punishment like this has tremendous force. We're social animals, and the idea of being shunned or pushed out of our communities is something we're hard-wired to avoid at all costs.

It doesn't work on Mary, though. She makes a mockery of the authorities by turning up for her punishment absolutely wasted. One letter from the time says that "she wept bitterly and seemed very penitent, but it is since doubted she was maudelin druncke, being discovered to have tipled of three quarts of sacke [wine] before she came to her penance".[10] (*Maudlin drunk* – what a great phrase.) According to her biography, she says "they might as soon have shamed a Black Dog as me", and that she would have happily done the penance in "all the Market Towns in England." The book also tells us that she gets revenge on people who come to gawk at her by sending out her pickpockets to cut holes in their clothes: "My Emissaries were very busie . . . in revenge of this disgrace intended me, spoiled a good many Cloaths by cutting part of their Cloaks and Gowns."[11] She says she got the idea from a story she'd heard about a pickpocket gang who would deliberately get one of their members sent to the pillory so that they could cut the purses of the watching crowd while they were distracted. She also claims that the punishment doesn't work on her at all: "This dealing with me therefore was so far from reclaiming me to the sobriety of decent apparel."[12]

Indeed, Mary only gets bolder. In 1614, she sets up an actual shop where you can buy back things that were stolen from you. How on earth does she manage to get away with this one? Even with the legal system as corrupt as it is at the time, this seems a step too far. But there are a couple of levers Mary can pull to keep the eyes of the constables away from her shop. Firstly, there's as yet no law against receiving stolen goods, so she can just say, *What, me? I'm just a humble pawn shopkeeper. I had no idea*

37

these were stolen goods, none at all! Secondly, she knows everyone in the underworld, and so she is able to sacrifice a pawn every now and again to keep the watchmen satisfied. For example, in 1621, a man named Henry Killigrew visits Mary's shop to get back his stolen purse. Mary promptly identifies the thief as a woman named Margaret Dell, who is arrested.[13] You'd better stay on Mary's good side if you don't want to be handed over.

Mary's last great deed in the historical record is a £20 bet she makes with a friend that she can ride through what was then the whole of London, from Charing Cross to Shoreditch, dressed as a man. Now, Mary has a pretty good set of men's clothes, and so if she puts on a big hat and a high collar, she can probably sneak through the city without alerting people that she is really a woman in men's clothes. But that's not Mary's style at all. Instead, she hires a trumpeter and someone to carry a banner to draw as much attention to herself as possible en route. Still, she makes it nearly the whole way without being remarked on at all – everyone just thinks she's a bloke. But when she gets to Bishopsgate, she spots a woman she knows in the crowd. Mary's biography calls this woman "a plaguey orange wench" – a fantastic insult that I shall be peppering into ordinary conversation forthwith. The orange wench calls out Mary's name, alerting the crowd, which "set the people that were passing by, and the folks in their shops, a-hooting and hollowing [hollering] as if they had been mad."[14] It seems that Mary is really afraid the crowd will hurt her, because she ducks into a nearby pub to escape the heat, and hides out there until she gets a lucky break – a wedding party comes down the road, distracting the crowd and allowing her to make a quick exit to Shoreditch, where she finally wins her bet.

Despite her wild life of crime, Mary made it to the respectable age of 74. Three years after her death, a book called *The Life and Death of Mrs Mary Frith* appeared on the market, supposedly written by Mary herself as a sort of deathbed confession of all her misdeeds. Sadly, Mary probably didn't write it. Most likely it's written by someone looking to cash in on a bit of true crime, like those TikToks where an AI face with an AI voice reads you an *I was kidnapped and locked in a basement for three years* story. But it does seem to be a collection of well-known tales about Mary's life, some of which (only some, mind) do agree with other sources from the time.

And still she's a figure that we can't stop thinking about. She's been played by Helen Mirren in a revival of *The Roaring Girl,* and she's a favourite subject of books about girl power and eccentrics right up to me writing these words now. She stands out so much in her own time that 400 years later we're still fascinated by her story, like a missing tooth you can't stop poking with your tongue. She wears the trousers, both metaphorically and literally, in her own life, and never stops telling her own story the way she wants it. Wearing the trousers isn't just for the men.

CHAPTER 6
LADY HESTER STANHOPE

*teaches us that you might have to travel long
distances before you find a home of your own.*

It was once said that Hester Stanhope (1776–1839) is "not like the common race of women, and does not submit her conduct to the common rules of life."[1] That's written during her lifetime in 1812, and to this day no one's managed to sum her up any better. Finding herself suddenly without family in middle age, she casts propriety to the wind and travels the world, not dressing, speaking or behaving like anyone expects her to. Out of everyone in this book, she's probably the most classically eccentric. She *Eat, Pray, Love*s her way across Turkey, Egypt and Palestine, and becomes one of the first European women to see the Syrian city of Palmyra, before finding her home after years of travel in an abandoned monastery in the Syrian mountains. There, she shelters hundreds of refugees, lives among dozens of cats, and finally, as her last eccentric act, walls herself in.

First off, with anyone from Europe going to southwest Asia, we need to talk about "Orientalism". "The Orient" is a super-vague term that kind of means "everything east of Sofia, plus sometimes North Africa", and is often used by historians telling Hester's story to refer to the Arabic countries she visits. The scholar Edward Said (1935–2003) wrote that the Orient is associated with Islam, which Christian Europeans often see as a sort of Professor Moriarty to their Sherlock Holmes – a great mortal enemy that's the opposite of everything they stand for. Brutal, rapacious, untrustworthy, dark and polygamous, while at the same time holding a powerful fascination because of its ancient archaeology, its biblical lands, its sexy slave girls and its cool swords – so the thinking goes. According to Said, Hester was part of a kind of first wave of

Orientalists that he called the "expert-adventurer-eccentrics", as distinct from the second wave, who went east as representatives of a conquering British or French Empire.[2]

Hester herself doesn't believe that English people are superior to those of the "Orient" – in fact, she says that "If they were to give me £100,000 a year to live among the boot-whipping, silly visiting people of England I would not do it. Here if I sit under a tree and talk to a camel driver at least I hear good sense."[3]

But a lot of the Europeans who visit Hester and write about her absolutely do believe they are superior to the Arabs. For example, French writer Alphonse de Lamartine (1790–1869) writes about the Arab world as if it's a spooky, mystical country full of easily duped people and not like a normal place: "This Arab land is the land of prodigies: everything sprouts there, and every credulous or fanatical man can become a prophet there in his turn." He then states that European countries should take it over and rule it as a colony: "This sort of suzerainty [lordship] thus defined, and consecrated as a European right, will consist principally in the right to occupy one or another territory, as well as the coasts, in order to found there either free cities, or European colonies."[4] So something we have to keep in mind when we're learning about Hester is to be wary of the people who write about her, especially at the time. These writers sometimes like to paint her as either striking awe among the locals with her magical white superiority or as more in touch with mysticism than ordinary Europeans by dint of having lived in the "Orient".

Hester is born into the upper crust of English society. Her father is the wealthy Earl Stanhope and her mother is the daughter of an earl. Despite their extremely consolidated social power (or maybe because of it), her dad is a bit of a maverick in his own right – he believes that there shouldn't be a king or an aristocracy even though he is an aristocrat himself. He calls himself "Citizen Stanhope" and tries to sell off his family mansion to fund the building of a new kind of marine vessel powered by steam – a "steamship", if you will. His son and heir, Lord Mahon, is not best pleased at this attempt to give away his inheritance, and the whole thing blows up into a family feud that sees Hester leave her parents and never live with them again. Instead, she goes to live with her uncle, who just so happens to be the Prime Minister, William Pitt the Younger (extremely normal family).

Since her uncle William doesn't have a wife, Hester ends up acting as the lady of the house, organizing the servants and throwing parties for his political friends. She lives with him in Downing Street, advises him on the Napoleonic War, and is such a shrewd operator that he tells her, "If you were a man, Hester, I would send you on the Continent with 60,000 men, and give you carte blanche and I am sure that not one of my plans would fail."[5]

And then – this is going to sound like I'm making it up for dramatic effect, like it's the sort of thing that happens in bad novels, not in real life, but it's true – in 1795, Hester visits a man in an asylum. His name is Richard Brothers, and he claims to receive prophetic visions from God. He tells her that one day she will travel to Jerusalem, spend seven years in the desert, and eventually become "Queen of the Jews".[6] Now today, yes, we can tell that this is #problematic – the idea that you can just turn up in a foreign country and the people there will be so easily overawed that they'll name you their queen is a fantasy – but Hester is completely taken by this. She never forgets it, and the idea that she is destined to fulfil a prophecy of some kind becomes her own fervent religious belief.

In 1806, her uncle dies. He's in debt, so he's not leaving her anything in his will, but Parliament gives her a really decent pension to live off as a thank-you for all the unpaid work she did running Downing Street. She's now financially independent, a rare thing for a woman of the time, and without a family, so like many singletons before her, she thinks, *I should see the world while I'm still young.* (She's currently 30.) She doesn't travel alone – she's got a whole retinue of servants, guards and her physician Dr Meryon with her, and along the way she picks up a young boyfriend, Michael Bruce, with whom she'll have a long affair as they travel together.

She heads to Constantinople (modern Istanbul) just like Lady Mary Wortley Montagu a few decades before (see Chapter 2). Here, she starts to learn about the Ottoman Empire. She visits the hot springs at Bursa, and there, also like Lady Mary, she visits a harem. She doesn't enjoy it quite as much, though – she thinks that all these women hanging out together and dancing while wearing so little is just too lesbicious, saying that she doesn't understand why women would get excited by anything "except by that which God created for the purpose, *a man*."[7]

Hester is having a great time on her trip so far, living in a beautiful house with ocean views, but it's all about to go horribly wrong. After Constantinople, Hester and her crew head by sea for Alexandria in Egypt. During the crossing, they hit a terrible storm, and their boat starts taking on water. While her boyfriend Michael, Dr Meryon and the sailors are furiously bailing them out, Hester grabs some fine crystal glasses and a cask of wine from her luggage, and runs around between them, giving them all a drink to keep their spirits up. After eight hours struggling against the water, the crew are exhausted, and the captain gives the order to abandon ship. The 27 people aboard get into a little lifeboat, and make for the only land they can see – a barren rock sticking out of the waves. Hester manages to save only a few of her possessions. Almost all her European clothes and £4,000-worth of jewels sink to the bottom of the Aegean Sea.[8] On the rock, the stranded seafarers scramble into a cave, where they survive without food or water for 30 hours before help finally arrives.[9]

An experience like that is bound to affect a person, but for Hester the change is pretty dramatic. After the shipwreck, she never wears European dresses again. Instead, she starts wearing local men's fashion. She has a stripy waistcoat, a sash with two guns and a sword, and, most extravagantly, gold-embroidered pantaloons. She says, "I can assure you that if I ever looked well in anything it is in the Asiatic dress."[10] The great thing for Hester about wearing Turkish and Egyptian men's clothes rather than European or Ottoman women's clothes is that none of the locals quite know what to make of her at first, so she finds she's afforded a lot more freedom and leeway than she would normally get. She loves Oriental clothing so much that even when they reach Egypt and she's able to buy English dresses again, she chooses not to. In fact, she goes even further, shaving her head, picking up a cashmere turban and purple trousers, and riding astride rather than sidesaddle.

On the way into Cairo, she sees someone else's company coming toward her in the other direction with an even bigger and more brightly swagged entourage than her own. It turns out to be that of the Ottoman Emperor's representative in Egypt, Pasha Muhammad Ali (1769–1849). Ali is a bloodthirsty but successful soldier. During his rise to power in Egypt, he got rid of his rivals, the Mamluks, by inviting them to a big banquet and having them all murdered like the Red Wedding in *Game of Thrones*. But to Hester, at least at first, he is charming and affable. He even gives her a horse, the first of many she'll receive as gifts on her journey. She gets a massive upgrade to her ride in Egypt, buying a tricked-out red velvet saddle and bridle with gold embroidery (honestly, no wonder she needs guards with her) and a whopping ten camels just to carry her servants' beautifully embroidered tents.

Hester should really stick to horses and camels, as she has very bad luck with boats. On her trip across the Nile to see the pyramids, the boat she's on collapses, but luckily one of the other tourists – and this isn't a joke – plugs the hole *with his turban,* which gives them just enough time to get to the other side of the river. Unsurprisingly, after that mess, Hester isn't in much of a mood to appreciate the majesty of the monuments at Giza.

Hester seems to have a knack for getting scary guys who might hurt her to help her instead. She meets another on the way to Jerusalem: Abu Ghosh, the local sheikh. She's been warned that he has a reputation for squeezing money out of tourists, but Hester has a great time with him, eating dolmades and rice, and Ghosh slaughters a sheep in her honour. It's with Ghosh that Hester hits on a tactic she'll continue to use to get on the good side of powerful men – just straight-up asking them to keep her safe from all the *other* dangerous guys. *Wow, there are a lot of perils out there for a wealthy single lady like me! Luckily I've got you to protect me.*

Rather than trying to avoid or run away from him, Hester asks Ghosh for some guards to protect her belongings, and not wanting to be rude to a dinner guest, he of course agrees and even offers to guard her stuff personally. Now it would be super-awkward, not to mention disloyal, to rob her. Ghosh considers himself a man of honour and Hester totally plays up to that. She arrives safely in Jerusalem, just as Richard Brothers predicted years before.

Later on her travels, in Damascus (in modern Syria), she performs the same trick again: she meets another pasha, who gives her another horse, and tells him that she wishes to travel next to Palmyra. He tells her this is a bad idea. *To get to Palmyra, you have to cross a desert inhabited by nomadic Bedouin people, who might rob or murder you. It's too dangerous.* But Hester wants to meet the Bedouins, as she knows that just as they could prevent her from reaching her goal, they're also the only ones who can help her cross the desert. So the pasha gives in to her, she sets off, and on the way meets a Bedouin chief, Muhana Al Fadil. She is completely taken by his way of life, saying that "for eloquence and beauty of ideas . . . they [the Bedouin] undoubtedly are beyond any other people in the world."[11] Once again, she finds that a man she's been warned about is instead welcoming and helpful, and with Muhana's protection, she makes it to Palmyra. Hester and her maids are the first European women ever to see the city. According to boyfriend Michael, the children of the city "came to greet Miladi Hester on her arrival. They began to dance, to the accompaniment of their own kind of music. . . . Nothing could exceed the beauty of this scene, the magnificence of the arch under which we stood, the picturesque group of old women among the columns, the cavalcade of warriors which followed Miladi Hester, and the imposing grandeur of the ancient ruins."[12]

Lots of Europeans are interested in Palmyra because of its historic ruins, and by this point Arab people are highly suspicious of Westerners coming to steal antiquities – the practice is pretty rampant in Egypt, for example, and Lord Elgin (1766–1841) has already made off with statues from the Parthenon in Greece, causing an international scandal. Hester is strongly against this practice and assures the sheikh that she's not here to pinch stuff. Years later, she'll meet an English bloke named William Bankes (1786–1855) – later a celebrated Egyptologist – who wants her to use her influence to get him into Palmyra so that he *can* pinch stuff, and she sends him on his way with a letter to the Emir saying not to hurt Bankes, but not to trust him either. Bankes ends up getting to Palmyra without the Emir, and gets immediately imprisoned.[13]

After the triumph of making it to Palmyra, Hester starts to slow down a bit. She heads to Sidon in Syria, where she finds a convent which will become her home for the next few years. By now, there isn't much money coming in anymore, so she gets rid of some horses and servants, and settles down. She spends her time learning Arabic and local religion. She never does get confident with written Arabic, but she does get a good handle on the local dialect. In terms of religion, the main group in the local area is the Druze, who have their own secret religion that's based on Islam, but with loads of other influences from Christianity to Zoroastrianism to Buddhism, all mixed together to create something entirely separate from all of them. Hester comes to believe that the Mahdi, a kind of Druze messiah, is about to arrive, and that one of her horses is a prophesied destiny horse that will one day be ridden by the Mahdi himself.[14] She gets into astrology and the occult, and consults with local holy men.

Finally, she moves further up into the mountains to another abandoned monastery near the village of Joun, which is where she will live for the rest of her life. The monastery seems extremely cool – there are dozens of feral cats, fruit trees, fountains and loads of space for horses and guests. The sad thing about Hester is that, just as she seems to have found somewhere to call home, she has a noticeable personality change. She starts to ramble, talking non-stop for hours on end. Her boyfriend and her doctor both leave her, and her pension is ended. She becomes obsessive, even cruel. She yells at her servants, whips them, throws things at them, and makes them work extremely long hours to impossibly high, unclear standards. Worst of all, she gives up her liberal principles and acquires an enslaved girl named Zezefoon, about whom, sadly, little has been written.[15]

On the other hand, she takes in hundreds of refugees from a rebellion that's broken out against Emir Bashir, sheltering the children and wives of executed rebels in her monastery and taking out loans to pay for their safe passage out of the region. She hides men from being conscripted to fight for Muhammad Ali's son, Ibrahim. Almost two centuries later, historian Lorna Gibb is still able to find people in the region who credit Hester for their families' survival.[16] Bashir even lays siege to her monastery, threatening to "cut into a thousand pieces" anyone who brings her water, but she stays firm, and the siege is lifted.[17]

By now her money has run out, so she's borrowing from anyone she can. She sells off almost all her furniture and stops making repairs to the building, so it starts to flood. In 1838, she sends British Prime Minister Viscount Melbourne a desperate ultimatum: *pay the debts I've incurred looking after all these refugees or* "I shall break up my household and build up the entrance-gate to my premises: there remaining, as if I was in a tomb."[18] And she's not messing about: a week before her doctor leaves her for the last time in August 1838, he sees the stones that have been collected ready for the mason to block up her gate with. Hester doesn't seal up the wall completely – she leaves enough space for water deliveries to get through – but she makes her intention very clear: the monastery will become her tomb.[19] And a few months later, it does.

Something else that Lorna Gibb tells us about Hester is that her retreat into the mountains was "that favourite subject for inclusion in late 20th-century anthologies." Okay, you got me. I'm extremely late to the party, understood. Unlike many in this book, Hester does often appear in compendia of eccentrics. But the tale bears retelling: it's irresistible, right? Fancy European lady with all the advantages in the world casts them aside to trek around the desert on a velvet-bridled horse and live in a monastery with a serious water ingress problem. But Hester didn't start travelling until she'd already been the right-hand woman of the Prime Minister during a continent-engulfing war, and once she did, it took her a long time to find contentment. You might have to travel long distances before you find a home of your own.

CHAPTER 7
WILLIAM BUCKLAND[1]

teaches us that once you've eaten a mole, that's what
everyone's going to remember about you forever.

William Buckland (1784–1856) is one of the founding fathers of palaeontology. In fact, he gets into the subject so early that the word *palaeontology* isn't even invented yet. He calls himself a geologist by profession, but even that word is peel-the-wrapping-off new, coined when he was nine years old. He writes the first full account of a fossil dinosaur, *Megalosaurus* (even though the word *dinosaur* doesn't exist yet, either). An incredible accomplishment that forever changes the way we think about our planet and our place on it, I'm sure you'll agree. But that's not what you tend to hear about in books that mention William Buckland. If you're enough of a weirdo in your personal life, you could make the greatest scientific accomplishments in history and it won't matter – all people will want to talk about is that time you ate a mole.

Born in Axminster in Devon, William starts getting into geology as a boy, exploring the local Devonshire countryside and the area around his school, Winchester College, where he collects fossils and rocks. Y'know, like a normal teenager. He gets into Corpus Christi College in Oxford and becomes a Fellow in 1808, teaching classics to the undergrads and making rock-collecting expeditions all over Oxfordshire on the side, riding around the country on horseback in his academic gown with his friend, the excellently named W J Broderip (1789–1859).

In 1813, William starts working two jobs at once, becoming both the Reader in Mineralogy and Oxford's first ever Reader in Geology. Geology at the time is a brand-new field, looked on with suspicion by some Christians who are worried about this new science challenging the biblical story of Creation. At first, William is keen not to upset the apple-cart, stressing to his colleagues that, *Hey, you might have heard about geologists dating rocks that are older than the Bible says they should be, but that's not anything to do with William Buckland, no sir!* He explains in his lecture *Vindiciae geologicae* that the strata of gravels around Oxford are good evidence of Noah's Flood from the Book of Genesis, a conclusion he will gently row back from over the course of his career.

His lectures are also well known in Oxford for being, well, *fun*. Rather than have some dreary robed chap droning on in Latin about dead Greeks, William brings in maps and drawings to show, and passes around his rock samples. He throws in jokes, and gets on all fours, showing how the various extinct animals of Oxfordshire would walk and run. Sometimes he even says, *It's such a nice day today – why don't we have lectures outside?* taking his students on horseback field trips to quarries and hills around Oxford. His lectures are so popular that it isn't just students turning up – famous figures of the day like Cardinal John Henry Newman (1801–90) and geologist Charles Lyell (1797–1875) drop in to see William do his impression of a *Megalosaurus*.

Lest you think the life of an early-19th-century geologist is all pleasant pony rides and swanning around in voluminous robes, William is also not afraid to get his hands dirty for his experiments – *really* dirty. In 1821, he does an excavation in Kirkdale Cavern where he finds the bones of all sorts of animals you wouldn't have expected to find in the middle of Yorkshire: hyenas, elephants, hippopotamuses, rhinos, oxen and bears. He isn't the first to find exotic animals in Britain. Farmers had been accidentally digging up mammoth bones since the dawn of agriculture – but in William's day, the most common explanation for them is that they were brought over by the Romans, perhaps to fight in gladiatorial arenas. But the remains of these creatures are in a cave. Why would the Romans have put them there? William shows that hyenas must have lived wild in the cave, dragging their prey in for safe-keeping and a more relaxed dining experience. He even gets modern hyenas and feeds them ox bones, diligently going through their poo afterwards to show that the bone shards that come out the other end are just the same as the pieces of ox bone from the cave – they can only get that way by passing through a hyena first. Never let anyone tell you that palaeontology isn't glamorous.

In the following year, 1822, William receives a letter from a woman in Wales whose daughter, Mary Theresa Talbot, along with John and Daniel Davies, has been finding mammoth bones in Paviland Cave near

Swansea. When William visits the location in January 1823, he finds the oldest fossilized human remains then discovered, although he doesn't realize it. Just 15cm (6in) below the surface of the cave lies a partial skeleton, missing the head and most of the right-hand side, covered in a red ochre earth that has stained the bones bright crimson. We now know that the man to whom this skeleton belonged lived 35,000 years ago in a period that eggheads call by its Greek-derived name, the Upper Palaeolithic, but which sounds much cooler when you translate it into English as the Old Stone Age. Palaeontologists have since found evidence of several much earlier human species, like *Homo heidelbergensis* and *Homo neanderthelensis,* living in Britain, but the man from Paviland is a fully modern *Homo sapiens* – one of the first we know of on the island. He would have lived in a hunter-gatherer society, when Britain was much more sparsely populated. Around the world, Palaeolithic humans like this one were figuring out cave painting, making it to Australia, and even taking up the art of fishing, but were yet to cotton on to farming and all that it entails.

Unfortunately, William doesn't know any of this. In 1823, we're still a long way away from the understanding that extinct animals like mammoths even lived alongside humans, let alone radiocarbon dating or human evolution. So he puts the Paviland man in the Roman period at a mere 2,000 years old. William also, after some wavering, decides that the skeleton is female, which has led to it being known as "the Red Lady of Paviland" even now, long after we figured out that it's not a woman. William even comes up with a couple of different ideas as to the Red Lady's life. Maybe she was a murdered Roman tax collector, stashed in the cave by her killers who were smuggling illegal goods into the province; maybe she was a sex worker following the Roman army into Wales. Maybe she was even a witch, using the animal shoulder blades around her to tell fortunes! Although William is wrong about most of the finer details, the discovery of the Red Lady alone would be enough to put him in the history books as one of humanity's great early contributors to palaeontology. But he's got more up his sleeve yet.

He's earning £200 a year from his two readerships – not amazing money, but enough to scrape by on as a single, middle-class man in Oxford. Then all of a sudden, the plum position of canon of Christ Church Cathedral opens up, and William's powerful friends lobby to make sure he gets it. This job comes with a whopping £1,000 a year plus house. Finally, he has enough money to marry, and he chooses the formidable Mary Morland (1797–1857). Mary is a geologist, scientific illustrator and naturalist in her own right, albeit one shut out of a formal Oxford education because the university doesn't accept women. Before she marries William, she's already developed a close friendship with another early geologist Christopher Pegge (1765–1822), on whom she makes such an impression that when he dies he leaves her his fossil and mineral collection, which she promptly brings to the new house. She teaches herself to mend and clean fossils, makes models of them for further study and illustrates William's books, which are in large part written by her from his dictation and edited by her.

Together they fill their home to the brim with cool rocks and exotic pets. Drop by the Buckland place and you might see guinea pigs running across the dining-room table, or a pony popping its head in at the kitchen door, and in the garden shed, a fox, jackdaws, magpies and chickens. Once, William is staying up late thinking about some fossilized footprints he's seen, and he gets his wife up in the middle of the night and asks her to make some dough. Once they have a freshly flattened roll of pastry, he gets his pet tortoise to walk across it so that he can compare the footprints. However, when he recreates this experiment a second time for his scientific and philosophical dinner-party guests, he doesn't make Mary repeat the baking. Instead, this time everyone pitches in, rolling up their sleeves and getting their fine suits covered in flour.

But William's big contribution to palaeontology, the thing that makes him a truly historic scientist, comes in 1824, when he publishes *Notice on the Megalosaurus or great Fossil Lizard of Stonesfield*. In it, he details several odd bones, beautifully illustrated in his paper by Mary, that have washed up in the Oxford Museum's collection over the years that belong to no animal yet known to science – a huge lizard, nine metres (30ft) long, with massive, sharp teeth. He describes and names this dinosaur *before we even have the word dinosaur*, calling it *Megalosaurus*, which means "big lizard" (it's a pretty vague name for a dinosaur, but like I said, we don't really know about dinosaurs yet). William doesn't even have the whole thing. All he has is a bit of the spine, hips, one back leg and a jaw with some teeth in it. Like with the Red Lady of Paviland, he doesn't get everything right first time. He thinks that *Megalosaurus* walked on all fours and was amphibious, a bit like a huge crocodile, whereas we now know that it walked on two legs and was shaped a bit like a *Tyrannosaurus rex*. But before the discovery of *T. rex* in the US in the 1870s, *Megalosaurus* is *the* carnivorous dinosaur, pictured in books stomping around Oxfordshire, taking chunks out of smaller beasts left and right.

Unlike the Cretaceous *T. rex* though, *Megalosaurus* was a true Jurassic dinosaur, living 170 million years ago. That's so old that it's older than spider webs, older than flowers, *older than the Atlantic Ocean* – the continents were still joined together. This means that animals could walk all over and find themselves in what look like very different places to us today. For example, *Brachiosaurus* was in both Tanzania and Wyoming, and *Stegosaurus* remains are found in places as far apart as Lindi in Tanzania, Chongqing in China, and Swindon in England. In prehistoric times, Stonesfield in Oxfordshire, where William's *Megalosaurus* was found, was hot, humid and swampy. This is also the period when *Megalosaurus'* smaller theropod relatives started evolving into actual, honest-to-goodness birds like *Archaeopteryx* – so *Megalosaurus* shared Stonesfield with pterosaurs perfect for a mid-morning snack; even bigger, massive, lumbering herbivores like *Cetiosaurus*; and huge dragonflies 25cm (10in) wide (yes, unbelievably, scientists have found *dragonfly wings* preserved from that long ago!).

Today, the species that William called *Megalosaurus* is now properly called *Megalosaurus bucklandii* after its namer, and *Megalosaurus* fossils are being found as far away as Tibet. William twice becomes President of the Geological Society, as well as a Fellow of the Royal Society and President of the British Association for the Advancement of Science. His work is still referred to by palaeontologists and natural history museums 200 years on. But if you go looking up his story, you'll find authors focusing on his much weirder habits instead.

William Buckland has a much more bizarre hobby, which is – and I can scarcely believe I'm writing this – to eat his way through the animal kingdom. The Bucklands host dinner parties where they serve hedgehogs, toasted field mice, crocodile steak and puppies. If you're wondering, William variously reports that the worst creatures he's ever eaten are a mole and a bluebottle. The *strangest* thing William ever eats is recorded by writer Augustus Hare (1804–1903). In this story, William visits the stately home at Nuneham Park, Oxfordshire, and is shown the preserved heart of a French king. This part of the story isn't totally implausible. The practice of cutting out the heart to be buried separately from the body was once relatively common among European nobility, especially in the days before refrigeration when you might die weeks or months away from the church where your family is buried. That way, the rapidly mouldering body can be buried where you die, and the heart can be embalmed and brought home. We know that the heart of French king Henri III (died 1589) was buried separately from his body, and that as recently as 1795 Louis XVII's heart was removed by the surgeon who performed his autopsy, pickled in alcohol, and kept in a crystal urn before being buried in the royal basilica at Saint-Denis. Hare does not deign to tell us which French king's heart ends up being passed around the Nuneham dinner table on the fateful night, but whoever's it was, when William is shown it, he supposedly says, "I have eaten many strange things, but I have never eaten the heart of a king before," and before anyone can stop him, he reaches out, stuffs it into his mouth, and swallows it![2]

I should be clear that I don't find this story plausible. I can't find any French king's heart that's gone missing, Hare wasn't there himself to witness this event, and he's not the most reliable of writers. It is true that William has a very *varied* diet. But his gastronomic experiments aren't simply the result of idle curiosity – he may have a greater purpose in mind. William is an early member of London Zoo, which in 1825 produces a founding document detailing its main aim: "the introduction of new varieties, breeds and races of animals, for the purpose of domestication."[3] In other words, when it is first founded, the zoo wants to be a kind of garden centre for the animal kingdom, finding new animals both to pull the plough and to end up being eaten. It makes a certain kind of sense. As the British Empire is expanding, British scientists and naturalists are realizing just how many different species there are in the world, and at the same time just how few of them are domesticated. Perhaps, they wonder, there's an animal out there that would be better at making wool than a sheep, or would make sausages faster and tastier than a pig? Surely it can't be that the few animals we decided to domesticate thousands of years ago just *happen* to be the best and most profitable ones for the purpose? Maybe there are animals out there that can make things we haven't even thought to use yet, so let's put them all together in a big park where we can study them and find out if and how they can be useful. Perhaps William hopes that his culinary adventures in the animal kingdom might yield cheaper, more plentiful food for London's poor, or easily transportable foodstuffs to be grown in Britain's colonies – though it's hard to see how "French kings' hearts" could be a scalable resource.

Despite all his geological and palaeontological work, William Buckland went down in history as the man who was mega-weird at dinner parties. Whatever achievements you have, however far you push the bounds of science, beware: if you've got a funny habit, especially if it's a bit gross, that's going to be the thing that people remember about you; what is worse, some jerk might make up a story about you eating human body parts after you've died and *that* might be the thing that everyone remembers about you. So next time you're at a dinner party and someone's passing around the heart of a deceased European monarch, just say no!

CHAPTER 8

ELEANOR RYKENER

teaches us that people are more interested in juicy
gossip than in enforcing their moral codes.

It's 1394 on a busy street in London, and a person is caught having sex behind a market stall with a paying customer, a man named John Britby. When she's first arrested, the person gives her name as Eleanor Rykener, but later admits that she was born John.

Her story comes from a single court transcript held in the London Metropolitan Archives, detailing a time when she was interrogated at the Guildhall. We don't have a birth certificate or a tombstone or a diary. The only time she appears in the historical record is in this one short document, which attracted no attention for years until it was rediscovered in the 1990s by historians Ruth Mazo Karras and David Lorenzo Boyd.

Which pronouns should we use to describe this person? We don't have anything written in Rykener's own hand, so we don't know what she went by. We don't know whether she thought of herself as a woman, or as a man using a female alias, or as something else. The court transcript describes her as a man throughout, and that's generally how academics have treated her in the past; but it also says that she spent time alternately living as Eleanor, wearing women's clothes, and as John, wearing men's, so perhaps it would be best to use the singular "they", or even alternate between "he" and "she". You could make a case for either of these approaches, but in this book I'm going to favour the approach taken by Dr Mireille Pardon of Berea College, Kentucky, who points out that this is someone who was born "John", whom the court calls "John", and yet who gets up in front of the court officials and introduces herself as "Eleanor", which must be a terrifying thing to do in a time when crossing gender lines means not just incurring the wrath of society, but also that of God. In doing so, she tells us how she wants to be seen, and she chooses her female name; so, I'm going to use "she" here.

When Eleanor is hauled up in front of the court at London's Guildhall, we don't know if she is coerced into testifying, but we do know that she is not herself on trial for a criminal offence. Neither prostitution nor sodomy is illegal at this time, and so the secular court in which Eleanor finds herself has no jurisdiction over these crimes. Buggery won't be illegal in England for another 150 years. Instead, medieval England has two court systems running in parallel – the secular courts that answer to the king (or in this case, to London's Lord Mayor), which dish out justice for crimes ranging from murder to stray livestock; and the ecclesiastical courts run by the Church, which deal with moral issues like adultery, heresy, missing Sunday services, and particularly for Eleanor, sodomy, fornication and prostitution.

Now, just because the ecclesiastical courts are not the king's courts doesn't mean they're not to be feared. The Church courts can have you fined, whipped or excommunicated. They can order punishments designed to humiliate you, like having to stand at the door of your parish church on Sunday, telling everyone your crime as they come in for Mass. But we have no record of Eleanor ever running up against the Church courts. The secular court at the Guildhall is not interested in her moral failings but in what *juicy gossip she can dish*. They want to know who she is, what she does, and they especially want her to name and shame all the priests and nuns she's had sex with.

Although we're denied an internal exploration of Eleanor's gender, which might be what we're most interested in today, we do get a short recounting of her fascinating life. She says that she lives and dresses as John, until one day she is given women's clothing by a woman named Elizabeth Brouderer in Bishopsgate, in London's East End. Brouderer is a notorious procuress operating under the guise of a legitimate embroidery businesswoman, and she inducts Eleanor into the world of women's work. A woman can do many different kinds of work in medieval England, but what she does is often dependent on the job of the man supporting her, be that a father or a husband. Thus if your husband is an apothecary, then you're an apothecary too. If your husband is an armourer, then you're an armourer too. These trades are strictly controlled by medieval guilds which prohibit women from joining unless they are the widows of members continuing their husbands' profession, so there are a lot of jobs that you can *only* get through your husband. But there are a few which are considered almost entirely "women's work", and both sex and embroidery fall under that umbrella. So these are jobs that John can't get, but Eleanor can. Brouderer teaches her both.

Sex work is regulated in medieval London. Officially, it's only supposed to take place outside the city walls, in places like the south bank of the river, where the nights are wild and the laws don't matter, and where Mary Frith (see Chapter 5) will sell stolen goods 300 years later. Southwark is owned by the Bishop of Winchester, who sees no contradiction in being both a man of the Church and a landlord to brothel keepers. Indeed, the area is so well known for its bordellos that the women who work in them are nicknamed "Winchester Geese". In reality, there are also a few thoroughfares within the city walls where prostitution is openly tolerated, if not entirely legal. These often have tell-tale names, ranging from the charming (Love Lane) to the filthy (Gropecunt Lane). There are some laws protecting sex workers from the worst predations of brothel keepers, who are forbidden to beat their staff or make them work while sick, but if your brothel keeper is a respected man, it will be difficult to bring a case against him.

It's not always clear if Eleanor's clients know her sex or not. She calls some of her clients "ignotos", meaning "unsuspecting", and certainly without bedside lamps or street lights or the standby light on the TV, it might be dark in her bedroom, but repeat clients surely must know what they're getting, right? However, there is some deception to her work, just not in the way you might expect. Blackmail seems to be just as much part of the job as needlecraft. Eleanor tells the story of one of her early clients, a rector named Phillip. Men of the Church are supposed to be celibate in this period, so this is particularly juicy gossip for Eleanor to be dropping before the court. Eleanor steals two gowns from Phillip, and when he demands their return, she tells him, *I'll have you know, my husband is a very important man, and if you want them back, you'll have to sue him.* She also describes how a favourite scam of Brouderer's is to send a customer to bed with Brouderer's daughter, Alice, only to switch Alice out in the morning for Eleanor. Brouderer would then tell the customer that actually Eleanor was the one that they had "misbehaved" with, presumably for the purposes of further blackmail.

Once she's got the hang of the job under Brouderer, Eleanor travels around Oxfordshire, moving from town to town, picking up odd jobs and a string of sexual partners, sometimes as John, sometimes as Eleanor. She works as an embroiderer and a barmaid, but also mentions a long-term relationship she had "as a man" with Joan Matthew, a woman.

Included in her list of partners are Oxford scholars like Sir William Foxlee, Franciscan monks called Brother Michael and Brother John, and also "many nuns" and "women both married and otherwise", but she says her favourite clients are clergymen, because they pay better.[1]

Eleanor's story is almost unique, but not quite. There are some other accounts of queer people and people blurring gender lines in medieval England, from ordinary working-class folk right up to the king himself. In 1235, Henry de Bracton's *De Legibus et Consuetudinibus Angliae* (On the Laws and Customs of England) lists the three genders as "male, female, or hermaphrodite".[2] The 13th-century French *Roman de Silence* tells the fictional story of Silence, who is born female but decides to live as a man. He trains as a knight and a minstrel and goes on adventures, becoming a hero and an exemplary person. There's also the Christian story of St Marinos, who is raised as a woman but decides to live as a monk. He passes so completely for a male that for a while he is even expelled from his monastery because they believe he's impregnated a local girl. He could disprove their story by outing himself, but he stays quiet, living as a beggar and raising the stranger's child rather than reveal himself; his true status isn't discovered until after his death. There are also real-life cases like that of Joan of Arc, who is burned to death in 1431 for refusing to wear women's clothes just 36 years after Eleanor's trial – such a short time later that Eleanor might still be around to hear of it.

Medieval kings like William II, Richard I and Edward II have also been studied by queer historians. William II never marries and has no children. Chronicler Orderic Vitalis (1075–1142) states that there are "loathsome Ganymedes" at his court who "abused themselves with foul sodomite-things."[3] Before Richard I gets the English throne, he is very close to the French king, Philip Augustus, and one chronicler writes, "Richard, duke of Aquitaine, son of the king of England, remained with Philip, the king of France, who so honoured him for so long that they ate every day at the same table and from the same dish, and at night their beds did not separate them. And the king of France loved him as his own soul; and they loved each other so much that the king of England was absolutely astonished at the vehement love between them and marvelled at what it could mean."[4] The writer characterizes the strength of feeling as surprising and unusual, but not immoral. King Edward II has a low-born favourite at court named Piers Gaveston. There's no proof that their relationship was sexual, but at the time people certainly thought it was unusually close, with one chronicler saying that the king "straightaway felt so much love for him [Gaveston] that he entered into a covenant of brotherhood with him and chose and firmly resolved to bind himself to him, before all mortals, in an unbreakable bond of love."[5] When Edward gets married, he spends so much time paying attention to Gaveston during the wedding that his wife's family actually walk out partway through!

However, what Eleanor doesn't have in the 1390s is the modern terminology we use to talk about queer people today: *lesbian, gay, bisexual, transgender*. The word *gay* has existed since the 14th century, but it doesn't gain its meaning of *homosexual* until the 1920s. *Bisexual* is coined in 1824 to mean "having both sexual organs", and the meaning doesn't flip to refer to "being attracted to both genders" until 1914. *Transgender* is very new indeed, coming from the 1970s, and even the older word *transsexual* is only from the 1950s. Of all of the terms for which LGBTQ+ is an abbreviation, *lesbian* is the oldest. Originally it just means "from the Greek island of Lesbos", meaning you can have Lesbian wine! But Lesbos is also known for the female Greek poet Sappho, whose love poems are addressed to both men and women. People have been saying "is she . . . you know . . . from the island of Lesbos?" since perhaps the 1730s, but the main meaning really was just "from Lesbos" until the 20th century, when the term "female homosexual" gained general currency. And indeed, *heterosexual* only goes back to 1894, and isn't in widespread use until the 1960s. These days, we generally talk about sexuality and gender in terms of identity. All our words refer to what you *are* on the inside.

In Eleanor's day, people don't think of who they're attracted to or who they sleep with as part of their identity. Instead, sexuality is something you *do*. Just as we in the modern day don't think of certain people as being more susceptible to, say, adultery, in medieval society sodomy is thought of as a vice that anyone might fall prey to. Indeed, historian Randolph Trumbach argues that before the modern era, people generally assumed that most men had some kind of attraction to young, beautiful men, just as we often assume that men might have some kind of attraction to women who aren't their wives – they're just not supposed to act on it.[6]

So if you're asking, "Was Eleanor non-binary? Was she a bi man in drag? Was she a trans woman?", then I'm afraid there's no definite answer. It seems like even the mayor's court didn't know what to make of her. We have no record of her ever being prosecuted for a crime, or indeed of anything of her at all outside this one short transcript. Once the ink was dry on the court document, she disappeared from the historical record. The officials asking her questions were simply not as interested in her gender as they were in the names and whereabouts of her clergy clientele. If Eleanor could reach through history and tell you anything, it would probably be to keep your blackmail records handy if you should ever need them – find good enough dirt on someone else, and your own crimes will be overlooked: *people are more interested in juicy gossip than in enforcing their moral codes.*

CHAPTER 9

JAMES CHUMA AND ABDULLAH DAVID SUSI

teach us that going for a walk can do more good than you think.

One of the most famous British explorers is Scottish missionary David Livingstone (1813–73), who travels all over East Africa trying to convert the locals to Christianity, end slavery and determine the source of the Nile. He scores nought out of three on those, but he is still fondly remembered, and he does end up finding out a lot about Africa that Europeans didn't know yet. He's the first European to get from Luanda on the west coast (in modern Angola) to Quelimane on the east coast (in modern Mozambique), along the way becoming the first European to see the Mosi-oa-Tunya, which he names "Victoria Falls". To this day, although most African places named after Europeans, such as Rhodesia (now Zimbabwe) and Leopoldville (now Kinshasa), have been renamed, there are still schools, hospitals and towns named after David. He compiles vast amounts of notes on African geography, botany and anthropology, and without James Chuma (c1850–82) and Abdullah David Susi (c1850–91), chunks of this material would not have survived. When David dies on the shore of Lake Tanganyika, he's been out of touch with Britain for years, and his notebooks are yellow with age and falling to bits. They might easily have rotted by that lake with him. But James and Abdullah, two of his employees, pick up his body and his notes and walk 2,250km (1,400 miles) across the continent *with a dead body* so that David Livingstone and his writings can make it back home.

Chuma is from the Yao people of southeast Africa. He is rescued from slavery as a child by David, who puts him in a school in India, where he decides to get baptized and is given the Christian name "James".

David calls him a "boisterous roaring laughter-provoking boy" who "reads frequently".[1] Abdullah Susi is from Chupanga in Mozambique, and he first joins the team when David employs him as a woodcutter. Abdullah doesn't get baptized until after Livingstone's death, when he gets the Christian name "David" (but to avoid confusion here, I'm going to call Susi "Abdullah" and Livingstone "David"). They're both recruited for David's 1866 expedition through Tanzania to locate the source of the Nile. If you're picturing a group of three intrepid heroes hacking through the undergrowth with one machete between them, let me adjust that for you – the first three months see more than 200 people joining the caravan for at least part of the trip, including Indian soldiers and boys, porters from the Comoro Islands, an Arab guide named Ben Ali, and local Makonde people, plus buffaloes, camels, mules, donkeys and dogs.[2]

By all accounts, David isn't a great leader. People desert his expeditions a lot, and he's not above hitting people to make them obey him. After one boy, Baraka, refuses to work, David writes that "a gentle chastisement would not do and I gave it him in earnest till he was satisfied he had made a mistake in ringleading."[3] By June 1866 he's getting increasingly frustrated with some of his party, writing that his soldiers keep abusing his camels and the boys are refusing to do their work. After the soldiers kill his last buffalo, he reluctantly pays them to leave. By mid-September the Comoro Islands men also refuse to go any further after hearing about raiding parties up ahead. By the end of the month, the huge party that David began with has been whittled down to just ten people: himself, six boys from India and three Africans, including James and Abdullah.

It doesn't get any easier with a slimmed-down crew, either. By the beginning of 1867, they're being slowed by heavy rain, food shortages and unreliable guides. They have to keep stopping for weeks any time someone gets sick, but in April they finally reach Lake Tanganyika. After that, they set off toward the Luangwa River in Zambia, and by November they're heading to Ujiji in Tanzania and then to Lake Mweru in Uganda.

In April 1868 tensions flare up in the party. James and Abdullah have both found girlfriends that they don't want to leave behind, and everyone is getting tired of this interminable tramping around. They tell David they don't want to go any further. David is furious, and even fires his gun at Abdullah before leaving both him and James behind. They go their separate ways for a whole year before being reunited in a village David calls Kabwabwata on the shores of Lake Mweru, when both James and Abdullah rejoin the party. Despite their differences, James and Abdullah soon become loyal to David, following him through adversity and triumph (mostly adversity). They're still getting stuck for months at a time while they wait for supplies to reach them and for illnesses to pass, and by April 1873 David is thoroughly sick, too weak to walk or ride. James and Abdullah make a kind of stretcher called a *kitanda* to carry him on, but even then he's in so much pain that they have to keep putting him down to rest. Slowly, finally, they make it to a place they call "Chitambo's village", where they lay him down in a house. Before dawn on 1 May 1873, Abdullah enters the house to find David has died.

This is the moment when things get really tense. All sorts of stuff can go wrong here. The head of the village, Chitambo, might fine them severely for bringing someone to his village to die. The other servants might make off with David's stuff or even destroy it. They might decide to head home, leaving James and Abdullah unable to carry everything back by themselves. But it's at this point that James and Abdullah take charge and truly come into their own, becoming what David's editor, Horace Waller (1833–96), will call the "captains of the caravan".[4] Taking a big risk, they call everyone in the party together to open David's luggage, so that all his valuables can be counted up with everyone present, to prevent anything from going missing. Together, they choose the member of the group with the best writing skills to be the scribe and make a full inventory: this is Yamuza, another member of the Yao people, who is also known as "Jacob Wainwright".

Next, they arrange for David to get a proper funeral, and prepare the body for the long journey home. They open his chest and remove his heart and viscera, pulling out a blood clot "as large as a man's hand" in the process.[5] These they bury in the village. Jacob Wainwright reads a Christian burial service, and they also find an African mourner to give a local-style funeral. Horace Waller gives the translation of the mourner's song as "Today the Englishman is dead/Who has different hair from ours:/Come round to see the Englishman."[6] Maybe it sounds better in the original language? (David is from Scotland, not England, but to be fair, he calls himself and his expedition "English" all the time, so the mourner probably wasn't to know.) Then they pack David's chest cavity with salt, douse his face in brandy, wrap him in fabric and tree bark, and then cover all that in tar. Finally he's ready to go.

Hoisting the body on sticks and carrying it on their shoulders, the party then heads for Zanzibar. Along the way, they have adventures of their own. They cross the Luapula River, which is not a simple wade-across job: it's 6.5km (4 miles) wide. A lion kills their donkey in the middle of the night; one of their party accidentally shoots a local in the leg and they watch the surgery the victim receives to set the bone. One night when they're very tired and looking for somewhere to rest, they find a place they call Chawendé's town, which won't let them in. They look around for wood to build their own shelter outside, but they can't find anything, so they force their way through the gates and start a fight that turns into a shoot-out. They drive out the locals, who go to get help from nearby villages, besieging James, Abdullah and their party inside the walls. In response, James and Abdullah's party start burning down houses and firing on people outside, killing several and seizing the village for themselves for a week before moving on.

Mostly, though, the people they meet along the way are only too happy to help them. Chiefs give them gifts, guard their belongings and allow them hunting rights on their territory. Partway through the walk, they start doubling back on places they've already visited with David, so people remember them and are happy to grant them hospitality.

After months on the move, they hear about a British party nearby who are looking for David, and they double their pace to catch up. The British party is led by a Lieutenant Cameron, and they tell him their story. Cameron tries to convince them to bury the body right there in the Manyara region of Tanzania, but they refuse – even though the country around them is beset with war between different peoples, they believe it's worth the risk to try to get David home. However, they can't stop Cameron's men from rooting through David's stuff and making off with his scientific instruments – compasses, barometers, sextants and so on. They quickly leave Cameron and his men behind.

As they make their way through Tanzania, the territory becomes more dangerous, and they're worried that people will steal or destroy David's body, or think that it's bad luck to be carrying a body around (to be fair, it's not an indicator of someone who's doing *great*) and chase them off. So as a diversion, they make a fake body out of grass, shroud it in cotton, and hold a very solemn funeral for it, hoping to make people believe that they've buried David. Then they take David's actual body and hide it among the rest of their stuff.

Finally they reach the coast at Bagamoyo in Tanzania, from where they get a boat to Zanzibar. If you try recreating their journey today, Google Maps will tell you it's a 325-hour walk from where they buried David's heart to Bagamoyo – a distance of 1447km (900 miles). That's in the best of circumstances, with no rest, illness, conflict or food shortages, and with modern roads and bridges. In the 1870s, James and Abdullah's route is a whopping 2,250km (1,400 miles) long and takes them nine months.[7]

From Zanzibar, the Royal Geographical Society is able to collect David's body and take it back to Britain. James and Abdullah don't follow it immediately, although Jacob Wainwright does, and he is a pall-bearer at David's funeral in Westminster Abbey on 18 April 1874 – carrying him right to the end. James and Abdullah follow a few months later. Horace Waller credits the survival of David's last year of writings "in the first place to his native attendants".[8] Sorting through them is a huge task. David had filled notebooks "to the last inch of paper"[9] with titbits he collected about the names of rivers, map sketches, drawings of African plants, quotations from books, pressed flowers, and notes on the size of the Moon. Horace could easily have given up in exasperation at these unsorted, yellowed, scruffy notebooks, but James and Abdullah were "at my elbow so long as I required them to help me amidst the pile of MSS [manuscripts] and maps. Their knowledge of the countries they travelled in is most remarkable, and . . . I found them actual geographers of no mean attainments."[10] Once, when Horace has questions about a particular river system, Abdullah goes away for a while with a pen and paper and returns a few hours later with a sketched map of all the rivers in the area.

While in England, James and Abdullah wear English-style suits for the first time, although adding the customary cloth cap or top hat seems to have been a step too far for them. They stay in the country for a few months, during which they are presented to the Royal Geographical Society and given medals for their intrepid and dauntless efforts. Both will go on to lead exploration and missionary expeditions, commanding hundreds of men from different parts of Africa with their leadership skills and command of many languages. Abdullah joins the explorer Henry Morton Stanley (1841–1904) on his trip up the Congo, during which they found what is now the capital of the Democratic Republic of the Congo, Kinshasa. James works on one of the most successful African explorations of the 19th century with Joseph Thomson (1858–95), who says that there is "certainly none equal" to him as a leader of caravans.[11]

When James and Abdullah first set out on their journey with a tarred, disembowelled corpse, it might have seemed like a mad idea (well, it *was* a mad idea), but it brought them fame, prestige and work at the top of their profession, and helped to preserve accounts and knowledge that would otherwise have been lost. All that from a walk in the woods? So the next time your FitBit is yelling at you for your low step count, or you're pondering whether to take the car, remember: going for a walk can do more good than you think.

CHAPTER 10

BLACK AGNES

teaches us to keep our castles well dusted.

It's 1338, and Black Agnes' castle, Dunbar, Scotland, is hemmed in on all sides. In front of her is the English army, and behind her a precipitous drop into the North Sea. She's surrounded, with no big army of her own, but she still manages to keep her castle, drive off her foes, and look fabulous while doing it. How does she manage this? Well, she keeps the castle walls well dusted, of course.

The 13th and 14th centuries aren't a great time for Scotland. In the 1290s, the succession goes completely up the spout after Scottish King Alexander III dies falling from his horse, leaving behind only a three-year-old girl to take the throne, who herself dies at the age of just seven. So Scottish nobles do what all nobles do when there's a succession crisis: they start feuding among themselves and pushing their own claims to the throne.

Into this mess steps the English king, Edward I (reigned 1272–1307). He says, *Don't worry, Scotland, I will help you.* He offers to give one man the military backing needed to take and keep the throne. But of course, there's a catch: he wants all of Scotland's castles, and to be the new Scottish king's overlord. When the new king does something the English don't like, Edward brings in his army, deposes him, and seizes the Scottish royal regalia. For the next hundred years or so, English kings are in and out of Scotland, pillaging and fighting battles, while Scottish heroes like William Wallace and Robert the Bruce are trying to beat them back. By the 1330s, when our story takes place, we're down to two main claimants to the Scottish throne: the English-backed Edward Balliol and the Scottish-backed David II. Unfortunately, David is still a child, and so isn't in much of a position to be fighting wars. In 1335,

English king Edward III (reigned 1327–77) invades Scotland in order to install his puppet Edward Balliol on the throne. And in January 1338, two English nobles, Richard Fitzalan and William Montagu, lay siege to Dunbar Castle, Agnes' home.

Agnes (*c*1312–69) is the Countess of Dunbar, but she's sometimes known in history books as "Black Agnes" because, as one 16th-century source says, "sho was blak skynnit [she was black-skinned]."[1] She probably wasn't "black" in the sense that we'd think of today, but perhaps she was dark-skinned compared to the very fair colour expected for medieval maidens. She's the daughter of the Earl and Countess of Moray, and sometime around 1320 she marries the Earl of Dunbar and moves into Dunbar Castle.

Dunbar is in a strategic location in the southeast of Scotland. If you're an English army marching toward Edinburgh, the capital, you basically have to deal with Dunbar first – if you try to go around it, its men will march out and attack you. The castle is a forbidding place, built on a crag of rock, surrounded on three sides by the sea. It's been used as a fort since at least the 7th century. When the English arrive in 1338, Agnes' husband is away fighting elsewhere, so it's up to her to defend her home. We don't know whether she was afraid or eager, but a siege is a pretty terrifying prospect for both sides.

Sieges are actually how most fighting works in this period. Rather than having two armies in the middle of a field running at each other like you see in movies, instead you have a castle with possibly hundreds of inhabitants (much more expensive to film than a field), and an army camping outside its walls, trying to get in. Sieges are a test of endurance – who can last the longest? If you're the one in the castle, all your farmland is outside the walls, so it's not easy to get food. But if you're the besieging army, well, you've got to keep everyone fed too, and your knights only owe you a certain number of days' service per year. If your siege goes on too long, they might say, *Well, that's my time up! I'm going home!* Also, you're a big army camping in one place for a long time with no proper sewage system, so every day the siege continues, the likelihood increases that some horrible disease is going to rip through the encampment.

In an effort to speed things up, a besieging army will bring siege equipment like catapults, trebuchets and battering rams. These are specialized pieces of technology that have to be operated by people who are trained for them. Sometimes armies even dig tunnels underneath the walls, and the castle will have its own counter-tunnellers trying to find the enemy excavations – absolute nightmare jobs in an age without electric lighting or mechanical digging equipment. While the armies wait for the walls to be breached, the besieging knights, who can't operate the siege equipment and won't dig tunnels, might be sent to do *chevauchée*, burning crops in the countryside, setting everyone's house on fire in the surrounding area and looting everything they can in order to deprive their opponents of resources. Meanwhile the people inside the castle play a tense waiting game. Convention of the time states that if you're being besieged and you surrender, you have to be treated with a certain amount of respect as reward for not having wasted the besiegers' time. But if you refuse to surrender, all bets are off. The invaders are allowed to pillage the castle for booty and kill anyone inside that they please, sparing only the clergymen and the chapel.

Agnes refuses to surrender, and so the English put up their siege engines – great catapults that can launch massive stones at terrifying speed toward the walls, and battering rams to knock down the doors. Agnes is undeterred. Rather than cowering in the cellars, she goes up onto the battlements, sometimes while missiles are raining down and she could easily get her head knocked clean off her shoulders. After a bombardment, she sends a lady-in-waiting up in her finest clothes and beautifully dressed hair to pull out her lace handkerchief and casually flick the settling dust off the walls. According to one account by the Scottish clergyman Andrew of Wyntoun: "They threw great stones, both hard and heavy, at the walls; but they did no damage to them. And once they had shot, a young lady, dressed prettily and well, wiped the wall with a towel so that they could see and be the more annoyed."[2] This has two effects: partly it really infuriates the English, who can tell when they're being made fun of; and partly the immaculate dress is a message: *We're not struggling. We're doing so well that we can swan about in fancy dresses and spend time on our hair! We've got plenty of supplies here to outlast you.* And the message is sent without uttering a word. Not that Agnes can't do snappy comebacks if the occasion calls for it. When William Montagu pulls up a huge battering ram called a "sow", she yells down, "'Beware, Montagow, for farrow shall thy sow!'"[3] – "Your pig will bear a litter"; in other words, his actions will have consequences.

Perhaps you had to be there.

She also tries to trick Montagu. At one point, someone in Dunbar is sent out as a double agent, pretending that he'll let the English in through the gate in return for a hefty wodge of cash. Montagu agrees and eagerly goes over to the gate, sees it wide open, but just before he can go in, a smaller fish named John Copeland wanders in through the gate instead. Thinking that Copeland is Montagu, the defenders spring their trap, slamming down the portcullis behind Copeland. They don't manage to catch Montagu, but they do now have a pretty good hostage, and Montagu heads back to the camp, furious that he's been tricked.

But for all her bravado, Agnes is badly in need of supplies to keep her people going. If she can't get what's required by land, she can try to get it by sea. Montagu has thought of that, and has stumped up a huge amount of money to get two galleys from Genoa, Italy, to blockade the castle on its seaward side. Luckily for Agnes, she has an ally in the shape of the highly successful Scottish guerrilla warrior Alexander Ramsay (c1290–1342). Under the cloak of night, Ramsay sneaks past the Genoese ships in a small boat, brings much-needed supplies to the castle, and then sneaks back out again. The English captains see Agnes on the walls, not looking any thinner or more tired, still dressed in her best, and they're dumbfounded. *How is she doing this?* Eventually, Edward III himself has to come to see this lady in person. When he gets there, he and his captains agree to give up on Dunbar. After more than four months, Agnes is victorious. The siege costs the English £6,000 and is a complete waste of time.

Agnes isn't the only medieval lady who fought in battle. Although war in this period is primarily considered a man's activity, a perhaps surprisingly large number of noblewomen also get stuck into the fray. This is because of how the job of a noble is seen at the time. Medieval writers divide people into three classes, not by how much they earn, but by their role in society. So instead of working class, middle class and upper class, we have "those who work" (farmers), "those who pray" (the clergy), and "those who fight" (the nobles). Ideally, each class supports the others. Those who work feed everyone, those who pray save everyone's souls, and those who fight keep everyone safe. Therefore, if you are a member of the nobility, your entire job is to go to war to protect the people who live in your territory. And if you're a bloke, then you'll be trained for it from a young age, but when there are no men around, the women in this class are expected to step up too. In the 11th century, Isabel of Conches, a French noblewoman, "rode armed as a knight among the knights."[4] In the English civil war that followed the death of Henry I in 1135, the Empress Matilda leads armies against Stephen, her cousin and the rival claimant to the throne, negotiates treaties and mints her own currency. Petronella of Leicester participates in the revolt of 1173–4 against English King Henry II and is captured wearing armour. Dame Nicola de la Haye takes part in the Siege of Lincoln in 1217, and the 15th-century writer Christine de Pizan says that any noblewoman "ought to know how to use weapons and be familiar with everything that pertains to them. . . . She should know how to launch an attack or to defend against one, if the situation calls for it. She should take care that her fortresses are well garrisoned."[5] She could be writing about Agnes.

At the same time, Agnes' dusting and her insistence on dressing in fine clothes, even in the midst of a siege, shows that she's not willing to give up being ladylike, either. Medieval Scotland, as seen in Hollywood movies like *Brave* and, well, *Braveheart*, is often stereotyped as a very macho culture, where big beardy warriors lob cabers around. Scottish sociologist Barbara Littlewood writes, "The heroes and villains of our popular histories, with the exception of Mary [Queen of Scots], are invariably male", and "popular representations of Scottish men continue to celebrate the inarticulate (except if drunk, or discussing football), physically competent (except if drunk, or dealing with the weans) man's man."[6] There's not a lot of space in these stories for fancy ladies like Agnes, but history shows that her strategy works well.

While keeping your castle supplied and trying to capture the enemy was vitally, materially important, it was the feminine touches in Agnes' strategy that were really demoralizing to the English. So if you want to follow her example when you're being besieged on all sides: don't let them see your weakness, carry on as if nothing is wrong, come up with a few snappy ripostes and keep your castle well dusted.

CHAPTER 11

MARGERY KEMPE

teaches us to get a second pair of eyes on our projects early.

Margery Kempe (*c*1373–after 1438) is an illiterate, middle-class woman from Norfolk who, despite several disadvantages, manages to write what's been called the first autobiography in the English language, known as *The Book of Margery Kempe.* In it, she describes intense religious visions where she not only sees Jesus Christ, but hears, touches, and sometimes even smells him, too. The visions lead her to give up her ordinary life as a housewife and travel widely throughout Christendom, living off the charity of others and speaking to as many religious people as she can. Finally, toward the end of her life, she enlists the help of a scribe to write down her extraordinary adventures. It is difficult enough to write a book, let alone one entirely through dictation. But to add to her misfortune, the scribe inconsiderately drops dead partway through the work. She takes his notes to a second scribe, hoping to continue the book, only for him to tell her, *You've been scammed, love – this is gibberish.* The first scribe's notes are completely illegible. She has to start again from scratch. If only she'd had a trusted friend who could have read it over early on, so much work wouldn't have been wasted.

As a very early autobiography, Margery's book hasn't quite nailed down the expected formula yet. It's not always clear what order the events she describes happen in. Things we'd consider hugely important, like when she was born, or the names of her children, she completely omits. But from what we can piece together, she is born sometime around 1373 in the town now known as King's Lynn, then known as Bishop's Lynn or simply Lynn. Her father is a local bigwig: he's been mayor five times and also an MP, an alderman, a coroner, a Justice of the Peace and a chamberlain. She tells us how important her dad was in order to compare him unfavourably to her husband, who is nowhere near as important. Oof.

She doesn't tell us much about her childhood, so we can only speculate on how she is raised, but one thing we do know is that although her dad is presumably pretty well-off, she isn't taught to read. If she had been, it would have been unusual for a girl in the 1370s. Tuition on reading might be available through your local cathedral or friary, but it's often expensive, far from home, and meant for boys only. By 1400, the literacy rate for men in urban areas of England is only about 20 per cent, and the number is much lower for women and men in rural areas.

There's a common misconception that medieval people married young, in their teens, but Margery is about average in marrying at the age of 20. It's true that the nobility sometimes marry off children as young as 12 in order to lock down important alliances, but those marriages are thankfully rare and usually limited to the very upper echelons of society. Most ordinary people are married in their twenties. Margery and her husband, John Kempe, start having children at an astonishing rate. They have a whopping 14 of them. Fourteen! You'd think that, therefore, her children would be a big part of her life, but she hardly ever mentions them in her book. We don't know how many survive infancy, what their names are, or if any are still living with her when she writes her book. We don't know if 14 children means 14 pregnancies, or if she has sets of twins or triplets.

What we do know is that her first pregnancy is hard. She's very ill during it, and afterwards she only gets worse. She stops eating properly and begins to have visions: terrifying visions of demons breathing fire, pulling at her and attacking her, and convincing her to deny her religion, slander her friends, and even try to kill herself. She starts self-harming. She bites her own hand so hard that it leaves a scar, and she cuts her chest with her own fingernails. These days, we would treat this as an illness: Margery might be diagnosed with postpartum psychosis, for example, which can cause hallucinations and depression. But if we were able to ask Margery herself, she would argue that this isn't a medical problem – it's a religious one.

Margery attributes this awful time in her life to a particularly Big Sin to which she hasn't admitted. She sends for a confessor to get it off her chest, but when he arrives he's so unkind to her that she can't bear to tell him. She doesn't tell us what the Big Sin is, either, leaving the path open for centuries of speculation. What we do know is that throughout her life she often struggles with sexual sins: finding a nice young man at church really hot, or wishing she had never married her husband so she could stay chaste. Perhaps her Big Sin is that she and her husband had sex before marriage, or maybe it's an affair that she doesn't tell us about, or maybe her Big Sin is getting married in the first place, when she believes she should have stayed a maiden.

Whatever it is, her anguish is suddenly calmed by a vision of Jesus, sitting on the side of her bed, who asks, "Daughter, why have you forsaken me, and I never forsook you?"[1] She says she becomes "calm in her wits", stops trying to hurt herself, and is able to eat normally again.

You might think that this is the vision that completely changes her life and leads to her becoming devout, but it seems like actually for years she considers the vision a bit of a one-off. *Huh, that was weird. Oh well – back to my normal life as a middle-class woman.* She carries on having kids, and actually tries to be an entrepreneur for a while, getting into different businesses like brewing and milling, but nothing really works out for her, and it seems like she doesn't start having visions again until years later.

But eventually they do creep up on her, and she becomes very devout indeed, even for the time. She goes to church every day, she wears a hair shirt under her clothes as penance, she fasts, and she develops a horror of sleeping with her husband. She says that the thought of it "was so abominable to her that she would rather . . . have eaten and drunk the ooze and muck in the gutter than consent to intercourse."[2] These days, we don't necessarily associate a lack of sex with holiness, but in Margery's day the connection is strong. Monks and nuns take vows of chastity alongside their vows to give up their worldly possessions, and in one of Margery's visions, God Himself tells her that "maidenhood be more perfect and more holy than the state of widowhood, and the state of widowhood more perfect than the state of wedlock."[3] She tries to convince her husband to free her from her marital obligation to have sex with him, but he refuses, and she cries whenever they do it.

Her visions become so strong that she starts weeping *a lot* – weeping for joy at how great Heaven is, and weeping for sorrow at Christ's crucifixion. This isn't a subtle little moistening of the eyes; this is howling – "violent sobbings with loud crying and shrill shriekings."[4] Imagine sitting in church, trying to listen to the priest, with someone behind you bawling their eyes out, their wretched sobs echoing off the stone walls. No wonder neighbours start to get annoyed with her. One asks her, "Why do you talk so of the joy that is in heaven? You don't know it, and you haven't been there any more than we have."[5] And it's not just going to church and having visions that make her cry. Seeing a woman carrying a baby will make her cry because it reminds her of the Virgin Mary. Seeing a handsome man will make her cry because it reminds her of Jesus. Finally, after three or four years, she convinces her husband that these visions are real, and that they must live chastely from now on. She leaves home and begins to travel.

She starts visiting churches and monasteries around the country, talking to spiritual people like the mystic Julian of Norwich and the Bishop of Lincoln. We often think of medieval people as living in their own village their whole lives, but it's not true! They do travel, for a few reasons, and one of them is to go on pilgrimage, which is kind of the closest thing medieval people have to going on holiday. While Margery finds lots of willing conversation partners, many of them think she's weird and annoying, and possibly even a heretic. Women are not supposed to be preaching, and the country is on the lookout for anyone who might disagree with church teachings. She's constantly being arrested and rearrested and interrogated. But she always manages to talk her way out of trouble, and it helps that the accusations of heresy slide right off her. In fact, she is resolutely orthodox in her beliefs, even if she puts them into practice in unexpected ways. Eventually she starts travelling further. She makes it to all the major Christian pilgrimage sites – Jerusalem, Rome and Santiago de Compostela – as well as some of the B-sides, like Canterbury, Danzig and Aachen. And it's in Rome that she has her most incredible vision of all. She gets married to God Himself.

God appears to her in a vision and announces that He will marry her. Margery seems, honestly, a little overwhelmed. She's used to seeing Jesus, who she openly thinks is pretty hot, but the Big G himself? It's a little scary. The wedding guests are Jesus, the Holy Ghost, Mary, the apostles and the saints, and God says his wedding vows: "For fairer, for fouler, for richer, for poorer."[6] And afterwards, God tells her that they must now live as man and wife: "I must be intimate with you, and lie in your bed with you."[7] Margery, tastefully, doesn't describe the wedding night.

It's an incredible life for a medieval mother of 14, and she knows it, so in 1436 she decides to write a book about her life. Because she's illiterate, she hires a scribe to whom she dictates the story of her religious life. He dies partway through, and when she takes his notes to a new scribe, he tells her that they are totally illegible – just scribbles. Maybe the guy had really bad handwriting, or he wrote in a style that was unknown outside his local area, but either way, the old notes are useless. Margery could have given up at this point. Scribes are expensive, and evidently owning pen and ink is no guarantee that you know what you're doing. Anyone who's found themselves taken for a ride by a shady car mechanic or a cowboy plumber will know Margery's plight all too well. Finally, though, she does manage to find a scribe who's willing to put up with her crying enough to help her start again, and they manage to complete it together.

We don't know what happens to Margery after the book ends. She disappears from the historical record. So she was right to record her life – otherwise we wouldn't know of her at all. There must be many more women and men out there with amazing stories that are simply lost to us, so we're really lucky that hers has survived. The printing press hasn't arrived in Britain yet, so her original is handwritten, and anytime someone wants a copy, they have to transcribe it by hand. That means there aren't many copies. A couple of extracts from her book become popular enough to survive, but they're mostly the bits that are pure religion, and not the juicy autobiographical story that connects them. For centuries, her complete book is lost, and no one outside a few medieval nerds in museum archives have even heard of her. Until the 1930s.

In 1934, at the house of the Butler-Bowdon family near Chesterfield, Derbyshire, the book was rediscovered sitting in a cupboard. Supposedly, the family had some friends over to play table tennis, and someone stepped on the ball and broke it. They opened a cupboard, rooting around for another set of balls, and instead, out fell something much more valuable: *The Book of Margery Kempe,* seen for the first time in centuries. Of course, no one at the ping-pong game knew what it was, but one of them worked at the Victoria & Albert Museum in London, and was able to ask around until the text was eventually identified. These days, Margery's book is popular enough to be printed in full by Penguin, and anyone can read her remarkable story. Her book is on the syllabus for lots of medieval history courses, bringing her name to new generations of scholars. We've never found a second copy of her book; the one that was found in that cupboard behind the ping-pong balls now sits in the British Library, where it can be looked at and admired. But we were so close to losing her story entirely that this should be a reminder: whatever you're working on, save a copy regularly, keep a back-up somewhere and get a second pair of eyes on it as soon as you can.

CHAPTER 12
LA CHEVALIÈRE D'ÉON

*teaches us that just because you're a middle-aged
lady in a bonnet doesn't mean you have to stop
kicking people's arses at sword fighting.*

La Chevalière d'Éon (1728–1810) has the kind of life that seems like it's
been ripped straight from the script of a swashbuckling period piece.
A spy for the French king, inducted into the highly confidential circle
"Le Secret du Roi" working to plan an invasion of England; a sword-
swinging, handsome dragoon captain and a famous fencing master
whose matches were attended by the British Prince of Wales – this is the
kind of life that would be cool enough to get into this book on its own.
But on top of all this, after having lived as a man for decades in the public
eye, in the 1770s d'Éon announces that actually she's been a woman the
whole time! She signs letters "Mademoiselle d'Éon", gets a new wardrobe
of silk dresses, and insists on being referred to as a woman. But she
doesn't give up her sword fighting, and carries on being a fencing master
all the way through her middle age, showing up to tournaments wearing
full skirts and a bonnet.

Okay, before we talk about La Chevalière d'Éon, we need to decide
what name and pronouns to use. "La Chevalière" isn't a name, it's a
title, meaning "the knight". Her name is actually (deep breath) Charles-
Geneviève-Louise-Auguste-André-Timothée d'Éon de Beaumont.
You might notice that some of those names, like Charles, seem like
boys' names, and others, like Louise, seem like girls' names. In her
autobiography she claims to have been given both boys' and girls' names
"in order to avoid any error",[1] which feels like something she's saying
as a joke rather than a completely serious reason, but either way, I'm
definitely not writing out the whole name each time. Ordinarily in this

book I've been trying to use people's first names in order to help us feel a bit closer to them, like this is a gossipy story I'm telling you in the pub, but in this case I'm going to be calling her by one of her last names – d'Éon (pronounced "DAY-on") – for the sake of brevity and in order not to exceed my word count. Happily, it's also what she was generally called in life, too, so it has that in its favour.

In terms of pronouns, I'm going to use "she" and "her" throughout. I mention this because historians have hotly debated what pronouns are appropriate for her and what her internal concept of her own gender would be. Some institutions, such as the British National Portrait Gallery, sidestep the issue by writing out "d'Éon" every single time, giving the text a weird feeling, like they're trying to get her attention by repeating her name over and over. However, partway through d'Éon's life, she does make a conscious decision to live as a female from then on. Not only that, but she tells everyone that she has always been a woman, only living as a man for convenience. So we're going to honour that choice and call her "she", even during the parts of her life when she's living as a man. Otherwise I'm going to have to swap pronouns halfway through and it'll be confusing. All right, let's go!

D'Éon is born in Tonnerre, Burgundy, France and raised as a boy. She's very smart: she gets a law degree and then starts writing the first of 15 books that she'll publish over the course of her lifetime. She's noticed by French King Louis XV (reigned 1715–74), who sends her on a diplomatic mission to Russia. She's in St Petersburg during the reign of the Empress Elizabeth (1741–62), who throws a cross-dressing party every Tuesday. The men come as women, and the women come as men. Apparently, the empress herself passes really well as a bloke. One attendee said, "As she was tall and powerful, male attire suited her. She had the handsomest leg I have ever seen on any man."[2] We don't know for certain if d'Éon is invited to these parties, but it's definitely something that's going on at court while she's there. She later claims to have dressed as a woman in order to inveigle herself into the Russian court as a lady's maid, but as great a story as that is, unfortunately it's one she made up later to make herself sound cooler (apparently being a famous duellist and spy wasn't cool enough).[3]

She joins the French army during the Seven Years' War (1756–63), an immensely complicated global conflict that we don't need to get into here. All we need to know for now is that Britain and France are on opposite sides, and France loses. During the war, d'Éon fights as a "dragoon", which is someone who turns up to the battle with a horse, but who isn't quite as specialized in horseback fighting as someone in the cavalry – dragoons sometimes use the horse to get *to* the battlefield, and then get off and shoot or stab their enemies from the ground. Dragoons are very cool, as you can tell from the fact that the name sounds a bit like "dragon", and they have a uniform so snazzy that d'Éon hangs on to hers for decades afterwards.

In 1762, she is sent on a diplomatic mission to Britain to draw up the peace treaty. She's given the fantastic title of "Minister Plenipotentiary", which is basically an interim ambassador, and she helps to produce the Treaty of Paris which ends the conflict. Under the agreed terms, France has to give up a lot of colonies to Britain, but not as many as the French feared, so all in all d'Éon is considered a success. And France isn't beaten yet. During her time as a diplomat, d'Éon also spies for the French king, sending back reports on Britain's weak spots should the French be able to muster an invasion force. This is a plan so secret that most of the French king's ministers don't even know about it, and it has the codename "Le Secret du Roi" (incredible name, so cool, would be a great movie title). Louis sends her letters about Le Secret, asking her advice on how to carry it out, and d'Éon does such a good job in her role that he awards her his highest honour, the Order of St Louis, an exclusive royal club. Members get to wear a fancy medal, and d'Éon can now call herself a knight.

As you might imagine, someone who's doing so well in her job is pretty furious when Louis passes her over for the permanent ambassador job in favour of a stupid aristocrat, the Comte de Guerchy. Meanwhile the king is stewing about having to foot the bill for d'Éon's prolific party-going and book-buying habits. So the French foreign minister tells her, *Thanks for stepping in while we appointed a proper ambassador; now come back to France.* And d'Éon replies, *Oh, you're firing me? Well, wouldn't it be awful (for you) if all these letters you've sent me about invading England accidentally find their way into the wrong hands? That'd be terrible (for you). (Not for me, though – I'd be fine with that.)*

This is pretty treasonous. Threatening the king? She's on really shaky ground here. To shore herself up, she kicks up a public stink about losing her job, to make sure she can't be quietly bumped off without people noticing. She publishes a load of letters between herself and other French officials. The letters don't actually give away any state secrets, but they were supposed to be private letters, so this is a clear threat about what she *could* publish if she felt like it. She accuses the new ambassador of trying to poison her, and the French get so embarrassed about the whole thing that they even float a plan to just kidnap her off the streets of London, bundle her into a carriage and drag her back to a French prison.

The British press have a field day with all this, going on about how awful the French are being to poor old d'Éon, but luckily for her she is in a liberty-loving land that would never do something like poison or abduct one of its own citizens. She even threatens to have France's new ambassador prosecuted for attempted kidnapping and attempted murder. So eventually the king of France gives in. *How about you carry on being a spy for me in London, and I'll give you 12,000 livres a year to live off, and no one needs to go public about any secret invasion plans?* Perfect. D'Éon has got everything she wants.

For a few years she's absolutely living it up in Georgian London. She goes to fancy parties, becomes a bit of a celebrity in high society and buys a lot of books. You think you have a book problem? By 1777, she has a whopping 6,000 volumes on all kinds of subjects,[4] but she's especially interested in women's rights. She collects what historian Gary Kates calls "the largest private collection of proto-feminist works of any known 18th-century book collector". And she's not just buying them to look at – she starts writing about the position of women in society herself, stating, "Men, who by their strength and their gallantry seem like lions and tigers, have seized authority, all political positions, all honours, all worldly riches, leaving women only the pain brought by having babies."[5] And remember, she's on a government pension, so effectively the king of France is paying for her to read and write about feminism and go to parties all day.

Now rumours are swirling around London that she's not the man she's been living as at all – she's secretly a woman! She's always had a baby face – she never has a beard, for example – but these rumours are quite new. They gather steam frighteningly quickly, though. People start printing cartoons of her sex being tested, or of her getting married to various political figures of the day. One newspaper even prints a joke story that she's had an illegitimate child and left it on the steps of the House of Commons.[6] And as soon as people hear the rumour, they're placing bets on whether it's true or not. This seems utterly bizarre today, but in 18th-century London people will lay down hundreds of pounds on absolutely anything. The ledger of the members' club Brooks's reveals one man betting £150 that there will one day be electric telegraphic communication between America and Britain, and another that he will successfully shag a woman in a hot-air balloon 1,000 yards

(900m) above the ground (the ledger doesn't record whether these bets were successfully cashed in – a massive loss for historians and nosy people everywhere).[7]

At first, d'Éon is furious about these rumours – not so much because she's offended that people think she's a woman, but because she considers the behaviour "indecent",[8] which, to be fair, it is. People are making bets worth thousands of pounds that can only be settled by her showing someone her dangly bits, basically. She starts marching into coffee houses and demanding to duel people who are placing bets on her (no one dares take her up on this), and she gets increasingly worried that someone is going to assault her in order to settle a bet. But after a few years, she starts leaning into the rumours, and indeed, making sure that the French court hears about them and believes them. We're not really sure what changes her mind. Perhaps as a man, she's a politically inconvenient exile, being sent less money every year by a king who really wants her out of the way, but as a woman, she would be seen as less of a threat. Perhaps the rumour matches an internal belief about how she would like to live in the world and so she just decides to go for it.

The new French king, Louis XVI (reigned 1774–89), realizes that this can give him a way out of being held to ransom by d'Éon. If she does start living as a woman, she won't be able to participate in politics or war anymore – the threat she poses will be neutralized. So Louis tells her, *Okay, you can come back and we won't imprison you for treason, but you have to give us back the secret documents and live as a woman from now on.* As in, you legally *have* to be a woman. After years in Britain, d'Éon finally gets to go home, and even keeps her Order of St Louis. Just before her return, all the people who've laid down money on her true sex panic. *If she goes, we're never going to settle this bet!* So, unbelievably, just before she leaves for France, her gender is decided by a court after one of the gamblers sues his bookie. An important judge called Lord Mansfield (who absolutely has better things to do with his time, and says as much in court) presides over a case where the jury finds that people who bet that d'Éon is a woman should win their bets. So d'Éon has her gender change legally recognized by an English court – in 1777.

When Louis XVI tells her that she has to live as a woman from now on, he is dead serious. At first, d'Éon carries on wearing her men's suits and her dragoon uniform, but soon after arriving in Paris she's *assigned* a dressmaker. In the 2020s, we're used to transgender people experimenting with gender presentation *before* deciding that they want to officially transition, but with d'Éon it seems to be the other way round

– she's legally a woman well before she actually starts wearing women's clothes. She's dressed by none other than Queen Marie Antoinette's stylist, Rose Bertin, the trendsetter for half of Europe, and d'Éon makes her debut in dresses on 21 October 1777, when she appears at an official's home in women's clothing for the first time and starts signing her name with the feminine "La Chevalière d'Éon" rather than the masculine "Le Chevalier d'Éon".

Although she's now dressing as a woman, she doesn't want to give up her military career and sword fighting. She tells Rose, "You have killed my brother the Dragoon. I am in great pain over it. My body is like my mind. It cannot be content with being embroidered in lace."[9] And although she will carry on wearing dresses for the rest of her life, she doesn't give up everything about living as a man – she refuses to change her "appearance or speech",[10] and she carries on doing little gentlemanly things for ladies, like filling up their coffee cups for them. When France gets involved in the US Revolutionary War (1775–83), she even asks if she can put together a troop of female soldiers and go and crack some British heads, but the government turns her down.

In 1785, tired of being watched and told what to do by the French government, she returns to London, still as famous as ever. But she's struggling financially. Louis XVI was never great about sending her money on time, but after January 1793 he's in no position to send her anything at all anymore, it being pretty difficult to write a cheque without a head (he was guillotined then during the French Revolution). D'Éon has to sell her books and do sword-fighting tournaments to make ends meet. We still have loads of posters for these demonstrations, and there are even drawings of her in action, bonnet and all. She markets herself as a great Amazon warrior or as a follower of Minerva, the Roman goddess of wisdom and war. One advert for her demonstrations says that she fences "agreeably to the best and most approved Method now practised by the first Masters in Europe."[11] She carries on doing these until she's almost 70, and in the end it isn't old age that stops her from sword-fighting but an injury she gets in her last tournament in 1796. Her final years are spent in a shabby, run-down apartment that she shares with a fellow elderly lady, Mrs Cole. Neither of them has much money, and they often have to do without coal for the fire.

You might think that people in the 18th century would not accept d'Éon swapping her gender, but although there is a lot of ridicule of her in cartoons, most people seem not to mind how she presents herself. By the 1790s, her story is that she was always a woman and that she'd been raised as a boy so that her father would have an heir: this becomes the accepted narrative. She's held up as an example of what talented women can do if they're given the opportunity. In her sixties, she attends a dinner party where she is given an eloquent toast by the radical English politician John Horne Tooke (1736–1812): "On the right sits a lady who has been employed in public situations at different courts, who had high rank in the army, was greatly skilled at horsemanship, who has fought several duels, and at the small sword had no equal, who for 50 years past, all Europe has recognized in the character and dress of a gentleman."[12] Neither femaleness nor age could stop La Chevalière from kicking arse – even in her long skirts, she could still swing a sword with the best of them.

CHAPTER 13

IRA ALDRIDGE

teaches us that if you don't like the role
you've been given, you can change it.

Being an aspiring actor is hard. It's such a competitive field that you're lucky to even get a callback, never mind an actual job. And when Ira Aldridge (1807–67) is starting out, he's got it even harder than most. As an African American in the 1820s, there's basically nowhere for him to get a foot in the door. Theatres in the US are segregated, and even in Britain there aren't exactly a lot of great black characters being written. But Ira Aldridge overleaps these barriers to become one of the most decorated thespians of the 19th century. He's piled up with honours from all over Europe, women send him adoring fan mail, and one writer calls him "the greatest actor of the present age."[1] How does he do it? Well, if you don't like the parts you're being offered, you can change them.

Ira is born in New York as Frederick William Aldridge – "Ira" is a nickname that he'll later go on to use as his stage name. As a young man, he dabbles a bit in amateur dramatics, and decides he wants to become a professional actor. The problem is that it's basically impossible to be a black actor in the US in the 1820s. No white company will have you – even the audience in an American theatre is segregated, never mind the cast. The only place you can really do it in New York is at the African Theatre, run by free black people, but that gets forced to close after white audiences riot at its shows. You'd think an obstacle like this would be pretty well insurmountable, but Ira clears it by simply leaving the country and heading for Britain. Imagine crossing an ocean to a country you have no connections in, to try to start up a career as precarious as acting – and then imagine doing that in 1825, when it was still sailing ships and weeks-long crossings.

Who knows what Ira's plan is if this doesn't work, but amazingly it does. He gets his first professional job at the Royalty Theatre in London at the age of 17, a frankly astonishing debut that would make any RADA student jealous. He then goes to the Coburg Theatre (now the Old Vic) to play the lead in an explicitly anti-slavery play titled *The Revolt of Surinam*. The fact that he's a black man playing a black character is specifically touted as a draw for the show, which says on its poster that it is "supported in its principal Character by a *Man of Colour,* and one of the very race whose wrongs it professes to record."[2] On top of moving to a new continent and starting a new career, he somehow finds time in the same year to get married to an English woman named Margaret Gill.

Audiences love him, but the critics range between lukewarm and outright racist. One reviewer says that "owing to the shape of his lips, it is utterly impossible for him to pronounce English in such a manner as to satisfy even the unfastidious ears of the gallery" while also complaining that he's not black enough. He says that the theatre managers who cast Ira "might, if they were bent on having a blackamoor, have procured one whose complexion was more *foncé* [dark]."[3] Some white men won't let their actress wives share the stage or even share the bill with a black actor. One biography tells the story of an American man arguing with a Dublin theatre manager about putting his wife on the same stage as Ira.[4] The manager keeps Ira on the bill, but that sort of thing only needs to happen a few times to be really detrimental to an actor's career. The actor J B Howe performs alongside Ira in Croydon and is horrified to see white women in the company flirting with him. He writes, "I can remember the feeling of repugnance I experienced at the adulatory congratulations bestowed upon him by the fair members of the company."[5]

So Ira's doing all right in London, but he knows he could be getting better reviews. He starts touring the country, going to theatres in Brighton, Chichester, Salisbury and Exeter, building up his experience on the stage with a huge variety of roles. Theatres in the 19th century don't do a single play for weeks on end like they do today – they want a new show every night, to keep people coming back. This means that actors in Ira's day have to remember way more lines than your average actor today – Ira might be doing up to 16 parts in the span of 10 days.[6]

A lot of these early parts are black characters, often in plays about slavery. Ira plays the title role in *Oroonoko,* Zanga in *The Revenge,* Hassan in *The Castle Spectre,* and Gambia in *The Slave.* Even though there's not a lot of choice if you're only playing black roles in the 1820s, Ira is still very choosy about what parts he plays. He tries to steer clear of foolish or stupid black characters, focusing instead on playing ones with some air of dignity, even if they're the villain or a victim. There aren't a lot of black heroes on the Victorian stage, but at least he can avoid being the butt of the joke (mostly – he does do some early minstrelsy, where the joke is *Don't these people talk funny?*). Sometimes he even has racist plays rewritten to give the juiciest parts to the enslaved characters, like with the play *Obi*, which is originally about a dangerous black man threatening the stability of a happy plantation. In Ira's version, he gets a tragic backstory about being kidnapped from Africa and losing his wife and children, making his villainous actions a lot more understandable and relatable. The character says, "They dragged me from my native land; can I forget? Can I forgive? Never."[7]

By 1833, Ira's back in London, now an experienced actor, playing the most famous black role in English theatre: Othello. Ira's probably the first black actor ever to play the part in London. In this period Othello and indeed all black characters are usually played by white actors wearing blackface make-up (burnt cork to darken the skin) and black gloves. Several commentators of the time note how refreshing it is to see an actual black person in these roles. The *Manchester Guardian* observes that Ira's performance in *The Slave* is done "without having the slightest occasion for having the cosmetic assistance of burnt cork"[8] and *The Athenaeum* remarks on how much more expressive Ira can be with his hands since he doesn't have to wear gloves: "Slight as this may seem, to the critical observer it is wonderful what additional animation this unwonted sign of life gives to the entire man".[9]

But still, generally the critics and the audiences have very different opinions of his performance. During the curtain call, he is "called for by the unanimous acclamation of the whole house, who, upon his appearance, rose en masse to receive him with bursts of applause, waving of hats, &c., &c.",[10] but the disgust of the critics is getting more obvious. *The Athenaeum* says that "it is impossible that Mr Aldridge should fully comprehend the meaning and force of even the words he utters" while, somehow, *in the same article*, claiming "we have no ridiculous prejudice against any fellow creature, because he chances to be of a different colour from ourselves."[11] (Literally anyone will say "I'm not racist, but . . . . ") *The Figaro* basically conducts a full campaign to end Ira's career, claiming that it has "hunted the N***** from the boards of Covent Garden" and vowing to "inflict on him such a chastisement as must drive him from the stage he has dishonoured, and force him to find in the capacity of footman or street-sweeper that level for which his colour appears to have rendered him peculiarly qualified."[12]

It's worth remembering that slavery hasn't even been abolished in Britain yet: that won't happen till 1834. In fact, at the same time as Ira's Othello is telling the audience about being "sold to slavery, of my redemption thence" in Covent Garden, just down the road in Westminster, Parliament is debating the bill that will ban slavery in British Caribbean colonies. Ira's pretty clear on which side of the aisle he stands; during one curtain call he looks forward to "the prejudice . . . fast dying away, when one man should be deprived of a hearing on the stage, because his face was of another colour, seeing the black man and the white were both the work of the same Creator."[13]

Some critics are fans of Ira, though: one review states that "his entire representation of Othello is a masterly performance, as cleverly executed as it is originally conceived."[14] Buoyed up by this taste of Shakespeare, Ira does another tour around the country, this time building up his repertoire of white Shakespearean characters: Richard III, Macbeth and Shylock. People who think that race-bending or race-swapping is a new thing to gratify the wokescolds should know that Ira Aldridge was out there doing it in the 19th century! Written accounts from the time report that Ira does these roles wearing pale make-up to make himself look white. We do have photos of him in his costumes for some of these parts, and speaking for myself, I can't really see it, but they are old black-and-white pictures, so maybe it's just hard to tell. Either way, these are roles that theatre managers wouldn't normally think to cast Ira in, so he's learning professional make-up techniques in order to expand the kinds of roles he's allowed to do.

His Shylock is especially well thought of. A Jewish character in Shakespeare's *The Merchant of Venice*, Shylock is usually played in the early 19th century as villainous and scheming. Ira gives this play the same treatment that he gave *Obi*, making Shylock much more dignified and sympathetic. One writer says that Ira "deeply understood the character and so he played it as an exploited, despised Jew . . . . [Shylock] is the bearer of the sorrow and tragedy of his hunted people."[15]

In the late 1840s, Ira performs in *The Black Doctor,* which is a pretty racist play by modern standards, but for the time it's surprisingly progressive in that its enslaved characters are serious, tragic figures rather than stupid comedy minstrels singing happy songs. Ira plays Fabian, a black doctor in a French Caribbean colony who falls in love with his former master's daughter, Pauline. He knows that they can never be together, but his hopes are kindled when he hears Pauline try to help her black maid, Lia, marry a white man. *Maybe Pauline's cool with black and white people getting married!* he thinks. When Pauline is threatened with being forced into a political marriage to a man she doesn't love, Fabian plans to kill both Pauline and himself to save them both from it. He repents at the last minute, Pauline confesses her love for him, and they secretly get married. Pauline's aristocratic family then moves to France just in time for the aristocrat-beheading French Revolution, and Pauline is about to be shot by the revolutionaries when Fabian takes the bullet for her. Again, we see just the sort of character that Ira likes: a one-dimensional black villain (who threatens to kill a white woman) being fleshed out with noble motivations and a tragic ending.

In 1850, Ira does it again with *Titus Andronicus,* a play that hasn't been performed for more than 100 years (it's way too much of a gore-fest for 19th-century audiences). Ira plays Aaron the Moor, who in this version is completely rewritten to be a heroic character rather than a villainous one. Shakespeare's plays are treated more like fairy tales in this period – available for rewriting as much as you like – rather than as canonical texts that you must stick to. You can tell Ira's getting bored with doing *Othello* over and over, and wants to add another great black part to the theatrical repertoire. And the great thing about his plan is that he isn't just helping his own career here – once the play's been rewritten, then other black actors in the future can take those roles, too, and create bigger careers for themselves.

This is a lot of work, though, and Ira's still struggling to get long-term engagements in British theatres, so in 1852 he decides to tour Europe. This is where his career rockets. On the Continent, they absolutely love him. In Leipzig, he meets the royal family; in Saxe-Coburg, he's invited up to the royal box to meet the duchess; in Prussia, his *Othello* is attended by the entire royal court. In Moscow, the students at the university are so thrilled to see him that they unhitch his horses from his carriage and pull him about the city themselves! He starts getting properly rave reviews, too: the *Preussische Zeitung* reports that "After this Othello it would be an anticlimax to have to see an ordinary Othello again",[16] and in Danzig a critic says that "Ira Aldridge is the greatest dramatic artist we have ever had."[17] He brings the work of Shakespeare to places that have never seen it before, like Novi Sad in Serbia, and when he meets the famous Swedish opera singer Jenny Lind (1820–87) she tells him that she's sorry she will have to miss his performance, as she's worried that he will overpower her with so much emotion that it will hurt her pregnancy! The King of Prussia gives him a Gold Medal of the First Class for Arts and Sciences, the Emperor of Austria gives him the Medal of Ferdinand, and in Saxe-Meiningen he is given the Royal Saxon House Order. He must have clanked as he walked onto the ship back to Britain.

It's also while in Europe that he starts getting some truly obsessed fangirls. It turns out Beatlemania and Swifties are nothing new; women are going nuts for Ira Aldridge in the 1850s. A woman called Emily tells him that "Every moment of my life is filled up with the thoughts of you, what would I not give to be but just for an hour beside you, to tell you again and again how dear you have been to me."[18] Another writes, "Oh God, is it possible that you, a stranger, a man who I only know at a distance, and that I shall perhaps never see again, can be so dear to me, that I should have just chosen you, whose language I do not know, whose country is far from mine and whose words of tenderness and love I can hardly understand."[19] The most devoted fan is probably Matilda from Budapest, who asks Ira to find her a job as a governess or a lady's companion near his house so that she can see him regularly, and who even offers to marry any eligible bachelor who lives near Ira so that "I would leave my mother on friendly terms and I could see you my grand Aldridge."[20] But the very best piece of fan mail has to be from the lady who tells Ira about a fantastical dream she had about him, which entirely consists of them "sitting side by side eating cheese" (to be honest, eating cheese with Ira Aldridge sounds like a great evening).[21]

Before we wrap up, I simply must tell you about Ira's greatest feat, which is something he's not famous for at all. In the 1850s, there's an enslaved family called the Wilsons from Baltimore in the United States who escape and run away to New York, where they're recaptured. They're about to be sold away from each other when Ira hears their story and sends the Society for the Manumission of Slaves in New York enough money to buy freedom for all of them – father, mother and three children. I had to dig pretty deep into researching Ira before I even found out about this, buried halfway down a 1950s biography.[22] His career on the stage is fun to talk about and is what's in sources from the time, but even the greatest acting in the world is a pale achievement compared to freeing five people from slavery, and I'd like to see more biographers mention it.

By the 1850s, even *The Athenaeum* (the magazine that was totally not racist) was forced to admit that it had "formed a favourable opinion of his talents."[23] He commanded fees of 400 roubles per night at the Imperial Theatre in St Petersburg at a time when well-known actors there would normally have got no more than 100 roubles a *month,* and he was absolutely loaded down with medals, orders and honours from across Europe. When Ira started his career in the 1820s, no theatre in his home town would have him, so he travelled across an ocean to find one that would. Rather than stick to stereotypical comedic black parts, he sought out roles with more depth and weight. When he tired of those, he played white characters, or had small black parts rewritten to be bigger. If you're not satisfied with the roles you're offered, why not just create the ones you want?

CHAPTER 14
THE REBECCA RIOTERS

teach us not to underestimate the value of a skirt and a pinny.

The first few years of the 1840s see huge riots and public disturbances across southwest Wales, especially in Carmarthenshire. The protestors are angry about unfair taxes and tithes, low wages, and especially tollbooths. They can dismantle an entire tollbooth overnight, wait for the authorities to rebuild it, and then tear it down again. They claim to be led by a mysterious figure called "Rebecca", and to protect their identities they often dress in outlandish costumes, most often women's clothing. Within a few years, the tollbooths have been removed, and few of those who did the damage are ever prosecuted. For the Rebecca Rioters, putting on their wives' dresses and aprons really does get them surprisingly far.

From the mid-18th century, roads increasingly become privatized, meaning that keeping them smooth and not overgrown is not the job of local government, but of private companies called "turnpike trusts", which must make profits. So one day, a road that you've been using all your life suddenly has a gate built across it, with a small house next to it, and the company charges you to open the gate. The period between 1750 and 1772 is known as a time of "turnpike mania", during which no fewer than 500 turnpike trusts are established all over the United Kingdom. By 1809, a fifth of the country's roads are privatized. So you're not just paying for the odd road here and there every few days – you might be stopping at multiple tollbooths on a single journey. They might cost you two or three pence per mile. Also, tollbooths aren't required to give you change, so you'd better have the exact amount on you, or else you might be paying more than the asking price.

By the 1840s, these turnpikes have been extremely unpopular for years due to their high prices. There aren't as many roads as there are today, so trying to go round a different way might add hours to your journey, if it's possible at all. They can hike up prices without notice for no reason, and upcharge you for all sorts of weird extras. One man from Cwmffrwd called, somehow, James James, goes through a tollbooth twice on the same day and is charged more the second time. When he asks why, he is told that there's a surcharge because this time he's carrying a kettle. *Yeah, just your standard kettle fee. Normal thing to have.* And when it goes to court, the judge finds in favour of the turnpike company! Judges are often invested in the turnpikes, so they don't have much incentive to force companies to lower their prices.

In 1839, this anger boils over into a riot at the hamlet of Efailwen. The Whitland turnpike trust decides to put up some new gates in the area, and the one at Efailwen has barely been built before a group of locals turns up to pull it down. They're wearing bonnets and nightgowns, and they're being led by a man named Thomas Rees, also known as Twm Carnabwth (c1806–76), dressed as a woman called "Beca". No one quite knows how the Rebecca character comes about, but it might be a Bible joke based on a verse in the Book of Genesis (24:60) which mentions a gate: "And they blessed Rebecca, and said unto her, Thou art our sister, be thou the mother of thousands of millions, and let thy seed possess the gate of those which hate them." Some Rebecca Rioters have other disguises, wearing strange masks or fake horsehair beards, and sometimes Rebecca's followers adopt female personas of their own, with names like "Miss Brown" and "Miss Cromwell". Imagine seeing a motley crew of blokes in disguise coming toward you with their sledgehammers on a dark night: the prospect is terrifying, even with the bonnets! After they destroy the Efailwen gate and burn down the tollbooth, the turnpike trust rebuilds it. Rebecca comes back, and her followers destroy it again. The trust rebuilds. Rebecca destroys it *a third time.* No one is ever prosecuted for the destruction of the Efailwen gate.

The idea catches on, and other gates and tollbooths all over southwest Wales start getting visits from "Rebecca" and her followers. The beauty of it is that Rebecca can be played by anyone, so you never know where she's going to strike next. St Clears, Swansea, Llangadog, Cardigan, Lampeter, even as far away as Montgomeryshire – nowhere is safe from Rebecca's outstretched hand. On 27 May 1843, two men in women's clothes calling themselves "Rebecca" and "Charlotte" break into a toll house operated by a man named Henry Thomas. They hold him and his family hostage while Rebecca's followers completely dismantle the house, methodically taking off the roof and even removing the windows. In another incident, a man named Walter Jones has been urging people to carry on paying the road tolls even when a tollbooth has been destroyed, and threatens to identify the rioters. One night, he and his wife are woken by the sound of his windows smashing, and bullets whizzing in. Luckily, no one is hurt.

Rebecca's followers also start targeting things other than tollbooths, like unfair rents, workhouses, fathers who abandon their children, and bailiffs. Landlords are a particular target. According to historian David J V Jones, rents in some parts of Wales at least double in the 40 years prior to the Rebecca riots, and in some places triple.[1] People feel that in the past, landlords were richer and more important than them, yes, but that was balanced out by them giving to the poor and to charity (including maintaining the roads so that they didn't have to have tollbooths) and being heavily involved in the local community. Whereas, the feeling is, by the 1830s landlords are more absent – many are living in other parts of the country and sucking up the profits from local farms. Some don't even visit the farms themselves – they get an agent to do it. One unpopular landlord, Edward Abadam, finds two of his hayricks on fire, and when he goes to his fishpond to get water to put them out, he finds that Rebecca's followers have drained it. He loses 60 tons of hay worth about £200. Another landlord, William Chamber, has five separate arson attacks on his possessions during the course of the Rebecca Riots. A landlord's agent named C Thomas Herbert Cooke is riding home one night when he finds about 40 people standing silently in the road, dressed in white with veils covering their faces, and carrying guns and sticks. Wisely, he turns his horse around and goes another way. Landlords and clergymen who speak out against the riots get threatening letters from "Rebecca", and if you particularly displease her, her followers have the *ceffyl pren* (Welsh: "wooden horse") – a cart that they can put people on to parade them around town in a public humiliation (this one is a favourite for dealing with deadbeat dads).

Then the authorities decide to clamp down. If you walk past a tollbooth without paying, even when the gate has been destroyed, you can get a heavy fine, and if you don't pay the fine, you can go to prison. When two men, John Harries and Samuel Bowen, refuse to pay their fines, warrants are put out for their arrest. When the constables get to Harries' house, they find a mob of people armed with scythes, guns and farm tools. The constables quietly turn around and go back home.

The magistrate who sent them is furious. *Well, go back with more men, then!* So they band together about 40 men and try again. This time, when they get to Harries' house, they seize his goods in order to sell them off to pay his fine, but as they're leaving, Rebecca's followers turn up again – 300 of them, wearing masks, horsehair beards and aprons. They force the constables to turn over their weapons and return the goods. Then they march the constables back to the magistrate's house and force him to tear down one of his own garden walls.

And then, in Carmarthen, the Rebeccaites plan a truly massive protest for 19 July 1843. All around the county town, people get anonymous letters from "Becca", telling them to go to the uprising: "Be you personally present on horseback and every male in your employment must appear. No excuse will be taken. Non-compliance will bring vengeance on your head and most likely you will be *launched into eternity without the least warning*"[2] (my italics, 'cos, wow, that's a great line). On the day, hundreds, possibly thousands, of people parade through town with a band of musicians they've hired especially for the occasion. The magistrates are ready for them – the police are guarding the town hall and the local prison. Nevertheless, the crowd storms the workhouse, releasing inmates and orphans, and throwing bedding from upper-storey windows. Then the army is called in. Mounted soldiers turn up with swords drawn, ride into the workhouse yard and *shut the gates behind them*, trapping everyone inside with them. People try desperately to climb over the walls to get out, and dozens are arrested. But Rebecca can't be stamped out. That night, 150 people dressed in skirts and masks destroy three toll-gates in the Teifi valley, and the riots carry on stronger than before. Sometimes newly built toll-gates last only for a matter of hours before Rebecca and her followers turn up to pull them down.

In all, there are more than 530 Rebecca riots, including 293 attacks on toll-gates. In the summer of 1843, the riots get so pervasive that there are multiple attacks in a single day. Sometimes a judge will make examples of Rebecca's followers: for example, in August, a group carrying reaping hooks, led by a man in a long red coat, turn up at the house of an elderly man named Daniel Harris in the middle of the night and tell him to sign a note giving them £20 to buy guns for Rebecca. When the case comes to court, seven of the men are transported to Australia for ten years, and their leader for 20 – a huge sentence. But in general, juries are reluctant to convict Rebecca's followers, even when there are multiple witnesses against them, and on at least one occasion, even when the defendant confesses while drunk. Only a tiny number of the presumably thousands taking part in the Rebecca riots are ever convicted. By the end of the summer, hundreds of tollbooths have been pulled down. The *Planet* newspaper reports that "Property has been destroyed in Wales, life has been endangered, the law, and officers of the law, have been set at defiance; discontent has taken up arms, it has boldly assumed the vigour of insurrection, and little seems to be required to make the entire country break out into open rebellion."[3]

In the end, what stops the rioters isn't slapping harsh sentences on them, or calling in the army. What stops them is agreeing to their demands. The moral of the story, surprisingly, is that riots work! In August 1844, the government passes the South Wales Turnpike Trust Amendment Act, which basically renationalizes the roads. All the turnpike roads are bought up and consolidated under a local government scheme called the County and District Roads Boards. Tolls don't go away, but they're standardized, and won't be hiked up to ridiculous levels; and the money thus raised goes into actually keeping the roads in good repair rather than just lining investors' pockets. People aren't being charged for kettles anymore, that's for sure. And it's not just the tollbooths that they take a look at – an amendment to the Poor Law means that single mothers who've been deserted now have the power to summon the father of their child before the magistrates and make him pay maintenance. Loads of Welsh women take advantage of this. For example, in a single week at the Newport petty sessions, Martha Griffiths, Margaret James, Elizabeth John, Martha Morgan, Elizabeth Howell and Elizabeth Owen are all able to make claims in order to raise their children.[4]

On top of getting legal protection, the Rebeccaites also see the economy turn in their favour. Between 1843 and 1867, agricultural workers' wages rise by 50 per cent.[5] There are new factory, mining, shipbuilding and railway jobs, and even gold rushes in America, Australia and Canada, so if you're a farm worker, you can get higher wages by threatening to take one of these lucrative opportunities elsewhere, or by actually taking them. And if your wages are rising, then even if your landlord hasn't reduced your rent in response to the Rebecca riots, it doesn't matter so much. There is the odd riot in the 1850s and 1860s, but after the new turnpike law, the uprising mostly fizzles out.

To this day, we don't know the names of most of the participants. It seems that after 1844 many of them hung up their aprons, handed their bonnets back to their wives and threw away their horsehair beards. "Rebecca" got her wish. Never underestimate the power of a skirt and a pinny.

CHAPTER 15
JULIUS SOUBISE

*teaches us that being able to charm rich old ladies is
just as important as being good at stabbing.*

Julius Soubise (1754–98) starts life very low in the pecking order, with
the humblest of beginnings as an enslaved child from the West Indies.
From there, he rises to become what historian Peter Fryer calls the "fop
among fops": a showy dresser, superb sword fighter and nationally
acclaimed horseback rider, even as a teenager. He moves in high society
circles, dresses in lace and jewels, and casually drops money at the
gambling tables every night. How does he achieve this? Two important
life skills: winning the heart of a rich older lady, and being able to slice
the nose off anyone who looks at him crooked.

Julius is born into slavery on the Caribbean island of St Kitts, the son
of an enslaved African woman and a free European man. When he's
just ten years old, his owner, British Royal Navy Captain Stair-Douglas,
brings him to England, where he meets a relative of the captain who
will change his life. The Duchess of Queensberry loves him so much
that she successfully begs the captain to give Julius to her, whereupon
she promptly frees him. It's the duchess who gives him the name "Julius
Soubise" in the first place – on the ship's documents, he's listed as
"Othello". She names him after Charles de Rohan, the French Prince de
Soubise, and raises him as a member of the nobility, as if he were her
own grandson.

As such, Julius gets a proper education, and even some lessons that
aren't on the usual curriculum: sword fighting and horse riding. On top
of that, he learns the violin, and he gets public-speaking lessons from
the greatest actor of the day, David Garrick (1717–79). One writer who
knows Julius says, "He grew fast, was engaging in his manners, and

soon manifested a disposition for gallantry. He was taught to fence, and talked of becoming a general".[1] He's good-looking, too: famous artists like the Englishman Thomas Gainsborough (1727–88) and the German Johann Zoffany (1733–1810) ask him to model for them, and he even writes sonnets!

Not all the duchess's friends think that this education is a good idea. One, Lady Mary Coke, writes: "I could not help thinking those exercises too much above his condition to be useful, & wou'd only serve to give him expectations that cou'd not be answer'd."[2] Although she's definitely wrong that these studies are "above his condition", in Georgian England she's right to be worried that they won't be useful for Julius. The problem is that society isn't really set up to have a place for him. If you want an upper-class lifestyle, you need land and investment income so that you don't have to work, and you usually get those by inheritance. Julius isn't going to be inheriting any land, so he needs some method of funding himself that ideally doesn't rely on the duchess – who's already in her fifties – being around forever. Lady Mary is probably thinking that the duchess should get him an apprenticeship in a trade – maybe train him up to be a tailor or a milliner – so that he can earn a living for himself. It's not like you can make a living off horse riding – right?

You can if you're as good as Julius. His riding and fencing teacher is the famous Italian master Domenico Angelo (1716–1802). The duchess tries to get Julius an apprenticeship with Angelo, to whom she offers a fat wad of cash, but Julius is so good that Angelo takes him on straightaway as a teacher at the school. The duchess turns up to Julius' lessons to see him show off, and Julius' fights are attended by La Chevalière d'Éon (see Chapter 12). The students at the riding school love him, and Angelo's son says that "his colour and humble birth might have made him repulsive to his high-born pupils, on the contrary, these circumstances seemed to excite a greater interest in his favour. His manners were engaging, and his good nature gained him the affection of every one who came to the house".[3] Julius plays the violin well enough to make the odd bit of money playing in London's Vauxhall Pleasure Gardens, the Disneyland of the 18th century, and his singing "would have fitted him for a *primo buffo* [comic singer] at the Opera-house."[4]

It's also worth having a bit of a look at the duchess too, since she pretty much deserves a chapter in *Mavericks* to herself. Catherine Hyde, known as Kitty, often appears in compendia of "eccentrics" merely for acting like a normal person while rich: in *The Emperor of the United States of America and Other Magnificent British Eccentrics,* Catherine

Caulfield writes that Kitty "was a beautiful and strong-willed woman who took little notice of the opinions of others" and that she would sometimes travel to a party "on foot, often walking several miles".[5] This is "trashy when a normal person does it, classy when a rich person does it" behaviour – can you believe she *walked?* To a *party?!* What whimsical, eccentric behaviour! Truly we must memorialize this in print centuries from now.

But Kitty really does stand out at the time among ladies of the court. Partly she's terrible at schmoozing people and instead is very blunt. She once invites the writer Jonathan Swift (1667–1745) to her house with the words, "I cannot say you will be welcome, for I do not know you, and perhaps I shall not like you; but if I do not, unless you are a very vain person, you shall know my thoughts as soon as I do myself."[6] Cool, thanks, Kitty! Partly she's very stubborn and refuses to let others tell her what to do. In 1732, there's a debate going on in the House of Lords, and they decide to close the ladies' gallery to the public so that members of the House of Commons can use it to watch the debate instead (notably, they do not attempt to close the *gentlemen's* public gallery – only the ladies' section). Kitty turns up with a dozen other noble ladies in tow, asking to be let in, and a guy named William Sanderson literally blocks the way, swearing that "by God he would not let them in." So Kitty and her friends lay siege to the House of Lords so that *no one* can use the gallery, taking turns at kicking the door so that the lords have to shout to be heard. Finally, the noise dies down, and the Lord Chancellor says, *Okay, I think it's safe to open the door for the Commons to come in,* whereupon Kitty and her gang are like, *Ahaaa! We're still here!* They barge through to the front row of the gallery and heckle the speakers for hours.[7]

Kitty is just the sort of person who would take a formerly enslaved child and educate him as if he were her son. She can't say no to Julius about anything, as society finds out when, at the age of 19, Julius suddenly gets really into "macaroni" fashion. He swans about in "powdered wig, white silk breeches, very tight coat and vest, with enormous white neck cloth, white silk stockings, [and] diamond-buckled red-heeled shoes"[8] and is never seen without a sprig of fresh flowers in his buttonhole. He rides around Hyde Park in his very own carriage, and starts getting reckless spending Kitty's money. Angelo says that "He had a constant succession of visitors, and his rooms were supplied with roses, geraniums, and other expensive greenhouse plants, in the spring. He was equally expensive in his perfumes."[9] He loves perfume and flowers so much that people say you can smell him coming before you see him!

The macaronis are a subset of fops – elaborately dressed men – who come home from holidays in Italy and France and want to emulate European styles. Shunning the traditional English dish of roast beef, they name themselves after an Italian dish instead. They're distinguished by their short, slim-cut waistcoats and frock coats so short that you can – gasp – almost see their (trouser-covered) bums! They wear powdered wigs that are really tall in the front with a big fat ponytail at the back, and they're so into perfect symmetry that they sometimes wear a second, fake pocket watch to "balance out" their real timepiece.[10]

Dressing in macaroni fashion is an expensive habit, but Kitty buys Julius all the clothes he wants. Macaronis also come in for not a small amount of mockery in the press at the time, and as a black man Julius gets it particularly sharply. People make fun of him for dressing "above his station" – they find the mere idea of a black person wearing aristocratic styles to be ridiculous. Cartoons are drawn of him and people call him the "Mungo Macaroni", "Mungo" being the name of an enslaved character in a popular play.

Julius could have gone on being a fabulous dresser and amazing swordsman around town, not caring what the cartoonists think, raking in money as a riding tutor to poshos, and that alone would definitely be enough to get him into this book, but now our story takes a dark turn. It's at this point that we should gently remind ourselves of what we said at the start – that just because someone is interesting does not make them necessarily good, and just because we can learn *something* from their lives, doesn't mean I'm suggesting we should emulate them in *all* things. So, bearing that in mind – Julius is sent away to India following an allegation in the press of attempted rape.

According to a press report at the time, "He enticed one of the house-maids . . . to call at a house in the Strand, where he had previously secreted himself, and . . . threatened the girl to murder her, if she refused to yield up her person."[11] The article goes on to claim that Kitty tried to pay the maid to hush her up, but she is determined to go public, and so Kitty sends Julius out of the country to escape prosecution.

When I first read this story, I didn't want to believe it – the last 200 years are full of examples of black men being falsely accused of assaulting white women – but as a historian, I can only tell you what the record says, and that there is just the same amount of evidence for the rape allegation as there is for the funny House of Lords story above. Since Julius gets out of the country, the case never comes to court, and so the newspaper article is all we have to go on.

What we do know is that in 1777 Julius does indeed make a hasty exit from England, and travels to Bengal in India, which is under the control of the British East India Company (EIC). The EIC was founded in 1600 to import pepper from Indonesia and Papua New Guinea, but by the time Julius makes his flight into exile it controls huge chunks of the Indian subcontinent. It has bases in places like Chennai, Kolkata and Mumbai, hires soldiers to drive out rival European companies and forces Indian rulers to accept its trade terms. In 1764, the EIC defeats the Mughal Emperor and rules his territory for profit, stripping it bare of assets and using the money to train up tens of thousands of soldiers with the latest tactics and equipment.

Unlike in later years of the British Empire, under the EIC there's no pretence of "bringing civilization" to India – it's just trying to make as much profit as possible. A few years before Julius arrives, a famine hits Bengal. Normally, Indian rulers lift taxes in famine years, but in the Bengal Famine of 1770, the EIC sends out soldiers to take taxes from starving families by force, bayoneting and hanging people who can't or won't pay. By the end, people are dying in the street, selling their farm implements and even their children for food, and there are reports of cannibalism. Somewhere between 3 and 5 million people are killed, and at the 1772 AGM, EIC shareholders vote to increase their dividend from 10 per cent to 12.5 per cent. By the time Julius arrives, the British government has realized that this isn't tenable and buys a 50 per cent share in the EIC in order to get the company under control, making it the first time the British state actually gets its hands dirty with colonialism in India.

Once Julius leaves England, records of him get scarcer, but there are some things we do know. Ignatius Sancho (c1729–80), the first known black voter in Britain, tries to get him to reform his free-spending ways and straighten up. He writes to Julius, "Let me, as your true friend, recommend seriously to you to make yourself acquainted with your Bible. . . . Use your every endeavour to be a good man."[12] Ignatius is speaking from experience here: when he was young, he was pretty wild too, and once lost all his clothes at a gaming table.[13] Ignatius especially wants Julius to pay off his debts, telling him, "Send over 20*l*. [pounds] to discharge your debt at . . . the sadler – it was borrowed money, you know", and warning another of his friends, Jack Wingrave, "against lending [Julius] money upon any account, for he has everything but – principle, he will never pay you."[14]

Julius badly needs money. Kitty dies only two days after he leaves England (*probably* just a coincidence – she's in her seventies by now), so without the duchess to bankroll his cravat habit, he picks up a new patron, the fabulously named "Memory" Middleton. (His real first name is Nathaniel; "Memory" is a nickname he picks up after his boss, head of the EIC Warren Hastings [1732–1818], gets impeached in 1787 and Nathaniel suddenly "can't remember" anything that might make his boss look bad on the witness stand.)[15]

Spending the rest of his life in India, Julius uses his horsemanship to get a job training up new horses for the government. He has "a large salary"[16] and generally does pretty well for himself. He advertises in Indian newspapers, and teaches both men and women to be cool, sword-swinging horseback riders. He gets married and has at least two kids, although we have no record of his wife's name outside of "Mrs Soubise".[17]

Julius Soubise ended up a long way from where he started, on the other side of the world and at the opposite end of the social spectrum. Without being born into land or money, he was able to secure this life for himself firstly with an overpowering amount of charisma to get Kitty Hyde to patronize him, and subsequently by being great at riding and fencing so that he could manage without her. Charming older ladies and swinging a big sword around: two important life skills to master.

CHAPTER 16

ETHEL MACDONALD

teaches us not to let anyone pick our battles for us.

Ethel MacDonald (1909–60) is a working-class girl from industrial Scotland who decides to do something revolutionary. When the Spanish Civil War breaks out in 1936, Britain forbids its citizens from going to help, but she disregards that rule, goes to the republican side and reports what's going on in socialist Spain for Scottish newspapers. Her anarchist radio broadcasts are listened to around the world, especially in the US. When the communist secret police scour Barcelona in search of anarchists, she helps to smuggle anti-fascist fugitives out to the UK. The papers dub her "the Scots Scarlet Pimpernel". After a while, she too escapes back to Glasgow. When she's called up for National Service in World War II she refuses to go, and the authorities decide it's best to leave her alone. Ethel is someone who chooses her own battles her whole life, no matter what she is supposed to do.

Born in Motherwell, Ethel grows up surrounded by steel factories. Her dad is a coach painter who works for the foundries, hand-painting the sides of horse-drawn carriages and wagons with the company livery. She does well at school, and even takes elocution lessons (which are going to be a great help later when she's on the radio). But her destiny isn't to get a world-class education. She leaves school at 14, and historian Chris Dolan suggests that she might have got pregnant by an unknown American, who promptly flees back to the US without her. Ethel goes into hospital, has a miscarriage, and never has a serious relationship again.

After that, she starts working in a newsagent's, but one day, without saying a word to anyone, she simply disappears. These are Ethel's "lost years", when we're not sure exactly where she goes. We know that, despite having no money, she somehow ends up in London, where she gets a waitressing job. It's the 1920s, so she's wearing a little white pinny and a hat and bustling around between tables, but although she's a service worker, she's hardly subservient. When she gets a promotion to senior waitress, she finds out that she'll only be paid 16 shillings a week, as opposed to the 18 shillings a man would get in the same job. Ethel argues with the manager and leaves – whether because she's fired or quits, we don't know. Either way, she leaves London and goes back to Glasgow, where we pick up her story again.

In Glasgow, Ethel becomes deeply interested in anarchism. Although it sounds like wild, dog-eat-dog lawlessness, anarchism actually has a lot of writing and political thought behind it, and if you want to read some serious philosophy, you can try anarchist authors like Mikhail Bakunin (1814–76), Pyotr Kropotkin (1842–1921), Emma Goldman (1869–1940) and more recently Noam Chomsky (born 1928). Anarchism is a left-wing movement like communism or socialism, but with a particular focus on getting rid of any positions of power that people unjustly hold over others. "Anarchism" literally means "without leaders", and holds that people are perfectly capable of solving the problems in their own lives without kings, presidents and bosses telling them what to do. In this way, anarchists disagree, sometimes very strongly, with other left-wing movements that *do* have presidents or general secretaries or high councils. Ethel particularly doesn't like electing people to a Parliament – why would you choose someone to decide things for you instead of deciding them yourself? She says, "For many years now the workers have been fed on the idea that with the right persons in control with alleged working-class leaders arranging the affairs of the nations, social change, a betterment of conditions leading finally to complete emancipation would come about . . . . The more mighty the strength of these social-democratic organizations became, the further has been the distance placed to the betterment of the conditions of the workers."[1]

It isn't just Ethel looking for a new political philosophy in the 1930s: people all over the world are getting radicalized. The Great Depression (1929–39) hits the working classes hard. Around 100,000 Glaswegians are unemployed, and so many are forced to leave their homes after being denied benefits that the city is surrounded by "nomads" who camp out in the countryside. The reaction of those in charge is not to fix things by giving ordinary people money to spend to get the economy up and running again, but to cut wages and unemployment benefits so that they will be forced by poverty into taking any job going. But this doesn't make sense – the Great Depression wasn't caused by a wave of people who just quit their jobs for no reason and needed a stern financial incentive to get back to work. Hence the government's solution doesn't do anything, and in fact makes the situation worse. When the established political system can't resolve your problems, you tend to look elsewhere. On the left, membership of the British Communist Party doubles between 1935 and 1937, and on the right, fascism is also on the rise.

Ethel joins the United Socialist Movement (USM), a small anarchist group in Glasgow, and writes for their newspaper, *Regeneración*. She also volunteers at their Workers' Advice Bureau, where poor people can get legal guidance and someone to compose letters for them if they struggle with writing. Ethel's friend John Taylor Caldwell said, "It was a miserable little office with a table, one chair, no lighting, no toilet."[2] They are so hard-up that they can't afford typewriters and printing machines, so instead they borrow them from companies by spamming their "free trial" periods over and over (a time-honoured tactic). Ethel teaches herself to type so that there's someone at the USM who can work these new-fangled machines.

Anarchism never gets much of a foothold in Britain, but in 1930s Barcelona it's a different story. In 1936, Spain is pretty socialist during the period known as the Second Spanish Republic. It has a democratically elected government, communism is increasingly popular, and there's even been a short-lived workers' rebellion. And then in July 1936 a group of military generals start a full-blown coup. A young general named Francisco Franco, a member of the right-wing Falange, leads troops from Morocco across the Mediterranean and begins to move through Spain. His forces are known as the "nationalists", and they're very right-wing, conservative, and even fascist, whereas those fighting against them – republicans and revolutionaries – are a coalition of liberals, communists, socialists and anarchists.

We may be used to thinking of left-wing radicals as the ones who do rebellions, but this is the other way round – a fascist rebellion against a democratic government. Liberal countries like Britain and France declare themselves neutral, but fascist Italy and Nazi Germany feel no compunction about giving the nationalists guns, tanks and planes. The German air force, the Luftwaffe, even creates a whole group called the Condor Legion to send planes over to bomb republican Spain and utterly destroy the civilian town of Guernica.

In desperate need of help, Spanish communists organize the International Brigades, recruiting young working-class people to come to Spain from all over the world. Volunteers arrive from France, Britain, Poland, Belgium and even some brave souls from Italy and Germany. People come from further afield, too: Mexicans, Americans, Canadians, South Africans, Chinese, Mongolians, Palestinians, Iraqis, Egyptians, Filipinos and Argentines. One-fifth of the volunteers are Jewish. An estimated 40,000 people join the International Brigades altogether. The region of Catalonia and its main city of Barcelona is particularly anarchist: divorce is allowed, abortion rights are widened, feminist groups set up women's colleges, and anarchists run farms, organize defences, keep shops and businesses open, replace the police with civilian self-defence groups, and make sure the trains run on time. The Confederación Nacional del Trabajo (CNT; National Confederation of Labour), an anarchist group, runs the telephone exchange, anarchist flags are flown from buildings, and factories are run by their workers. Writer George Orwell (1903–50), himself an international volunteer, writes, "It was the first time that I had ever been in a town where the working class was in the saddle. . . . Waiters and shop-walkers looked you in the face and treated you as an equal."[3] Ethel simply has to see it for herself.

However, she doesn't have the money to get there (anarchist groups aren't typically rolling in cash), so she and colleague Jenny Patrick pretty much hitchhike the entire 1,600km (1,000-mile) journey from Glasgow. If they can't cadge lifts, they walk from town to town, meeting anarchist groups along the way and drumming up enough cash to catch the train or the bus to the next town along, where they repeat the process. Since the British government is officially neutral, they don't want people to go to Spain and interfere, and they clamp down most strictly on Brits heading off to help the republicans. But Ethel and Jenny make it to Barcelona in about three weeks, arriving in November 1936. Ethel hadn't told her family she was going.

In Barcelona, she uses the typing and newspaper-writing skills that she picked up at the USM to write articles on the state of the war for people back home. She sends them to Scottish weekly the *Bellshill Speaker*, earning her the nickname "The Bellshill Anarchist". But her efforts don't stop there. The CNT has a radio station to help its international volunteers communicate across language barriers, and in 1937 they choose Ethel as the voice of their English-language service. She says, "Are you, English-speaking workers, prepared to let this tragic force which means the rape of Spain go on? Are you prepared to lend yourselves to this mockery?"[4] She drums up financial support, criticizes governments that have remained neutral, and reports on the fall of Málaga, interviewing a British resident who has been forced to flee the city. She is particularly popular in the US, where her Scottish accent stands out as unusual and delightful. Ethel spends a blissful six months in her element, working for a cause she believes in among people who support her.

But by April, cracks are appearing in the alliance between communists and anarchists. Anarchist newspapers are suspended and printing presses seized by people supposedly on their side. Worse, communists and anarchists keep assassinating each other. On 3 May 1937, Barcelona's anarchist-run telephone exchange is stormed by socialists. The workers defend the place with machineguns. Ethel reports on the ensuing chaos: "Jenny and I passed groups of men and women running, rifles in hand . . . the only sounds were the heavy firing and the screaming of ambulances."[5] She now has more important things to do than radio shows. She spends her time keeping anarchist fighters supplied, filling their cartridge clips and cooking their meals. She sees dozens of people shot, and has to crawl below barricades, trying not to let her head poke out. Jenny manages to get out and heads to Glasgow, but Ethel doesn't want to leave and, anyway, she doesn't have the right paperwork, since she entered the country illegally in the first place. By now she's been blacklisted by the British government, and letters and money from home are slowing to a trickle.

British people start being arrested by communist forces, who, again, are supposed to be on their side. One, Bob Smillie, dies under what Ethel thinks are suspicious circumstances. Her friend Dan Mullen gets shot at and beaten by the police and has his leg broken. She visits anarchists in prison and at great risk to herself smuggles in letters and food for them. She sets up escape routes for prisoners to leave Spain by finding them civilian clothes and new papers, and persuading sea captains to take them aboard their ships. Then, in the summer of 1937, armed men burst into her house in the early hours of the morning, turn the place upside-down, and drag her away to a hotel that has been turned into a prison. You'd think the conditions in a hotel-prison would be pretty decent, but this is far from the case: there's only one toilet between 150 prisoners, and they get nothing to eat except rice, potatoes and bread.

While on the outside Ethel was smuggling letters in, now she starts smuggling letters out. She collects letters from fellow prisoners and puts them in her empty food cans. The guards who clear them away are unaware that they're delivering them to an ally of hers who sends them on their way, either to a French captain who takes them abroad, or to the British consul. Ethel sneaks out her own news updates, too. She speaks out against the injustice of her situation: "Comrades are placed in a cell and allowed no visitors for as long as the authorities wish. The length of their detention without trial is likewise. The cases are too numerous to cite of prisoners kept for months without communication and without trial."[6] Her faithful listeners and readers realize that something is wrong, and she is so beloved that they mount an international campaign to find her and get her to safety.

In mid-July, the prison releases her, and you'd think she'd take the hint and get out of Spain, but there are two things that stop her. Firstly, she still doesn't have a visa to leave, and secondly, she isn't going to let a little thing like being imprisoned without trial cow her spirit. She marches right down to the police station to get her confiscated things back, and when they refuse to hand them over she tells them what she thinks of them: "I protested and gave them a lecture",[7] she reports. Imagine being imprisoned by a repressive regime, getting out, and then going back to tell them off! She does manage to get back her passport and money, but nothing else, and she can't return to her lodgings for fear they're being watched. Instead, she goes into hiding, sleeping in a different place every night. Somehow, she manages to find yet more energy to help escaped prisoners. Rumours in Britain swirl around that she's been rearrested or possibly tortured. Questions are asked in Parliament; her family believes she's dead. But finally she gets a pass to leave from the British consul and takes a boat out of Spain. She heads to Paris, safe at last.

Ethel then tours Europe giving speeches about her time in Barcelona and the importance of democracy, liberty and justice. She speaks out against Mussolini, Hitler, Franco and Stalin. When she finally makes it back to Glasgow, 300 people turn up to her house to welcome her back. But the story doesn't have such a happy ending for Spain. In 1939, Franco's forces emerge victorious, and he's officially recognized as leader of Spain by the UK, France, Holland, the US and even the Pope. He goes on to rule Spain for decades until his death in 1975, executing an estimated two million people and banning opposition parties. As for Ethel, she never loses her anti-authoritarian streak. By 1939 she's had enough of armed conflict and denounces World War II as a struggle between oppressors. When she's conscripted, she sends her call-up papers back with a single sentence scrawled on top: "Come and get me."[8] They decide it's best to leave her be.

Ethel spent the rest of her life with her Glaswegian anarchist friends, running a publishing house until her death in 1960. To the end, no Parliament, no government, and no king could tell her what to do. She refused to let others pick her battles for her. Even 30 years after her Spanish escapade, her death was broadcast on the news, and when her friends came home from the hospital, their cab driver refused to take his fare out of respect for "the great Ethel MacDonald."[9]

CHAPTER 17
THE CHARTISTS

teaches us that the idea you think is too radical
today might be common sense tomorrow.

The state of democracy in 1830s Britain is pretty shoddy. In fact, you probably wouldn't recognize a country run this way *as* a democracy if it existed today. Only about one in six adult men have the vote, and no women at all. And so, thousands of working-class folk come together to demand change. They protest, they write articles, they pull down fences and they even riot in order to get the vote. To the upper classes, this is terrifying. Police officers and even soldiers are sent to break up Chartist marches, the demonstrators are denounced as dangerous radicals, and the movement ends seemingly without progress. And yet, over the following 80 years, almost all their demands get adopted. Today, any society that doesn't include them seems tyrannical to us. The idea you think is too radical today might be common sense tomorrow.

If you want to vote in the 1830s, it's not enough to be an adult man. The upper class do not trust the working class to vote "properly", and so the vote is given to men based on how expensive their houses are. If you live in an ordinary working-class house, or worse, you are homeless, you don't get to vote at all, so you don't get to change who gets to vote! This isn't the only thing the working class are fed up with. The Industrial Revolution is in full swing; people who were once reapers and ploughmen and wool-spinners, working according to the sun, are now expected to operate spinning cotton frames, feed steam engines, and turn up on the clock's time for their shifts. People move into cities, creating massive new conurbations like Manchester and Birmingham with slum housing, overcrowding, no green spaces, poor sanitation leading to cholera outbreaks, and soot constantly hanging in the air.

You'll generally be working six days a week, with no long holidays, only the occasional holy day off, like Christmas. There is no such thing as an old-age pension, so you work until you drop. Wages are so low that women in the textile industry are increasingly forced into factory jobs instead of their old work-from-home arrangements, meaning that children and housework are neglected. And working conditions in those factories are utterly abysmal – one source from the time calls them "cruel and tyrannical arrangements."

So in 1838, working-class groups all over the country organize and put together a six-point plan for a better, more democratic country. They call it *The People's Charter*, and these are their demands:

1 **Annual elections.** In 1838, an election might be called as infrequently as every seven years. You might vote for a candidate based on his promises about, say, Catholic emancipation or the Corn Laws, only for him to about-face once he's taken his seat in Parliament. If that happens, you're stuck with him for a decent chunk of your life. Out of all the Chartists' demands, this is the one that we would probably say is the least important now – can you imagine having to go through an election cycle *every year?* – but at the time it's seen as a crucial way for voters to hold their representatives to account.

2 **Secret ballots.** Yup, your vote isn't secret until the 1870s, meaning that voter intimidation is ridiculously easy. Some candidates, especially in seats with small voter populations, hire "cudgel men" (yes, that's literally their job title) to make sure the vote goes their way. It's not just the threat of physical violence, either: what if your landlord is running for a seat in Parliament? You could find yourself homeless if you vote the wrong way. The Chartists demand secret ballots, so that when the cudgel men come round you can simply lie to their faces and your landlord cannot know you voted against him.

3 **All regions to be equal in the electoral system.** Not all constituencies are created equal. In the 18th century, some of them are "rotten boroughs" where hardly anyone lives anymore. Most famously, the deserted town of Old Sarum, near Salisbury, Wiltshire, was a borough with just 11 voters, none of whom actually lived there, but it still had two MPs. All you needed to do to become an MP was literally buy the land, and now you're the landlord for all the farmers who are your voters. By 1838, the rotten boroughs have been abolished, but there are still thousands of people moving from the countryside to the cities, so a vote in a rural constituency with 30 families and their sheep is going to have a much

greater influence on the overall outcome of a general election than a vote in an overcrowded Sheffield constituency with several factories' worth of voters. The Chartists want equal-sized constituencies, where the country is divided up into chunks of roughly equal population. That is going to mean there are some urban constituencies the size of a single massive street, whereas some rural ones will be spread out over a huge area of farmland, but everyone's vote will count for roughly the same.

4 **All men eligible to be MPs.** It's not just the vote that working-class men are not allowed; they're also barred from becoming MPs. You have to own a certain amount of property to take your seat in the House of Commons, so anyone who's renting is right out.

5 **A salary for MPs.** Even if a working-class man is allowed to take his seat, how is he supposed to feed his family? The job of being an MP is unpaid. All current members of the House are living off rent from their tenants, and off their investments. They've never needed a salary – instead, they take the job so that they can influence laws to keep themselves rich. The Chartists argue that MPs should be paid, so that they can go to Westminster without worrying that their wives won't be stuck for bread while they're gone.

6 **The vote for all men.** The big one: all men over 21 should be able to vote, not just the ones who live in fancy houses. By this point in history, the US and France have had revolutions based on democratic principles (even if those principles didn't play out in practice), and Chartists have been avidly reading American and French thinkers who advocate "one man, one vote".

The People's Charter is first presented to the public at a rally in Glasgow in May 1838, when maybe 150,000 people turn up to hear speeches by activists from all over the country. The news spreads like wildfire, and Chartist societies start popping up across Britain, especially in the north. It's hard to imagine the scale of this today. 150,000 sounds like an extremely large number for a single rally, especially before modern public transport, but Chartist demonstrations regularly draw tens of thousands of people, and up to 200,000 isn't unheard of. In the following year Chartists take their first petition to Parliament. The petition (that is, the actual bit of paper) is 4.8km (3 *miles!*) long and signed by more than 1.2 million people. The House of Commons votes it down by 235 votes against to just 46 in favour.

If this huge mass of people is a little tricky to wrap our minds around, let's get down to a more human level and have a look at some individual

Chartists. One of the leading lights of the movement is Feargus O'Connor (1794–1855), an Irish landowner who moves to Oldham, Lancashire, where he sees the rotten heart of the Industrial Revolution. He describes his first meeting with Oldham cotton workers: "The pallid face, the emaciated frame, and the twisted limbs. . . . From that moment I became the unpaid advocate of my fellow man."[1] He's a really talented public speaker, which is especially important in a period where a large minority of the population is still illiterate. In fact, the whole Chartist movement has to be structured around the fact that its participants might not be able to read, so a really popular evening activity is to gather in a courtyard or a beer shop and listen to someone else read aloud from a Chartist newspaper. Chartists will even buy pamphlets they can't read, knowing that they'll be able to find someone at the pub to read it out to the room. Rallies feature many little podiums dotted about a park or a common, each with a local leader or activist giving a speech, like separate stages at an outdoor music festival (in the days before microphones, having many speakers going simultaneously is the only way you're going to hold the interest of 50,000 people). So in a movement like this, someone like Feargus, who has a great loud voice, is going to shine. But by 1838, his speaking tours aren't getting the attention he would like, so he decides to make his own newspaper.

It's called the *Northern Star*. Feargus writes a column for it every week, and he also prints accounts of rallies and meetings happening all over the country. By 1838, the *Northern Star* has a circulation of 10,000, and at its height it's outselling *The Times*.[2] Suddenly, activists who were working in their local town or city pretty much alone can now see other people doing the same thing as them all over the country. If you're fighting the Poor Law in Bradford, you can now learn about people who agree with you in Bristol and London and Newcastle. People name their *kids* after Feargus – that's how important he is to the movement.

The Chartists limit their ambitions to just getting the vote for men, but it's worth noting that people are thinking about female suffrage already in this period. Referencing the British monarch of the time, Victoria, Chartist R J Richardson says that "If a woman is qualified to be a queen over a great nation, [she] ought not to be excluded from her share in the executive and legislative power of the country."[3] And the Charter itself mentions women's suffrage, but comes to the conclusion that it has to be jettisoned to make sure men's suffrage is achieved: "Against [female suffrage] we have no just argument to adduce, but only to express our fears of entertaining it, lest the false estimate man entertains for this half of the human family may cause his ignorance and prejudice to be enlisted to retard the progress of his own freedom."[4] Despite being kinda thrown under the bus, lots of women are Chartists. Of more than 500 Chartist societies around the country, over 100 of them are women's groups. It isn't thought proper for women to do public speaking, but they can collect funds, make banners and organize meetings. Because women are doing most of the household shopping, they can boycott anti-Chartist shops; and in riots, they can throw stones and get arrested just the same as the guys. One leading member of the movement, Elizabeth Neesom (c1797–1866), even runs an entire Chartist school on Brick Lane in London, where activists' children could get a free or subsidized education.

Another leading Chartist is William Cuffay (1788–1870). He isn't the only black Chartist, but he is the most prominent. His father is born into slavery in St Kitts, but he later comes to Britain, where William is born. We think he might have some Ghanaian heritage, as the name "Cuffay" sounds like an anglicization of "Kofi", a name from the Twi language of Ghana. William's spine and shins don't grow straight, so he never gets taller than 1.5m (5ft), but he finds work as a tailor in London and in 1839 he joins the Chartists as a founder member of the Metropolitan Tailors' Charter Association.

One big debate within Chartism is if and when the movement should use violence. If petitions don't work; if Parliament refuses to give working-class people their rights, at what point should Chartists take those rights? Again, they are looking at the bloody revolutions in the US and France, and although they would like to get their way with words, they aren't very hopeful that just asking nicely will work. "Moral force" Chartists advocate peaceful methods only, and the motto of "physical force" Chartists is "Peaceably if we may, forcibly if we must." Whether or not the Chartists use violence, the government is certainly prepared to use violence against them. In November 1839, 7,000 Chartists march through Newport, Monmouthshire, and are confronted by soldiers. Twenty-four of the protestors are killed, 125 arrested, and 21 charged with high treason. As the movement continues to bring petitions and is continually ignored by Parliament, William reluctantly becomes more of a physical force kinda guy.

It all comes to a head in 1848, when Chartists organize a huge march through London with their biggest petition yet. The plan is to start off north of the River Thames on Tottenham Court Road, cross to the south bank at Kennington Common for speeches, and then cross back to the north to deliver the petition to Parliament. This thing is huge – there is a whole carriage just for the petition, written on five *bales* of paper. But the march doesn't go smoothly – once the crowd gets to Kennington, Chartist leaders like Feargus reveal that they've been working with the police to disperse the meeting there, before they get to Parliament. The petition is put into cabs to drive to Westminster, but the people won't be going with it. Feargus tells the crowd to go home. William is shocked and furious. He denounces the leadership as cowardly, but there's not much he can do. If he does want to lead the crowd back over the river to Parliament, they will have to funnel themselves over Westminster Bridge, where they can easily be barricaded in and shot at. He reluctantly goes home.

In the aftermath, Feargus argues that he did what was best for the movement – that the crowd was too riled up to be trusted not to break things when they got to Parliament. He says, "The dogs of war would have been let loose, and this morning our cause would have been a laughing-stock."[5] William loses his tailoring job. His wife, Mary, has to take work as a charwoman, but when her employers find out who her husband is, she gets fired too. In response, they get radical. William and Mary start melting down old printers' type to make into bullets – the time for words is over. He does demonstrations for his fellow Chartists on how to use a pike, and advises Chartist women to fill bottles with nails to throw at soldiers and policemen from their windows. He becomes a member of an "Ulterior Committee" that is ready to back up their demands with force. They plan to start a full-blooded revolution, beginning with arson attacks on specific buildings around London. William really doesn't want it to come to this, but he is the committee's secretary. Suddenly, during one of their meetings at the Orange Tree pub in Bloomsbury, the police burst in and arrest the conspirators. As William is being read his rights, he says, "Oh, that's quite sufficient; as I am a Chartist I understand it." He is charged with "levying war on the queen" and sentenced to transportation to Tasmania for life.

The story of Chartism can feel like a big let-down. The Chartists' petitions were dismissed, their leaders imprisoned, and the movement thoroughly stamped out after 1848. Most of them did not live to see their demands accepted. But eventually they were accepted. A century later, almost everything that the Chartists wanted had become common sense. Secret ballots, universal suffrage, no property qualification for MPs – these things were so radical in the 1830s that their proponents were shot at and transported to the other side of the world, but these days, anyone who argues against them would be thought a dangerously anti-democratic maniac. Be careful what you dismiss as "too radical", because in 100 years' time you might end up on the wrong side of history.

CHAPTER 18

GERRARD WINSTANLEY

teaches us that the Earth was made for all to share.

Staying on the subject of things that were too radical for their time, did you know that a merchant tailor from Wigan invented communism two centuries before Karl Marx? In 1649, Gerrard Winstanley (1609–76) and a few like-minded friends get together on a hill in Surrey and try to build their dream society – a moneyless, classless Utopia. They grow food on land that everyone else has given up on as barren and worthless, and Gerrard writes thousands of words detailing his vision for the future, where everyone is equal and the land is shared by all.

We don't know much about Gerrard's life before the commune. He's born in Lancashire, and at some point he comes to work as a merchant tailor in London, where he marries surgeon's daughter Susan King. In the 1640s, his business goes belly-up. His customers fail to pay their bills, so Gerrard starts failing to pay *his* bills. In *A Watch-word to the City of London* (1649), he writes: "I was beaten out both of estate and trade, and forced to accept the good will of friends crediting of me."[1] In 1643, he and Susan move to the village of Cobham in Surrey and become farmers. Life is hard. He says, "my weak back found the burthen heavier than I could bear."

It's not just the day-to-day labour of planting and ploughing that Gerrard is struggling with. The whole country is at a historic low point. If you ever get to time-travel back in England's history, your last year of choice should be, well, any of the plague years, but 1649 has to be the next worst option. In a nutshell, King Charles I believes that, since he's king, God has decreed that he can do what he likes without consulting his Parliament. As you might imagine, Parliament disagrees. Both sides amass armies, and in 1642 the tension spills over into violence.

The whole country is divided, with some areas declaring for the king and others for Parliament. Brothers fight brothers, fathers fight sons. Gerrard's home in Surrey finds itself particularly pinched in 1647, when Parliament captures Charles and imprisons him at Oatlands Palace nearby. People flock to see him.

Surrey is a big Parliamentarian stronghold, so its residents are often expected to "free quarter" (give free accommodation to) Parliamentarian soldiers, or to pay for their lodgings elsewhere, and this is a huge financial burden. John Turner, a landowner from Bletchingley, a village in the same county, tells the House of Commons that the taxes and free quarter demanded by the soldiers are so strenuous that people are deserting the area, and his tenants' farms "lye at wast [lie in waste] for that he is not able to manage them."[2] Gerrard's village of Cobham lies on the road between London and the Parliamentary garrison at Portsmouth, so soldiers are always tramping through. Worse, some men in Cobham are rounded up and forced to join the army – "pressed" – in 1643, 1645 and 1647–8. And then in 1648, a famine hits. Bread gets so expensive that people riot, and bodies are found slumped in the road, starved to death.

On top of being pressed, taxed and starved to death, there's something else going on in 1640s England – enclosure. In Gerrard's day, all the land in the country is supposed to be ultimately owned by the king, who parcels it out to his friends – aristocrats, gentry and the Church – who in turn sublet it to people further down the class rankings. Most people live in villages where the farmland is owned by a few big players. But just because you don't *own* land doesn't mean you don't have *rights* to it. There'll be bits of your village known as "common land" – usually scrubby bits that aren't great for farming, but which you're allowed to put cows or geese on, or collect firewood from, or trap animals on. Without somewhere to collect firewood or keep animals, you might have no way of keeping warm or fed. Your village will generally have some people actually living on this common land, too – very poor people indeed. But gradually, over the course of centuries, this common land is being taken away. One day you'll turn up, and the local landowner will have put a fence around it. *Oh, you were using this land? Your father and his father, for generations? Do you have a piece of paper saying you own it though?* By the end of the 17th century, only 23 per cent of the country is unenclosed. With nowhere else to go, you might be forced to move to a town, or to pay more in rent so that you have some guaranteed land, or worse, become a vagrant, a crime punishable by having your ear burned through with a red-hot poker. So, y'know, there's a lot that people are mad about.

Finally, in January 1649, Parliament gives up trying to keep Charles under lock and key, and cuts his head off instead. At first, people all over the country get really excited. *The king is gone! We can decide for ourselves what society is going to look like now!* People come up with all sorts of different ideas, and debate them furiously. *Should we vote for a king? Should we put church leaders in charge? Who should get to vote, and how?* The whole country is really teetering on the edge of something here. A butterfly's fart might be enough to push England over the edge to build a long-lasting democratic republic over a century before the French or the Americans will try it in their revolutions. In Gerrard's day, almost all of these ideas are practically unprecedented – monarchies have been the norm in Europe for so long that no one's really tested any other way of running things.

Gerrard publishes his first writing in 1648. He cranks out four huge works in a single year about the nature of religion and morality. He believes that soon God will get rid of all conflict and crime, and everyone will work together in harmony on the land. No one will be an employer or an employee; everyone will be equal. He asks, "Was the earth made for to preserve a few covetous, proud men, to live at ease, and for them to bag and barn up the treasures of the earth from others, that they might beg or starve in a fruitful Land, or was it made to preserve all her children?"[3] He thinks it's immoral for lords and churchmen to lounge around reading books and drinking champagne out of each other's belly buttons (or whatever aristocrats do all day) while making other people work to eat. He argues that since the king, who owns all the land, is dead, we should go back to the system he supposes we had before monarchies, when the land belonged to everyone, and everyone worked it together for the common good. In October, he is briefly arrested for blasphemy and, to be honest, the stuff he's saying *is* completely against the orthodox doctrine of the time.

In April 1649, Gerrard and a small group of fellow idealists put his ideas into practice. They arrive at St George's Hill, a small piece of Surrey wasteland formerly owned by the Crown, and start farming it. One witness from the time says that "They invite all to come in & helpe them, and promise them meate, drink & Clothes. They doe threaten to pull downe & level all parke pales [fences] and lay all open."[4] They quickly acquire the nickname "Diggers" from all the digging they're doing, and they claim to number in the thousands already (there's probably only ever about 60 of them, even at the peak of their activities – awks).[5]

The St George's Hill settlement is never very big, but that doesn't stop Gerrard from having some truly gigantic ideas. In his ideal society, owning land, paying wages, and "the thieving art of buying and selling" would be abolished.[6] Everyone works on the land together, and all the harvested crops go into a big barn, where people can collect them for free when they need them. We'd still need some officials to assign people jobs and deal with disputes, but these people would be elected and there'd be an election every year, so if they get corrupt, they can be voted out quickly. In terms of who can vote, Gerrard is really radical for the time in believing that suffrage should be universal (at least, universal among those who want to participate – Gerrard thinks that if you want to hold onto your land, that's fine, but you don't get to vote over the rest of us who want to try the communism thing). He even believes that criminals and people with different religious beliefs should vote, which is another one of those things that sounds utterly normal now, but at the time marks Gerrard out as a fringe weirdo.

Gerrard also talks quite a bit about how education should work. He thinks all children should get some tuition, although unlike basically every school at the time, his ideal school won't teach the Bible. It's not that he doesn't believe in God – he's very devout – but he thinks that God lives in your heart, and all these sermons and Bible readings are shouting over what God wants to say to you. Instead, "it is profitable for the commonwealth that children be trained up in trades and some bodily employment, as well as in learning languages or the histories of former ages."[7] In Gerrard's Utopia, teachers would explain the growing of crops, mining, livestock, forestry and – a bit of an odd one out – astronomy. On top of the education for children, adults should get a day off every week to broaden their horizons, with study groups for law, politics, the news, arts and sciences, foreign languages, ethics and philosophy.

Pretty soon, all this utopianism draws the attention of local landowners, who really don't like this group of rowdy dreamers just farming wherever they feel like. The Diggers argue that St George's Hill was "waste ground" not considered good enough to farm, owned by a dead and overthrown king, but that doesn't cut any ice. Parliamentary General Thomas Fairfax sends a group of soldiers to see what's going on over there. The soldiers actually meet Gerrard, but they figure that he and his friends are not hurting anything. There are only about 20 of them, and "the business is not worth the writing nor yet taking nottis [notice] of."[8] Ouch. A short while later, Gerrard actually goes to meet the great general himself in London to explain what he's doing. He refuses to doff his cap, and when Fairfax demands to know why, Winstanley reportedly tells Fairfax that he is "but their fellow creature."[9]

Fairfax's men might think that the Diggers aren't a threat, but the local bigwigs disagree. On 11 June 1649, landowners William Star and John Taylor lead an attack on them. Over the course of the summer, Gerrard's livestock keeps getting pinched to try to drive him out. He'll wake up in the morning to find his cows gone, and he has to wander around the village farmland, trying to find them and bring them back. He says that someone attacked the cows "and beat them with their clubs, that the Cowes heads and sides did swell, which grieved tender hearts to see."[10] Cobham's church regularly preaches anti-Digger sermons, and on 17 June several members of the group are indicted for trespassing. Gerrard is fined ten pounds, nine shillings and a penny (you'd think they could at least round it down for him). He's charged with trespassing *again* in December, and landowner Francis Drake (no relation to the famous pirate of the same name) sends gangs after the Diggers to beat them up and burn down their houses.

After almost a year on St George's Hill, the Diggers give up and move to Little Heath in Cobham. And they do really well! By the spring of 1650, they're farming 4.4 hectares (11 acres) of grain, and have built six or seven houses. But they have the same problem again. The lord of the manor, Parson John Platt, lets cattle loose in the Diggers' fields and destroys their houses. The Diggers are facing assault and arson, and one Digger woman has a miscarriage after being attacked. They try to report these crimes to the authorities, but the charges are dismissed. After that, it seems like Gerrard quietly gives up on his commune. The Digger settlements fade out of the historical record, and Gerrard himself even drops off the map for a bit.[11] Maybe he's sent to prison, or maybe he's just keeping his head down and trying to rebuild a respectable life.

But as months pass and Parliament's army maintains its grip on the nation, all the radicals start to realize that the new boss is going to be the same as the old boss. Gerrard says, "We have parted with our Estates, we have lost our Friends in the Wars, which we willingly gave up, because Freedom was promised us; and now in the end we have new Task-Masters, and our old burdens increased: and though all sorts of people have taken an Engagement to cast out Kingly Power, yet Kingly Power remains in power still in the hands of those who have no more right to the Earth than ourselves."[12]

Gerrard stops writing and rejoins mainstream society. By the 1660s he's even become a minor member of the gentry himself. He gets bigwig jobs in Cobham like "overseer of the poor" and "churchwarden", and in 1671 becomes high constable for Elmbridge.[13] By the end of his life, he has a nice house in the fashionable London district of Bloomsbury.

If you go to St George's Hill today, you won't find any starry-eyed proto-communists there anymore. In an ironic twist, the hill is now home to a 390-hectare (964-acre) private gated community, the most expensive streets in Surrey, with mega-celebrities like John Lennon, Tom Jones and John Terry having lived there, as well as multi-millionaires like Theo Paphitis and Mian Muhammad Mansha.[14] It has a 27-hole golf course and a 34-court tennis club. It's so exclusive that even the Google Street View car can't get into it.

Although Gerrard's commune didn't get the success he wanted during his lifetime, his ideas have blossomed since. In the 20th and 21st centuries, land reformers all over the country credit him as an inspiration. *Winstanley,* a film of his life, was released in 1975 and in the 1990s activist group The Land Is Ours briefly occupied St George's Hill, just as Gerrard did 300 years previously.[15] To those who read Gerrard's words and carry on his work, one message is clear: the land is not meant to be parcelled off for the enjoyment of only a few. The Earth was made for all of us to share.

CHAPTER 19

MARY ANNING

teaches us to tread softly, for we tread on
long-dead beasts with teeth the size of our faces.

If you've ever been a child with a dinosaur fixation (approximately seven to ten years seems to be the age range at which the brain mysteriously acquires a knack for memorizing and pronouncing words like *pachycephalosaurus*), then there's a good chance you'll know about Mary Anning (1799–1847). Mary is possibly the world's greatest fossil hunter, and completely changes our understanding of the origin of species and the age of the Earth. And when she finds her first great ancient beast, a sea creature with huge, staring eyes and a face that seems to have grown longer purely to fit more teeth in, she is only 12 years old. She's known as the "Princess of Palaeontology"[1] and is an inspiration to dino-hunting kids everywhere.

Mary is born into a working-class family in Lyme Regis, a town in Dorset on England's south coast. Even while she's still a baby, she manages to be exceptional. One day, a lady named Elizabeth Haskings takes baby Mary and two other kids out to see a horse-riding display; it starts pouring with rain, and Elizabeth takes the children to shelter under a tree. (Don't try this at home, kids.) Lightning strikes the tree, and everyone is killed, except, miraculously, baby Mary. People at the time think that the lightning made her into a genius: one person said that she "from that time, from a dull child, became very intelligent"[2] (sidenote: who calls a baby "dull"? What's the infant done to you?).

Lyme Regis is a great place to go fossil-hunting. That's because 200 million years ago it was at the bottom of the sea. The top dogs were huge marine lizards like plesiosaurs and ichthyosaurs eating fish and shelly animals, while pteranodons flew overhead. Nowadays, every time there's a storm, the sea knocks chunks off the cliffs in which a practised eye can spot ammonites and gryphaea (devil's toenails) lurking under the surface.

Mary isn't the first person to go raking through Dorset's coastline for weird-shaped rocks. Her dad did the same thing, selling them to tourists as curiosities and taking Mary and her brother Joseph with him. But Mary's dad dies when she's just 11 years old, leaving the family not only in poverty but also with his debts. They spend five years on "parish relief" (the Georgian equivalent of being on benefits) and Mary never goes to school. In fact, despite finding incredible fossils that push forward the boundaries of scientific knowledge, Mary never makes it out of the working class, and only once even leaves Lyme. But one day, as she's walking down the street with an ammonite she's found, a lady stops her in the street and gives her half a crown for it. To an impoverished child, this is a huge amount of money. Mary then has an idea.

A year earlier, her brother had spotted something sticking out of a cliff. It looked like the head of a huge crocodile. Now Mary goes back to have a proper look. The Annings hire a team of workmen to get the head out of the cliff, and Mary carefully chips the rock away from the fossil at home, leaving behind the skeleton of what we now know as an ichthyosaur.

Ichthyosaurs look a bit like dolphins, with a bottle nose and a streamlined body, but they're not closely related – it's just that this is a really good shape for swimming and catching fish, so evolution has come up with it a few times separately. Ichthyosaurs even evolved the same dorsal fins and tails as dolphins all on their own, because those fins are just such a good idea! Unlike dolphins, though, you wouldn't want to run into one of these in a dark reef – they're fitted with long rows of sharp teeth, and have a bone in the eye known as a *scleral ring* about the size and shape of a pineapple slice, which gives their fossils permanent, unblinking grins. They're also not dinosaurs – again, they're just not very closely related. Instead, they are classed as reptiles, albeit reptiles that give birth to live young, a fact we know because we have found fossils of ichthyosaur mums, mid-birth, with babies halfway out. Ichthyosaurs are found all over the world, and people were finding *parts* of them for ages, but we'd always thought they were fish or crocodiles until 1811, when Mary and Joseph Anning find this whole skull and a bit of a torso – the most complete specimen ever found at the time.

Mary's ichthyosaur is sold to local collector Henry Hoste Henley for £23, and Henley sells it to William Bullock, who runs a natural history museum on Piccadilly in London. There, the prestigious Geological Society of London hear about it. They're a club that puts on lectures and passes around new discoveries for all kinds of rock-loving gentlemen, and counts among its members geologists, palaeontologists and natural historians who are still commemorated and celebrated in museums around the world to this day, such as Henry De La Beche (1796–1855), Charles Lyell (1797–1875) and our boy William Buckland (see Chapter 7). In fact, I'm delighted to tell you that William and Mary get on really well – William brings his kids down to Lyme to go fossil-hunting with Mary, they write letters to each other, and William makes sure that the British Museum buys Mary's best specimens (and pays a good price for them, too).

But this doesn't mean that Mary is immediately catapulted to fame and fortune. The family is still very poor – in fact, when fossil hunter Thomas Birch (1768–1829) comes to visit, he finds them on the point of selling their furniture. He actually sells off his own collection to raise money for them, saying that "I may never again possess what I am about to part with; yet in doing it I shall have the satisfaction of knowing that the money will be well applied."[3] Finding fossils is hard and dangerous work. If you're imagining a cheerful day by the beach with a little trowel, delicately popping ammonites into your hand, think again – Mary is out in all weathers, since immediately after a storm is the best time to find new fossils. She's heaving around huge lumps of rock for a living, and her dog dies in a landslide that only narrowly misses her.

Mary's next discovery is even bigger than the ichthyosaur – it's a plesiosaur. This is another sea lizard with a huge snake-like neck and massive flippers. Fossil hunter Thomas Hawkins (1810–89) calls it "the Great Sea-dragon, the Emperor of Past Worlds, maleficent, terrible, direct, and sublime."[4] (What an incredible phrase. Put that on my tombstone.) Like the ichthyosaur, this has never been named by science before, but in 1821, when Mary is just 22, De La Beche and William Conybeare (1787–1857) take a look at one of her finds and dub it *Plesiosaurus* (meaning "lizard-ish").

At the age of 24, Mary finds another plesiosaur, probably her best-ever find, as it's almost complete. It's bought by (deep breath) Richard Temple-Nugent-Bridges-Chandos Grenville, 1st Duke of Buckingham and Chandos, and is presented to the Geological Society by Conybeare at the same meeting where Buckland presents his *Megalosaurus* – frankly in the top 10 best-ever nights for fossil fans.[5] It's still a struggle for Mary to get noticed: Conybeare doesn't credit her in his speech, and French scientist Georges Cuvier (1769–1832) even accuses Mary of creating a fake (he hasn't seen the real thing, only a drawing of it, but I guess he thinks he knows better than Mary). But people do figure out that it's real and who found it, and after this, Mary starts getting well known in the world of natural history and geology. People come to Lyme Regis not only to see the fossils, but to see *her*.

Mary runs a little shop in Lyme Regis called Anning's Fossil Depot, where interested visitors can find her among shelves of curios for sale, perhaps cleaning a new specimen or writing letters to find a buyer for her next big thing. She's not the only person doing it in Lyme, either – the sisters Mary, Margaret and Elizabeth Philpot are also great fossil hunters and have a little museum of fossil fish. Even though they're quite a bit older than Mary, they become good friends, and Elizabeth in particular goes out hunting with Mary every day. Mary is impressively skilled at just *looking* at the rock and *knowing* there's a fossil underneath, where other people see only stone. She is also highly adept at identifying species: she can gauge the size of a creature just from the thickness of its vertebrae. One woman who knows Mary writes that "It is certainly a wonderful instance of divine favour – that this poor ignorant girl should be so blessed, for by reading and application she has arrived to that degree of knowledge as to be in the habit of writing and talking with professors and other clever men on the subject, and they all acknowledge that she understands more of the science than anyone else in the kingdom."[6]

Mary gets this knowledge partly from personal experience with fossils, but also by writing letters to the scientific community in London and keeping abreast of the latest developments. When a friend tells her about a visit she made to the British Museum to see the minerals collection, Mary writes back, "How I envy your daily visits to the museum! Indeed I shall be greatly obliged your sensible account of its contents: for the little information I get from the professors is one-half unintelligible."[7]

Mary's next great discovery is a relative of the modern squid that *still has ink in it*. It's dried up, but with a little water Mary is able to revive it, and Elizabeth Philpot makes sketches of fossils *in fossil ink!*[8] Mary is also the first to identify coprolite – fossilized poo. Sometimes she even finds fossilized animals with fossilized poo still inside them – yes, they were about to poo when they died – and Mary is able to pick apart the coprolite to find fish scales and teeth still in there.

At the age of 30, Mary discovers yet another new species – a fossil fish named *Squaloraja polyspondyla* and – my favourite of her discoveries – her first flying creature, *Dimorphodon*, a kind of pterosaur. William

Buckland gets a big gold feminist ally sticker for giving her due credit for this, writing that "In the same blue lias formation at Lyme Regis, in which so many specimens of Ichthyosaurus and Plesiosaurus have been discovered by Miss Mary Anning, she has recently found the skeleton of an unknown species of that most rare of curious of all reptiles, the Pterodactyl."[9] William then buys this fossil for the British Museum, and makes sure that they buy a plesiosaur off Mary, too.

Finally, in 1829, Mary gets her wish to see the British Museum for herself. She leaves Lyme for the first and only time in her life and heads to London, where she stays with two geologist friends in Marylebone. While there, she does all the tourist stuff – she browses the shops on Regent Street and potters around the mummies and the statues in the British Museum – but she also goes to see her great plesiosaur displayed at the Geological Society (although, as a woman, she is not allowed to attend meetings).

For the rest of her life, geologists do fund-raising to support her work, with the Geological Society giving her a pension and even Prime Minister Lord Melbourne being persuaded to donate £300 to the Mary Anning fund. She never becomes a member of the Geological Society (they won't admit a woman for another 50 years), but in 1846 she is made an honorary member of the Dorset County Museum, and in 1844, she's visited by none other than the King of Saxony himself (who is also a massive dinosaur nerd). By this time, she's used to posh gentlemen dropping by to see her – as she tells the king's doctor, "I am well known throughout the whole of Europe."[10] Today, you can visit the Natural History Museum in London or the Museum of Natural History in Oxford and still see Mary's ichthyosaurs and plesiosaurs hanging in pride of place.

When Mary started her career at the age of 12, dinosaurs hadn't been identified yet, and even the idea that animals could go extinct was unknown to science. The established view in Britain was that the Earth was just a few thousand years old, and that every creature currently living was one that God created in the Garden of Eden for the enjoyment of mankind. Mary's work upended that view completely. She discovered new animals that painted a portrait of a completely different world – one with gigantic, terrible sea monsters that hunted each other in ancient oceans and died millions of years before any human could witness them. By the time Mary died in 1847, Charles Darwin (1809–82) had come up with his theory of natural selection that he would later release to the world in *On the Origin of Species*, explaining a mechanism for new forms of life to evolve without divine involvement. Mary showed that the Earth that people think was created new for us was actually around for ages before humankind got to enjoy it, and that wherever you walk, there could be tremendous beasties hidden underneath your feet. So tread carefully.

CHAPTER 20
CAROLINE HERSCHEL

teaches us to turn our eyes to the starry heavens once in a while.

Caroline Herschel (1750–1848) is destined for a life spent looking downward. As a child growing up in 18th-century Germany, her parents and older brother Jacob tell her that the only things she'll ever be useful for are scrubbing floors and knitting stockings. But they can't dim Caroline's star. She becomes one of the best-known astronomers in Western Europe, discovering numerous nebulae and comets. The first woman to receive a Gold Medal from the Royal Astronomical Society, she gets visits from kings and duchesses, and has a crater on the Moon named after her. She becomes so famous that a letter can be addressed to "Caroline Herschel, Famous Astronomer, Slough" and it will find her.[1] And she does it all without formal training or, frankly, much encouragement from her family.

Caroline is lucky to survive childhood. She contracts smallpox aged four and typhus aged ten. The diseases leave her "totally disfigured"[2] (in her own words) and partially blind in her left eye, and they stunt her growth: in adulthood she is only 1.3m (4ft 3in) tall. She's also the only daughter left in the house (her older sister gets married when Caroline is five) in a big family of boys. So from a very young age, her parents use her as free servant labour around the house. This is fairly usual for girls in the 18th century, but what isn't usual is that her father tells her that her life will never be anything other than this. She shouldn't even bother looking for a husband, "saying as I was neither handsom nor rich it was not likely."[3]

While boys of the 1760s often feel that they become men when they get their first job, there are so few professional opportunities for women that usually a girl's only way to graduate from childhood is marriage.

With her parents telling her that that avenue is utterly closed off, there's not much Caroline can do to get out of her parents' house. One option is to become a governess: a live-in teacher for upper-class children. The life of a governess is poorly paid and difficult, but it is a path that Caroline could pursue – except that her mother will not allow her to learn French, an absolutely necessary skill for every governess to have. The decision seems bizarre and spiteful, with the only effect being that it traps Caroline at home to continue to do free labour for her parents. If she leaves the house, they'll have to hire a servant. On the other hand, her mother is happy for her to go to a knitting class, because that means the girl can knit free socks for the whole family.

One story in particular highlights how thoughtlessly the family treats Caroline. When she's six, she's sent out to fetch her dad and her older brother, who are coming home from a stint in the military. She's freezing cold and has a stomach ache, but she searches for them for ages before giving up and trudging home, only to find them all tucking into a hot dinner without her. They'd forgotten she was gone. Caroline still remembers this story in her eighties.

She desperately tries to learn something, anything, outside of how to do the most menial housework. She even gets up at dawn to sneak off to a neighbour who teaches her embroidery, just because it's marginally more interesting than the pillowcases and socks that her mother has her making. She longs for "acquiring a little knowledge and a few accomplishments; as might have saved her from wasting her time in the performance of such drudgeries and laborious works as her good Father never intended to see her grow up for."[4] But with her mother (and, after her father dies, her older brother Jacob) determined against her, it looks like she has no future at all – no marriage and no job except unpaid housework, forever.

However, in 1772, when Caroline is 22, the family gets a letter from her big brother William that will change her destiny. William is an organist and composer living in the English city of Bath, and he thinks that Caroline might have a future there as a professional singer in his concerts. Would she like to come? Caroline's never thought about being a singer before, but if it'll get her out of the house, *Yes, absolutely.* She starts practising as much as she can, waiting until everyone else has left the house and making sure to carry on sewing at the same time so that no one can come home and say, *Why has nothing been done around here? You're wasting your time singing when you should be looking after your family.* Even so, her mother and Jacob are constantly threatening to call off the trip. Caroline says, "By the time I had set my heart on this change in my situation, Jacob began to turn the whole scheme into ridicule . . . I was left in the harrowing uncertainty, if I was to go or not!!!"[5] To make absolutely sure that they will have no excuse they could use to make her stay, she knits a whopping two years' worth of stockings for her mother before she goes, and William generously pays Jacob enough money to hire a servant to replace Caroline.

Finally she is out of the family home. Once she makes it across the English Channel to William's house in Bath, she throws herself headlong into learning as much as she can. She studies English (which she can't speak at all before her arrival), mathematics and dance, with William giving her music lessons and taking her to his rehearsals. William tells her that she hasn't completely got out of housework – he also needs someone to run his household for him – but at least she has a maid to help her here, and she has the freedom to spend hours at the harpsichord. And her studies pay off! She makes her musical debut in Bath's Assembly Rooms in 1777, singing the Handel oratorio *Judas Maccabeus*, and by the following year she's climbed the ladder to become the first soloist.

But just as Caroline is making her way as a musician, William's like, *Yeah, I'm kinda bored of music. I'm really into this astronomy stuff instead.* He starts building his own telescope from scratch, which he makes Caroline help with (she isn't too thrilled) and they even move house so that they have more room for it. As William spends less time on music and more tinkering with his telescope, Caroline is left without her music teacher and without his concerts to perform in. She gives up her budding professional career as a singer in order to support his work. He stays up all night stargazing and spends all day polishing mirrors. Sometimes he's so lost in the star sauce that Caroline literally has to hand-feed him while he works on his mirrors, because otherwise he won't stop to eat. When she's not doing that, she's polishing mirrors herself, or sitting beside him and writing down his observations as he peers through an eyepiece.

At first, she's pretty angry about this – and rightly so. William is supposed to be helping her establish a career so she can be independent. She didn't move to England just to carry on being an unpaid servant! She writes, "I have been thoroughly annoyed and hindered in my endeavours at perfecting myself in any branch of knowledge by which I could hope to gain a creditable livelihood; on account of continual interruption in my practice by being obliged to keep order in a family on which I was myself a dependent."[6]

But to be fair to William, his telescope is really, really good. Most people in 1770s Britain use refracting telescopes with lenses inside, but such instruments have some downsides. Tiny imperfections in the glass can distort light in weird ways, and when colours pass through the lens, they're all refracted at slightly different angles, giving you a kind of hazy rainbow effect which is very pretty but makes it hard to see things in detail. Rather than lenses, William's telescope uses mirrors, which are a lot harder to put together but give much clearer images. You can also see things much closer with William's telescope. A decent model at the time will get a magnification power of about 200, while his gets over 2,000.[7] It means he can see with a clarity totally new to human eyes. In March 1781 he discovers the planet Uranus. These days scientists are finding new planets all the time, but until that day we only knew about Mercury, Venus, Earth, Mars, Jupiter and Saturn. William discovers the first "new" planet since humans started noticing there are other planets at all. In fact, it's so unexpected and unprecedented that at first William thinks it must just be a very weird, tailless comet.

Even when the scientific community realizes it's a planet, he doesn't come up with the name. William wants to name it "Georgium" after King George III (he's angling for a royal favour), and it's not until 1783 that German astronomer Johann Bode (1747–1826) suggests that "Uranus" would fit better with all the other planets named for Roman gods.[8] Even though Georgium doesn't stick, the king is flattered enough to appoint William Astronomer Royal, and so William and Caroline leave Bath and move to Datchet, a village near Windsor Castle. This is the last gasp of Caroline's dream of becoming a singer – there's no opportunity for her in the village. Instead, William ropes her into copying out star catalogues and astronomical papers for him, making him coffee to keep him up all night, and doing the grunt work of sweeping the sky for comets. It's in Datchet that, with nothing else to do, Caroline starts looking through a telescope herself, and keeping her own records of what she sees. To better calculate the positions and motions of the stars, she starts learning about logarithms, geometry and sidereal time (a kind of timekeeping particularly useful to astronomers because it's based on how the stars move rather than how the Sun moves). She also learns how to spot nebulae (dust clouds in space) and in 1783 she discovers a new one. By the end of the year, she has 14 new ones under her belt, at a time when only about 100 are known to science at all.[9] A very cool accomplishment to be sure, but at the time nebulae aren't well known outside the scientific community. Caroline has a few more years before she'll make an observation that'll bring her real fame.

Astronomy wasn't what Caroline would have chosen, but she absolutely commits to it. On one particularly dark night, she's running around making adjustments to William's telescope when she trips in the dark and lands on a big metal hook which drives itself into her thigh. When William and his assistants run over to help her up, she states "they could not lift me without leaving near two ounces of my flesh behind."[10] She treats the wound herself (she doesn't mention William helping at all – was he completely useless?) and when the local doctor finds out, he says "if a surgeon had met with such a hurt he would have been entitled to six weeks' nursing in a hospital."[11] By contrast, Caroline is back to work on the next clear night, a mere two weeks later.

Although the job of Astronomer Royal comes with a large amount of prestige (and a small amount of money), it is also extra work for William. Halfway through 1786, the king sends him on a month-long trip to an observatory in Hanover, and Caroline is left behind in Slough (where they move after their Datchet landlady threatens to raise the rent). She who has never been "Mistres of her Brother's house nor of her Time"[12] suddenly finds herself alone in the house with no one to tell her what to do. Of course, there's still housework to be seen to, but she isn't beholden to William's demands to keep notes for him and fetch him coffee, so she's able to get on quietly with her own observations. She reports, "the employment of writing down the observations when my brother uses the 30-foot [9m] reflector [the good telescope] does not often allow me time to look at the heavens."[13] She's fought her whole life to have control over her time, and almost as soon as William's gone, she discovers her first comet.

The effect is instantaneous. She becomes a celebrity in her own right, with people visiting the house just to meet her and look through the telescope themselves. Scientific journals publish notices on her findings, and French astronomer Jérôme Lalande (1732–1807) even names his daughter after her![14] Over the next ten years, she'll discover seven more comets in her own right, noting them down carefully in her "commonplace book".

When William comes home, he asks the king if his sister can have a small salary, too, and the monarch awards her £50 per year. To put that in context, it's a quarter of what William is earning from the king, and William himself notes that it's a lot less than a male assistant would be paid, writing to the king that if Caroline ever wants to stop working, hiring a new assistant "would probably amount to nearly one hundred pounds more."[15] But to Caroline it's "the first money I ever in all my life thought myself to be at liberty to spend to my own liking",[16] and it's a huge amount for a woman to earn. A high-end governess like Mary Wollstonecraft (1759–97) might earn £40 per year, but most governesses earn more like £20–30, and ordinary servants much less.[17] And for a woman to be paid for scientific work is almost unprecedented at the time, when there are very few scientific jobs going at all, and most scientists are enthusiastic amateurs.

In 1798, Caroline completes a star catalogue compiling all the observations she and her brother have made over the past decade and a half. Before Caroline's catalogue, British astronomers almost uniformly relied on the "British Catalogue": a list of stars put together a century earlier by previous Astronomer Royal John Flamsteed (1646–1719). Caroline and William both notice gaps and errors in this document, and so she painstakingly copies out all Flamsteed's stars in order, inserting the new discoveries of the past 100 years and correcting typos. Her *Catalogue of Stars, taken from Mr Flamsteed's Observations contained in the second volume of the historia Coelestis, and not inserted in the British Catalogue*[18] adds over 500 new stars and is instantly vital to the study of astronomy.[19]

Caroline is so indefatigable that she's still working on astronomy in her seventies. In 1821, when William gets too sick to work, she starts working as an assistant for his son, John, who *also* becomes a famous astronomer in his own right. (Although you'd think *he'd* be *her* assistant – surely he's the one who needs to build up experience?) At the age of 74, she finishes her final big work: another catalogue, this time of nebulae. Between them, Caroline and William have increased the number of known nebulae from about 100 to 2,500, so a new list is definitely in order. She calls it *The Reduction and Arrangement in the Form of a Catalogue, in Zones, of all the Star-clusters and Nebulae observed by Sir W. Herschel in his Sweeps*, graciously awarding William the lion's share of the credit.[20]

This is Caroline's last big astronomical work, but it's now that she really starts to get high-end recognition as a pioneer in the field. In 1828, the Royal Astronomical Society award her their Gold Medal. No woman will win this prize again for – get this – 150 years. In 1996, it is given to Vera Rubin (1928–2016), the astronomer who discovered that galaxies are filled with what we now call "dark matter". To date, only nine women have ever received the award. The Society make Caroline an honorary member in 1835, and in 1846 she is awarded a Gold Medal for Science by the King of Prussia. She lives to 97 – something that, were it not for her scientific achievements, would be an impressive-enough feat on its own for someone who caught two potentially deadly diseases in childhood.

Caroline was filled throughout her life with an ambition to do something great and to be recognized, and at every turn her family told her that was impossible. Her mother tried to stop her learning French and embroidery; her brother Jacob wouldn't let her go to England until they found someone to do the housework instead of her; and even her beloved William cut her singing career dead without, it seems, a passing thought. But she had her eyes on something higher, much higher, and through great patience and perseverance she achieved it. She is buried in Hanover, where her gravestone reads, "The eyes of her who is glorified here below turned to the starry heavens."

CHAPTER 21

PETER THE WILD BOY

teaches us that you might find kindness in unexpected places.

The year is 1726, and St James's Palace in London is abuzz with the news. Bewigged heads tilt toward each other behind paper fans. The murmur zigzags from maidservant to courtier to footman. Soon everyone knows. The King of England has found a boy raised by wolves in the German forest, stuffed him in a three-piece suit and stockings and brought him to court.

George I was never supposed to be king; there were more than 40 people in front of him in the line of succession to the British throne. The previous monarch, Queen Anne (reigned 1707–14), had done her best to produce an heir, going through a crushing 17 pregnancies without a single child making it to adulthood. As she aged and it became clear that she would die without issue, Parliament started to get antsy about the possibility of the crown going down a dogleg in her family tree and ending up on a Roman Catholic head. They were all good Protestants, and didn't want to lose their jobs, thank you very much. So they passed the Act of Settlement, which cut Catholics permanently out of the succession. To this day, no Catholic can inherit the British throne, even if they convert to the Church of England. This means that once Anne died, Parliament went down the list of her relatives, crossing off 41 family members before they got to George, Elector of Hanover, a distant but safely Protestant cousin in Germany. He was duly crowned King of England in Westminster Abbey on 20 October 1714.

Life at the Georgian court is full of sniping, scandal and politics. A wrong word or a misinterpreted glance can ruin your career. George brings with him a lot of German courtiers, which rather displeases the British courtiers, who think they're a load of foreign upstarts.

One German countess says that English women "hold their heads down, and look always in a fright, whereas those that are foreigners hold up their heads and hold out their breasts, and make themselves look as great and stately as they can", to which the English Lady Deloraine cuttingly replies: "We show our quality by our birth and titles, Madam, and not by sticking out our bosoms."[1] Burn.

Status, etiquette and manners are everything. If you want a position at court, you have to learn a whole host of rules about bowing, walking and even your posture. You should hire a dancing teacher to teach you how to bow or curtsy correctly, and practised eyes at court can spot a newcomer's awkward attempt a mile off. Even if the throne is empty, you should bow to it three times, and a lady who wishes to leave the king's presence should curtsy three times and back out of the room (somehow without tripping on her train or her heels). Maids of Honour are forbidden from crossing their arms, and no one may leave the king's presence without permission. You must not refer to anyone by their first name unless you know them very well indeed. If the queen wants a glass of wine at dinner, a page hands the glass to a Woman of the Bedchamber, who gives it to a Lady of the Bedchamber, who is the only one permitted to actually put it in the hand of the queen.

Knowing lots of arcane and labyrinthine rules helps distinguish those who've been brought up correctly from everyone else. It sounds silly, but it really is important to show respect to people around you, and you won't get far if you don't. These days, it's cool to be relaxed about etiquette, but at the Georgian court there is no such thing as cool. Treating your superiors and even your equals with deference is how you earn their respect.

So imagine how a boy will get on who was found living feral, with no clothes, no manners and no speech in any language.

In 1726, such a boy arrives at the Georgian court. He isn't there by dint of his birth or his parents' politicking; he was found in the woods around Hamelin in Germany. The accounts of his discovery are practically mythical. Some say that he's found living off grass and moss, or climbing up tree trunks like a squirrel, or walking on all fours. Some say he was raised by wolves. We don't know how he ends up in the woods, and accounts don't even agree on the time of year when he's found. What we do know is that he's somewhere around 12 years old, almost entirely naked, and speaks no language. As such, he cannot tell his discoverers his name, the names of his parents or carers, how he ended up in the woods or how long he's been there.

He's taken to George's Hanoverian court, Herrenhausen, and given a place at the dinner table, where he proceeds to shock the German courtiers with his dreadful lack of breeding. According to one author, "He had no notion of behaviour, or manners, but greedily took with his hands out of the dishes, what he liked best, such as asparagus, or other garden-things, and after a little time, he was ordered to be taken away, by reason of his daubing undecent behaviour."[2]

You might think that such an ill-mannered person, without speech or family to help him, would be the very antithesis of the type of person who is welcome at the haughty Georgian court. But on 8 April 1726 he makes his first appearance in the belly of the beast: at St James's, the most senior palace in Britain. Someone dresses him in a bright blue silk suit, which according to the fashion of the day comprises a long coat, a waistcoat and breeches, and is worn with stockings, and perhaps even a lacy collar or cuffs – definitely not forest attire. To keep his hands busy, he is given one of the Princess of Wales' gloves and a pocket watch to play with, but we can only assume he fails to make his perfect bow to the throne. Not only that, but he commits an even more shocking breach of the peace by putting his hat on in front of the king! (Monocles popping all around, one imagines.) He simply will not be constrained by the court's strict etiquette. He sits whenever he feels like it, eats with his hands, sleeps on the floor, laughs loudly, and even picks people's pockets (looking for snacks, not money). He is still unable to speak. Somewhere along the way, he is given the name "Peter".

This could go badly for Peter. We're about 150 years away from the golden age of freak shows at the end of the 19th century, but that doesn't mean that the folk of 1720s London are kind and accepting to people who are different. Without his own speech or a family to speak for him, Peter will find it difficult to make his way in Georgian society. Boys of Peter's age are normally looking for an apprenticeship in order to learn a trade. The parents of 14-year-old boys find a master for them to learn from – someone who's reached the height of their craft – and pay him a lump sum to take on their beloved offspring. The amount can vary wildly depending on the trade – a top-notch surgeon or a lawyer is going to charge a lot more than a tailor or a miller – but the whole procedure requires money and connections that Peter doesn't have. Without an apprenticeship, an orphan child's options are very limited. Without an address or a family, Peter could be considered a vagrant, and vagrants are thoroughly criminalized in the 18th century. Vagrancy is a vague crime. It doesn't apply just to people who are homeless or unemployed, it also seizes people who are employed, but in arenas that the authorities don't like, such as sex work. Vagrants can be arrested and sent to the local "bridewell", a correctional facility designed to punish the "crime" of vagrancy with backbreaking labour and whippings. If Peter manages to avoid the bridewells, his propensity for pickpocketing could get him into even hotter water. Three years before his arrival in London, Parliament passes the Waltham Black Act, otherwise known as the Bloody Code, creating a mandatory death penalty for all sorts of minor crimes. Stealing goods worth as little as one shilling – 1/20th of the week's wages of a skilled worker – can be met with hanging, and the legal system can and does hang children as young as eight.

However, Peter doesn't know it, but he's been thrust into the middle of a fierce political battle. The relationship between King George I and his eldest son and daughter-in-law, the Prince and Princess of Wales, is not exactly all-out war, but neither is it completely convivial. (We've met this Princess of Wales already in Chapter 2: she's Caroline of Ansbach, the one who takes Mary Wortley Montagu's advice to inoculate her children against smallpox.) The king is pretty shy and dislikes too much limelight, so the Prince and Princess of Wales do a lot of entertaining in his place. They speak better English and are more popular, which, of course, makes the king super-jealous.

Nine years before Peter's arrival, the court was rocked by the so-called Christening Quarrel soon after Princess Caroline gave birth to her fifth baby. The king attended the baby's christening to pay his respects, but did not speak to his son, the Prince of Wales, at all. The king then damaged the relationship further by giving his unwanted opinion on the subject of who would be a suitable godparent for the child, and a shouting match broke out during the service.

Ever since, the Prince and Princess of Wales have been banished from St James's to Leicester House, in what is now Leicester Square in the centre of London, and worse, they are forced to leave their children behind. Now London has two rival courts orbiting each other, poaching people from one to the other. Of the two, Leicester House has a reputation for being cooler. The Princess of Wales is especially popular. She's clever and funny and really into science. She's friends with the top scientists of the day like Gottfried Wilhelm Leibniz (1646–1716) and Isaac Newton (1642–1727), and collects antiquities and curiosities that she loves to show off. When these intellectuals hear about the boy raised by wolves, it sparks all sorts of questions which are the hot-button topics in philosophy of the day.

For example, the court is familiar with *Leviathan* (1651), a work of philosophy in which Thomas Hobbes (1588–1679) proposed an original "state of nature" for mankind before society came in and gummed everything up with etiquette, hierarchy and dinner forks. He argued that life in the state of nature was "solitary, poor, nasty, brutish and short",[3] a battle royale style free-for-all in which anyone might crack open your head with a big rock simply to feast on the delicious brain inside with absolutely no consequences, just total, unadulterated freedom. Hobbes argued that mankind gave up this freedom of the state of nature in exchange for the legal protection you get from living in society. These days you can't bash people's heads in with rocks anymore, but equally, no one can bash *your* head in with a rock anymore. So if Hobbes was right, then is Peter an example of the kind of "nasty, brutish" person you have to be when you grow up in the state of nature?

From a different angle, another English philosopher, John Locke (1632–1704), argued that we are all born with our minds a blank slate. We don't come preloaded with any information about language, relationships or morality – we have to gain all that through experience and education. So, people wonder, is Peter what a human looks like if you never write anything on that slate? In his 1726 pamphlet *Mere Nature Delineated*, Daniel Defoe (1660–1731) argues that it's *Peter* who's the sensible one for shunning modern society and going to live in the woods. He also suggests that humans might do well in the state of nature, but that they need art to earn a soul. "Mere Nature receives the vivifying Influence in Generation, but requires the Help of Art to bring it to the perfection of living."[4] This is a really unkind thing to say – that Peter doesn't have a soul – so we can only hope that no one says this to his face.

Even worse, in 1735 Swedish naturalist Carl Linnaeus (1707–78) publishes his seminal work, *Systema naturæ*, which classifies the natural world into the species, classes, orders and genuses we know today. He splits humans into six different varieties: *Homo afer, Homo americanus, Homo asiaticus, Homo europaeus, Homo monstrosus* (mythical monster-people that Linnaeus believes are real, with faces in the middle of their torsos or with one giant foot) and *Homo ferens*. "*Ferens*" means "wild", and Linnaeus' examples of *Homo ferens* are all feral children like Peter, who is even mentioned by Linnaeus as a pure example of the type: Linnaeus thinks that Peter is not even the same species as the rest of us![5]

However unkind the attention may be, all this buzz from writers and philosophers means that science nerd Princess Caroline is desperate to poach Peter for her own court. Suddenly Peter finds himself in demand from both St James's and Leicester House. Instead of ending up on the street, Peter is given fine clothes. The royal physician, Dr Arbuthnot, is told to look after him. The boy is taught to say his own name, to fetch and carry things, and to kiss his fingers in greeting. They even pay an artist to come and paint his portrait! To this day, visitors to Kensington Palace in London can see Peter's face among a crowd of Georgian courtiers around the walls of the grand staircase. This doesn't mean he avoids all the cruelties of the day – Dr Arbuthnot hits him on the legs with a leather strap when he doesn't behave properly, which must be particularly distressing for a child who might not understand what's being asked of him. Peter never does learn to speak more than repeating back single words, but he is accepted by the court, in a way. They understand that he's never going to make a useful servant or a brilliant courtier, but still he is kept on rather than being turfed out onto the streets or ending up in a horrible freak show.

Even after Caroline's death in 1737, Peter carries on being looked after. He is put in the care of one of Caroline's bedchamber women whose relative, James Fenn, owns a farm called Haxter's End near Berkhamsted, Hertfordshire. Peter is sent there, along with big annual payments for the family so they can provide for him. He lives out the rest of his long life on the farm, free to roam the countryside as he pleases. He does have a tendency to wander off and get lost, so he is given a collar with his name and address on, and the locals bring him back home whenever he goes missing.

In 1782, when Peter is in his sixties, he is visited by Scottish philosopher James Burnett (1714–99), who gives us one last glimpse of Peter's world. The man that Burnett finds in Hertfordshire is short – about 1.6m (5ft 3in) in height – with a beard, and very gentle. Burnett says that Peter can understand other people's speech, but that he still hasn't learned to speak himself. He loves music and folk tunes, and can sing and dance, although he doesn't sing *words*, only *tunes*. Burnett writes, "I think it is evidence that he is not an idiot, not only from his appearance, as I have described it, and from his actions, but from all the accounts that we have of him."[6] Peter dies three years later in 1785 and is buried in the local village at Northchurch. You can still visit his grave today.

The mystery of how Peter came to be in the woods around Hanover will most likely never be solved. Peter couldn't tell us, and whoever left him there probably didn't write it down on a paper that's waiting to be discovered in an archive somewhere. But despite his rough start, despite being an utter misfit in Georgian society and especially the Georgian court, he still managed to find a surprising amount of kindness among the stiff waistcoats and curled wigs of the royal household.

CHAPTER 22
SABRINA SIDNEY

teaches us that firing a gun at someone won't make them love you.

Plucked out of an orphanage at the age of 12 and whisked away by a strange man, Sabrina Sidney (1757–1843) is the subject of one of the strangest experiments in pedagogical history. Wax is dripped onto her bare skin, guns are pointed at her, and she's made to throw perfectly good clothes on the fire, all to see if it is possible to mould someone into the perfect wife. And it's done without anyone telling her what it's for or even that she's being tested. In the end, the experiment is an utter failure – you'd think you wouldn't need to say it, but shooting at someone doesn't make them love you.

Sabrina is born in Clerkenwell, London. We know nothing about her parents, because as a baby she is abandoned on the steps of London's Foundling Hospital, a huge orphanage that takes in hundreds of children. Although we can't say for sure why Sabrina is left there, babies generally arrive at the orphanage for one of two reasons: poverty or the shame of illegitimacy. So either Sabrina's parents can't afford to keep her, or Sabrina's mother is forced to leave her to avert a scandal, or both.

Although a Georgian orphanage is a pretty terrible place in which to find oneself, in some ways Sabrina is very lucky. Of the seven babies left at the orphanage that day, she is one of only three who survive infancy. Like all infants at the orphanage, she is farmed out to a foster mother for the first few years of her life. There's no such thing as formula milk yet, so in order to look after babies the orphanage has to find women who are breastfeeding and willing to take on an extra child for ten shillings a month. As a bonus, a foster mother who manages to get her charge to survive to the age of one year gets a further ten shillings. So Sabrina grows up in a very normal working-class farmhouse alongside children of her own age, doing all the normal things that need doing on an 18th-century farm. But at the age of eight, it's time for her to prepare, at a satellite orphanage in Shrewsbury, for a life without surrogate parents.

As with Peter the Wild Boy (Chapter 21), it's very difficult for parentless children to make their way in 18th-century Britain. Luckily, the Shrewsbury orphanage is able to secure apprenticeships for its charges. Sabrina seems to have been put on the "domestic service" track, training for a job as a maid in a rich person's house. She learns polishing and sewing and laundry, and, most importantly, to obey her betters at all times. These lessons will shape the course of her life. When she's 12 years old, a gentleman arrives at the Shrewsbury orphanage looking for just such a maid.

He is Thomas Day (1748–89), a wealthy man in his early twenties. He has his own estate with an annual income of £1,200. His friends are not just people who own factories, but people who design the machines that power the Industrial Revolution itself – men like Matthew Boulton (1728–1809) and James Watt (1736–1819), who invent and improve on steam engines and factory machines. Day says he is looking for a maid for his married friend, Richard Lovell Edgeworth (1744–1817), another inventor. The orphanage is only too pleased to oblige, and the girls are lined up for his perusal. After some deliberation, he chooses Sabrina. Normally the orphanage doesn't sign its girls over to random men miles away who send their mate rather than bothering to turn up themselves, but Day is clearly much wealthier and more powerful than the grocers and craftsmen to whom they usually apprentice their girls, so without doing their normal reference checks, the orphanage signs her over to Edgeworth with a binding contract for a whopping nine years, until she reaches the age of 21. No one asks her whether she'd like to go: she is bound to do what the orphanage tells her. Day is also the one who gives her the name Sabrina Sidney. He doesn't ask her opinion on that, either.

Day bundles the newly minted Sabrina onto a carriage, and takes her far away from Shrewsbury. But he doesn't take her to Edgeworth's house, as he'd promised the orphanage he would do. Instead, he takes her to a rented flat off Chancery Lane in London. A few weeks later, another orphan arrives at the flat, and again, Day has given her a new name. She is a year younger than Sabrina, and Day tells her to call the new girl "Lucretia". To be clear: even though 18th-century Britain doesn't usually care about orphans, what Day is doing is 100 per cent against the rules of the orphanage, which would not have signed Sabrina and Lucretia over if they'd known they would be living unchaperoned with an unmarried man. The orphanage is not normally afraid to sue people who are negligent or cruel to their apprentices, or who break their contracts. But they've also taught Sabrina and Lucretia not to question their social superiors, and they have not taught them how to write, only how to read. So even if the girls have the resources to speak out, they can't get a message back to the orphanage. Day knows he will get away with it. But even so, he doesn't dare tell them his true plan: to train both the girls up to be his perfect wife, and to choose the better one to marry.

Unlike the girls, Day grows up very privileged. He has a huge inheritance from his father, and goes to Oxford, where he reads a lot of Voltaire and Hume. Unlike many of the other students, though, he thinks it's sinful to fritter one's money away on fancy clothes and food. He drinks mostly water and refuses to wear powdered wigs, instead letting his hair grow long and lank, and not brushing it. He refuses to pick up elegant table manners and shuns luxury. As a teenager, he has a couple of disappointments in love, and he becomes frighteningly misogynistic, convinced that he will never be able to find a woman who hasn't been ruined by society. In his mind, all women of his own class are shallow, air-headed temptresses, and all working-class women are rough-handed, tanned and coarse. They're good for only one thing: "If the whole female Sex cannot furnish one single rational Woman, I must make use of them in that Manner for which alone Nature has perhaps intended."[1] When a girl his age turns him down, he rounds on her, writing, "I think I never saw so damn'd conceited a Bitch as Leonora."[2] If he can't find a woman, maybe he needs to create one.

So what kind of wife will Day make for himself? Well, she'll need to be happy living without luxuries, like him. She mustn't be interested in fancy clothes or food. He wants to live out in the countryside with no servants, but does that mean he's going to help with the housework? No chance – so she'll have to be able to do everything herself. And most of all, she must accept absolutely everything he tells her without question. A woman must never ask a man to do anything: "The most disgusting sight of all is to see that sex, whose weakness of body and imbecility of mind can only entitle them to our compassion and indulgence, assuming an unnatural dominance, and regulating the customs, the manners, the lives and the opinions of the other sex."[3]

So how would one go about training a woman to be like this? Both Day and his friend Edgeworth are big fans of philosopher Jean-Jacques Rousseau (1712–78), who has just written *Émile*, a blazingly popular book on child-rearing. Rousseau disagrees with the idea, widely held in the 18th century, that children are born with original sin that has to be beaten out of them with discipline and – well, literal beatings. Instead, he thinks that children are naturally good, and the best thing for them is to be shielded from the corrupting influence of society. Boys should be allowed to play out in nature as they please to learn hardiness and self-sufficiency, and they shouldn't be taught to read unless they ask to learn (he would have loved Peter the Wild Boy!). They should also be inured to fear by purposefully scaring them – making loud bangs, shutting them in total darkness, exposing them to creepy-crawlies, and so forth. It's important to note that *Émile* is not based on any science or even on anecdotal experience – the character of Émile is completely fictional, even though the book is written in the style of an instruction manual. But people go *wild* for this book, and start trying to raise their kids like Émile. The Prince of Würtemberg has his four-month-old daughter plunged into icy baths to increase her resistance to cold. Swiss banker Guillaume François Roussel forces his kids to forage their own food in the woods. All over Europe, parents get rid of their children's tutors and leave them to just sort of get on with it. To be fair to Rousseau, he does try to put the dampers on this a bit, and when people write to him asking for child-rearing advice, he sometimes tells them, *You know that the book isn't real, right?* "I cannot believe that you took the book which bears this name for a real treatise on education."[4]

Day's friend Edgeworth tries to raise his own three-year-old, Dick Edgeworth (great name), in a Rousseauvian way, and is shocked – *shocked!* – to realize that he's taught his boy to *think for himself*: "He was not disposed to obey . . . he had too little deference for others, and he shewed an invincible dislike to control."[5] Still, when Day tells Edgeworth his plan, Edgeworth eggs him on. But Day realizes that he is still going to get mega-judged by people around him if he keeps the girls in London, so he whisks them off to France, where they don't know anyone and, crucially, where the girls can't even speak the language. Edgeworth says, "From their total ignorance of the French language, an ignorance which he took no pains to remove, his pupils were not exposed to any impertinent interference; and as that knowledge of the world from which he wished to preserve them was at one entrance quite shut out, he had their minds entirely open to such ideas and sentiments, and such only, as he desired to implant."[6] This is scary behaviour. Folks, if someone tries to cut you off from everybody except themselves, run!

But Sabrina and Lucretia don't have anywhere to run to, so they spend their days doing all the housework and getting an education from

Day. Since he's into science, he teaches the girls a bit of astronomy and geometry, which they would never have learned at the orphanage, and he thinks things are going great: "They have never given me a moment's trouble... and think nothing so agreeable as waiting on me (no moderate convenience for a lazy man)."[7] (This is the most self-aware Day will get, so enjoy it.) He insists on trying to toughen them up by putting them in reckless danger, like riding a boat down a swollen river when neither of them can swim. The boat capsizes and luckily he's a good enough swimmer to rescue them before they drown. After a few months, he makes his choice: Sabrina is the lucky girl he is going to marry. He gives Lucretia a cash lump sum and sends her away to be apprenticed to a milliner. She eventually gets married and manages to live a normal life. Sabrina has to stay.

Day takes Sabrina back to England, to Lichfield, where they get into the local social scene. Day still hasn't told Sabrina his plan – but everyone in Lichfield knows. Here, his experiment gets more drastic. He starts trying to inure her to fear in the way that Rousseau outlines in *Émile*. He drips hot wax onto her back and arms, fires unloaded guns at her, stabs her with pins, gives her expensive clothes and orders her to burn them, and forces her to stand up to her neck in a lake (remember, she can't swim), all while ordering her not to flinch. He seems to forget the bit of his experiment where Sabrina is supposed to fall in love with him. (Also, what about inuring *him* to fear? Would he let Sabrina shoot at *his* head in the hope of making himself a better husband? The thought does not seem to cross his mind.) Day's friends report differently on whether Sabrina "passes" these tests or not. The poet Anna Seward (1742–1809), a Lichfield belle, says that she can't stop flinching, but Mary Anne Schimmelpenninck (fantastic name, stupendous: if you put it in a novel you'd get a note from the editor saying "no one's really called that – choose something less silly") says she gets used to it.

Again, this treatment is something that, even in Georgian times, you shouldn't be able to get away with. You're allowed to beat apprentices as a "correction", but stabbing them with pins and firing guns at them? No. This is not legal. But everyone who knows about Sabrina's treatment turns a blind eye to it. And as far as Day is concerned, she should just be grateful that she's not in the orphanage anymore. He later tells her, "I thought myself sufficiently entitled to make an experiment where, whatever else ensued, you would be placed in circumstances infinitely more favourable to happiness than before."[8] But he still doesn't tell her his plan to marry her.

Although no one steps in to help Sabrina, she does slowly realize that she is not being treated properly – that something is wrong with her place in the household, and this isn't how other girls live. And if Day doesn't realize that what he's doing is wrong, he at least realizes that it isn't working. Sabrina isn't the imaginary, wax-covered, cold-water-loving, inexplicably-attracted-to-him tradwife he thought she'd be, and his friends feel weird about him having a teenage wife-in-training that he acquired from an orphanage. A year after beginning his experiment, he tells Sabrina that she has failed, and he sends her away to boarding school.

On the one hand, Sabrina must be pretty devastated. Although this man badly mistreats her, he's her only protector and guardian in the whole world, and she does look up to him. On the other hand, boarding school is probably the best thing that can happen for her, and certainly better than Day trying to carry on with his experiment. There, she learns fine manners, how to write, and maybe some French too, although Day forbids the school from including her in their music and dance lessons (he thinks that dancing leads to frivolousness). Definitely no one's making her stand up to her neck in freezing water anymore. She actually has some time to make friends with girls her own age, and she learns skills that normally would be completely out of reach for an orphanage girl.

When she reaches the end of her schooling, Day brings her back to Lichfield. There, people notice that she's done so much better in school than she ever did under Day's "education". According to Seward: "The reader will not be sorry to learn the future destiny of Sabrina. She remained at school three years; gained the esteem of her instructress; grew feminine, elegant, and amiable."[9] Day tells Sabrina that she will face one last test to prove her worth to him. He still doesn't tell her that passing it means she will have to marry him. But Day forgets something he once knew – that if you want to take advantage of someone, it's much easier if you isolate them first. In Lichfield, Sabrina gets back in touch with her old acquaintances who finally, finally, tell her his plan. She is horrified. When she confronts him about it, he admits that it's true, although he does not admit that it's been his plan since she was 12 years old. Since Sabrina believes that Day is her legal guardian, she doesn't realize that she is allowed to turn him down. He tells her that he is leaving for a few days to make some preparations for the wedding, and gives her instructions on how to behave and dress in the meantime. Like all his other standards for her, he is incredibly picky about her dress. We don't know exactly what she does in his absence, but when he comes back he finds that she has disobeyed these commands somehow. We don't know if it is a small, accidental thing or a big deliberate thing, but either way Day is furious. He sends her away to a boarding house, and never sees her again.

To his credit, Day does give Sabrina a small annual income, but she is still thoroughly in the soup. The money isn't enough to live an upper-class life; since she hasn't learned a trade, she can't earn her own money, either; and as an orphan, she has absolutely no marriage prospects. She finally manages to find work as a lady's companion. A lady's companion is basically a maid, with all the expected duties of running the house, but who's upper-class enough to also be expected to go to parties and converse with her mistress. It can be a desperately lonely job, pretending to be friends with your boss, with basically no time off and no opportunity to make friends outside the house.

One day, Sabrina runs into an old school friend of Day's named John Bicknell. He's in his thirties and not doing so hot – he's got a reputation as a pretty lazy lawyer who just sits on cases and doesn't do anything; he's lost a lot of money on gambling; and he's got palsy. But he offers to marry her, and with no other options, Sabrina says yes. He also spills the beans on Day's entire shady scheme from the beginning – that he'd taken her from the orphanage under false pretences, that he'd planned to marry her from the start, and that everyone else knew and was hiding it from her. After many years, Sabrina finally knows the truth.

Sabrina is dealt a terrible hand in life – an orphan stolen away for mad science experiments. But she truly makes the best of her situation. She and John have two sons, one of whom is named after American abolitionist John Laurens (both John and Sabrina are opposed to slavery) and the other is named after Day's friend, Henry Edgeworth. After just three years of marriage, John dies of a stroke, leaving Sabrina with no money to bring up two children. But at this point life finally throws her a bit of good luck, and she's offered a job by a friend of a friend of her late husband, Charles Burney, brother of famous novelist Fanny Burney (1752–1840; fantastic name!). Sabrina works as the housekeeper and secretary for Charles' school, helping to educate dozens of boys. She gets practically adopted by the Burneys, who become the family she never had. She goes on holiday with them and sits with them at the dinner table. Unlike at Day's house, she's allowed to hire servants to help her run the school. Her story inspires whole novels like *Belinda* by Maria Edgeworth, *Watch and Ward* by Henry James and *Orley Farm* by Anthony Trollope. Both her sons become respected lawyers, and finally, at the age of 68, Sabrina retires to Bath. When she's 75, an artist paints her portrait. She's born a destitute orphan, and she dies in a comfortable townhouse, aged 86, with more than £3,000 to her name.

As for Day, he eventually found a woman willing to put up with him, although it wasn't one he'd moulded since childhood, but one who'd been through the finishing schools and society balls that he hated so much. This was Esther Milnes, and their marriage was, as you might expect, pretty miserable. He made her do all the housework and banned her from playing the harpsichord or writing poetry, which he thought women should not do. He rode horses around his estate, but in stark contrast with his treatment of Sabrina, he thought that he could tame the animals with love and kindness instead of following the more normal breaking-in practice of the time, and one day, his horse threw him off and killed him. Womp womp. He ended up being wrong about almost everything – about how to find a woman who loves you, about how to keep a happy marriage, and about how to train horses. But he never tried his experiment again, so perhaps Sabrina at least taught him this: that you can't make someone love you by firing a gun at them.

CHAPTER 23

RADCLYFFE "JOHN" HALL

*teaches us that trying to keep something secret might end
up backfiring and making it internationally famous.*

If you want to see how trying to censor, suppress and ban information often backfires and makes the information way more widely known than it would otherwise have been, look no further than the story of the 1920s English writer Radclyffe Hall (1880–1943), a pioneering queer author who dares to write about relationships between women.

Radclyffe Hall is born Marguerite Antonia Hall, and she goes through many nicknames in her life. Her close friends call her "John", after a portrait of one of her long-dead ancestors to whom she bears an uncanny resemblance. There is a bit of a fad among British lesbians of the time to have male nicknames, partly as a signal to each other, and partly to express their butch side. But for her pen name, she chooses "Radclyffe Hall", after her father. Since that's the name she wants to be known by in public, that's the name we're going to use for her here, too.

These days, Radclyffe is a bit of an icon among lesbians, and it's as a lesbian that she's often talked about by historians and literary critics. But she has a different term she uses to describe herself: a "congenital invert". If it sounds clinical, that's because it is – it's a term used by scientists studying sex at the time. These days we tend to separate gender and sexuality – a woman can be gay, but that doesn't necessarily mean that she'll be masculine, and vice versa. But the concept of an "invert" mushes gender and sexuality together inextricably, like two colours of plasticine. An inverted woman is one who takes on masculine traits, not only in dress, habits and name, but also in terms of being attracted to women, which is considered a masculine trait. Hall doesn't think every woman who has relationships with other women is an "invert"

– just the ones who also wear suits, cut their hair and take on male names. To her, women who have homosexual relationships but also marry men, wear dresses and have babies are more "normal".

Radclyffe has a pretty miserable childhood. Both her parents are abusive, and her dad leaves when she's very young. Later in life, she calls her mother "violent and brainless."[1] Her mum straight up *tells* her that she wanted to abort her but it didn't work. Radclyffe struggles with dyslexia at school, and as a young child doesn't have any friends her own age. She gets her first long-term girlfriend, Agnes Nicholls, at the age of 17, but when her mother finds out, she pulls Radclyffe's hair so hard it comes out.

When she's 21 she comes into a huge inheritance from her dad – enough for her to be independently wealthy for the rest of her life – and immediately escapes her mother's home. She gets her own house, and is finally able to dress how she likes. She wears a lot of tailored jackets and cuts her hair short. Photographs of her often show her only from the waist up, so it looks like she's always wearing a full suit of men's clothes, and she does like wearing breeches, but equally she is happy to wear skirts with her suit jackets. This is fashionable at the time, if a little counter-cultural. Some lesbians wear this style as a signal to each other, but equally, so many straight women dress this way at the time that it's got plausible deniability. Under the cloak of jackets, Radclyffe starts pursuing women, whether or not they're married.

The first great love of her life is singer and composer Mabel Batten (1856–1916). Mabel is 51 to Radclyffe's 27, and she's married (with grandkids!), but they fall in love, and after Mabel's husband dies they move in together. It's Mabel who first gives Radclyffe the nickname "John", and who introduces her to a circle of artistic and intellectual women among whom lesbianism is common. But in 1915, Radclyffe meets Mabel's cousin, Una Troubridge, and the two start spending *lots* of time together. Una comes over for tea, they go for long drives in the country, and Radclyffe even gives Una a ring with both their names engraved on it. Very subtle. Like Mabel, Una is married, but she tells her husband she wants a separation so she can live with Radclyffe.

In 1916, Mabel dies, and Radclyffe is wretchedly guilty. Did she make Mabel's last days on earth unhappy by cheating on her with Una? Did she let Mabel die angry with her? Is Mabel even, perhaps, watching her with fury from the afterlife? Desperately trying to assuage her conscience and get some closure, Radclyffe and Una seek the services of a medium – a spiritualist who, for a fee, supposedly contacts Mabel in the afterlife to reassure Radclyffe and Una that, *No, really, everything's fine! I want you guys to get together. You're such a great couple! The afterlife is full of ponies and puppies* (seriously, this is what the medium tells them[2]) *so I'm really happy. You'll love it when you get here!* Radclyffe is utterly drawn in by her contact with Mabel's spirit, and decides to become a medium herself. She writes a paper for the Society for Psychical Research, and the Society is considering giving her a seat on their council when one of its members speaks up and teaches Radclyffe an important life lesson.

St George Lane Fox Pitt (an utterly deranged name) is both a member of the Society and, crucially for Radclyffe, friends with Una's husband. He's been hearing about how Radclyffe is a skirt-chaser and a seductress who spirited away Admiral Troubridge's wife into an unholy lesbian relationship. He tells the Society that they must rethink their decision, saying that "Miss Radclyffe Hall is a thoroughly immoral woman. [She] has got a great influence over Lady Troubridge and has come between her and her husband and wrecked the Admiral's home."[3] Now, we might disagree with his moral judgement, but on the facts, he's not wrong. Radclyffe *is* having an affair with a married woman. So St George has a pretty good case here, if he can prove it. St George just so happens to be the son-in-law of the notorious Marquess of Queensberry – the guy who got Oscar Wilde sent to prison for gross indecency a few decades earlier, when Wilde made the mistake of suing *him* for libel. History could so easily repeat itself. But luckily for Radclyffe, St George doesn't have the doggedness or moral certainty of his famous father-in-law.

Radclyffe sues St George for slander. When the case comes to trial in 1920, Una's husband throws St George under the bus. He's like, *What? I never said anything like that about Miss Hall. Don't know where he got it from.* And without his friend to back him up, St George utterly fumbles his time on the witness stand. Instead of showing any proof that his claim is true, he completely backpedals, saying, *Um, um, that's not what I meant at all! Your honour, I was using the word "immoral" to mean "bad at writing scientific papers", a totally normal and common way of using the word! What a whimsical misunderstanding!* Radclyffe wins the case and is awarded £500 plus her legal costs. This is a Pyrrhic victory for her, though. Not only does St George never pay her what she's owed, but now everyone's heard the allegations of lesbianism, and the court of public opinion doesn't play by the same rules as a court of law.

Lesbianism becomes a hot-button topic in the news, and the Houses of Parliament begin to discuss criminalizing sex between women, something that had been quietly going on legally throughout Britain's history. Although homosexual behaviour between *men* is illegal in the 1920s, falling under the crime of "gross indecency", there's never been anything on the books about lesbian sex. With the subject in the news, Parliamentarians start to wonder if they should change that. You'll sometimes hear the urban legend that the reason sex between women was never illegal in Britain is because Queen Victoria didn't believe it was real, or alternatively, that government ministers didn't want to have to explain it to her. And while both stories are, don't get me wrong, extremely funny, they aren't true. Lawmakers simply don't feel as threatened by the spectre of sex between women as they do of sex between men – until Radclyffe's legal victory. In 1921 MP Frederick Macquisten suggests adding a new crime to the statute book called "Acts of Gross Indecency by Females". He thinks that women are losing their morals and running away to become lesbians instead of doing what they should be doing, which is having children. The reason why the amendment is defeated, though, is perhaps even funnier than the Queen Victoria story. It passes the House of Commons, but in the House of Lords, Lord Birkenhead stands up and tells the House that they shouldn't pass this into law, not because he's pro-gay rights, but because "you are going to tell the whole world there is such an offence, to bring it to the notice of women who have never heard of it, never dreamed of it. I think this is a very great mischief."[4] In other words, *Shhh! Don't tell them that lesbianism exists, or they'll all want some.* The amendment is quietly shelved.

By 1928, Radclyffe has thoroughly learned that trying to suppress information often only makes it better known, and now she uses it to her advantage. In that year, she publishes her most famous book, *The Well of Loneliness,* the only one of her novels to be overtly queer. The book tells the life of its protagonist, a woman named Stephen Gordon (her parents were certain she was going to be a boy, and once she was born they didn't want to pick a different name). Stephen is . . . not like other girls. As a child, she goes horse riding astride instead of sidesaddle, she's into the manly arts of bodybuilding and fencing, and develops an early crush on the housemaid. She asks her dad, "Do you think that I could be a man, supposing that I thought very hard – or prayed, Father?"[5] As she grows up, she finds herself incapable of falling in love even with a totally decent man, and is instead attracted only to women. Like Radclyffe, she realizes that she is an "invert".

Stephen starts off as the wanted child of wealthy parents, but her relationships with women mean that she is increasingly cut off: disowned by her mother and shunned by her neighbours. She meets other queer people – among them London writer Jonathan Brockett and society lady Valerie Seymour. During World War I she is driving ambulances in Europe when she meets Mary Llewellyn. Stephen and Mary fall in love and move in together, but they are rejected by society, and it makes Mary miserable. In the end, Stephen pretends to have an affair with Valerie in order to drive Mary away, believing she'll be happier with a man. Finally, deserted by everyone, Stephen suddenly finds her room thronged with company. She sees other queer people all around her – some who are dead friends, some historical figures, and even those who will come after her, crying out to be accepted by a world that has cast them aside. The novel ends with the words, "Give us also the right to our existence!"[6]

The book isn't particularly lurid. The closest Radclyffe gets to writing a sex scene is "That night, they were not divided."[7] As the title suggests, it portrays lesbianism as utterly miserable from beginning to end. Stephen gets very little joy out of her relationships. Instead, they're full of agonized longing, jealousy and being shunned by polite society. But it does put forward the ideas of sexologists like Havelock Ellis, Richard von Krafft-Ebing and Magnus Hirschfeld. They argue that "inversion" is a natural state, given by God, rather than a moral defect or the result of a neglectful childhood. Stephen can't change who she falls in love with, but she's still a good person. Radclyffe writes, "You can kill all the inverts but while they live you cannot make them other than inverted. They are and will always remain as God made them."[8]

So it isn't any pornography or sexiness in the book that gets people angry – it's the argument that queer people should be tolerated. In particular, Radclyffe finds an enemy in James Douglas, editor of the *Sunday Express*, who writes, "I would rather give a healthy boy or a healthy girl a phial of prussic acid than this novel."[9] He gets the attention of the Home Secretary, William Joynson-Hicks, who has the power to begin a prosecution against Radclyffe's publisher for obscenity. He asks his deputy Director of Public Prosecutions, George Stephenson, if a jury would convict, and Stephenson says, "A prosecution would undeniably give the book a further advertisement."[10] He's learned the same lesson that Radclyffe did in her slander trial, at least.

Radclyffe's publisher is printing her book in France and importing it into the UK, so Joynson-Hicks tells Customs to seize all copies coming through the border, and one month later both Radclyffe's publisher and her distributor are summoned to appear in court. Their plan is to pack the trial with star witnesses: famous authors and notables who will testify to the importance of freedom of speech and the literary merit of the book. It's tricky; even people on Radclyffe's side don't want to appear in court to defend a queer book. H G Wells, Arthur Conan Doyle and George Bernard Shaw all have excuses. Radclyffe does, though, get support from Virginia Woolf, who's prepared to speak from the witness box even though she privately thinks the book itself is "stagnant and lukewarm."[11] Not the most convincing ally you could hope for, but Radclyffe takes it.

In the end, it doesn't matter if the luminaries of 1920s literature line up behind Radclyffe or not; the judge refuses to hear any witnesses except a single police officer. He has already made up his mind. At appeal, the judge calls Radclyffe's book "more subtle, demoralizing, corrosive and corruptive than anything ever written."[12] Radclyffe and Una are devastated, and leave England, finding themselves a house in France, the same country that Wilde fled to after his conviction. However, all is not lost. Now, *The Well of Loneliness* is a *banned book*. The publicity and intrigue around it make it all the more exciting. The book is openly published in the US, and people find ways of sneaking copies onto bookshelves even in Britain. It becomes the most famous novel about queer women for decades, and makes the concept of lesbianism better known than it had been before. It crops up over and over again in lesbian coming-out stories for the rest of the century, as people read it and realize that there are others out there like them. It doesn't get published again in the UK until 1949, when a collected edition of Radclyffe's works is released. The Home Office threatens to prosecute the publisher again, but they never do, and the book has been continuously in print ever since.

Several scholars have noted that if *The Well of Loneliness* was about a man and a woman, then it would be a pretty unremarkable romance. In the middle of 1920s Britain, when writers like Woolf, T S Eliot and Dorothy Richardson were pushing the boundaries of literature with new modernist techniques, Radclyffe's writing style was old-fashioned. Woolf's own queer novel, *Orlando*, came out in the same month as *The Well*, but no one even mentioned banning that. If the Home Secretary hadn't tried to ban *The Well*, its market probably would have stayed small. In the 1930s, when discussing censoring a different novel, a Home Office memo stated, "It is notorious that the prosecution of *The Well of Loneliness* resulted in infinitely greater publicity about lesbianism than if there had been no prosecution."[13] At long last, the authorities learned their lesson: that trying to keep something secret might backfire and end up making it really famous.

CHAPTER 24
PAUL ROBESON

teaches us that just because it's not the Renaissance
doesn't mean you can't be a Renaissance man.

It's not often someone has both the skills and the opportunity to be a professional athlete, film star, singer, lawyer, civil rights activist and polyglot all in one lifetime. It's extra unfair if he also happens to be tall, popular and good-looking. But Paul Robeson (1898–1976) has all these gifts at once. He's a true Renaissance man – for the 20th century.

Out of everyone in this book, Paul probably has a claim to being the best known during his lifetime. At the height of his fame in the 1930s and 1940s, he is singing to sell-out crowds all over the world, and is named "America's No.1 Negro" by the *American* magazine. Some 12,000 people turn up to see a concert celebrating his 46th birthday in 1944, and that's not even a milestone anniversary! Paul is one of those people blessed with a frankly envy-inducing amount of talent. But unless you're into vintage music, you might not have heard of Paul these days, because in the 1950s his career is thoroughly scuppered by the FBI due to his anti-racist activism, and he spends the last 20 years or so of his life well out of the limelight that he deserves.

Paul is born in Princeton, New Jersey. Although Princeton is in the supposedly-less-racist North of the US, Paul later says that it is "spiritually located in Dixie",[1] the region south of the Mason-Dixon line. His father is born into slavery, escapes to the North like Ellen and William Craft (Chapter 3) via a network of safehouses known as the Underground Railroad, and becomes a preacher. When Paul is just six years old, his mother is horribly burned to death after a flaming coal sets fire to her skirt, and so he is raised by his dad alone. Paul's dad teaches him to walk a careful line around white folks, being always polite and self-effacing but never deferential or servile. Paul grows up during the height of the US system of apartheid nicknamed "Jim Crow", a system of both legal and informal segregation, where African Americans are barred from many restaurants, schools, libraries, water fountains, benches, waiting rooms, and even from voting, running for office and sitting on juries. African Americans who resist, or who are thought to be resisting, these rules might be threatened, beaten up or even lynched. Paul is taught from a very early age to be careful with white people.

He's also taught to work very hard. His dad expects him to get perfect grades at school, to be an excellent public speaker like him, to help out at the church, and also to take on side jobs from the age of 12 alongside his schoolwork. Paul's talent begins to shine from a young age. This is where he gets to play Othello for the first time in a school play, a part that he will return to several times over the course of his acting career. He becomes the only bass baritone in the school choir. He plays baseball, basketball, tennis and American football. He enters the state oratory competition with a speech about the Haitian hero Toussaint Louverture (1743–1803) that is so passionate and well delivered that the audience is moved to tears. He passes the scholarship exam for Rutgers University (his local Princeton University won't accept black students for decades yet), and becomes only the third African-American student ever to go there.

It's when he goes to college that people really start to notice that this kid is exceptional. He gets great marks on his papers, wins the class oratorical prize four years running, and is inducted into the Cap and Skull Society, a select group of only four senior students each year who best embody the values of the university. However, he still has to deal with a lot of prejudice. When he goes to try out for Rutgers' American football team, the white team members take every opportunity to give him a battering. He limps off the field with a broken nose, a sprained shoulder and bruises all over. Despite that, he goes back a few weeks later to try again. This time, team member Frank Kelly stamps on his hand, and Paul loses his temper. He knocks over three guys and lifts Kelly over his head, ready to smash him to the ground. Luckily, the coach steps in, yelling, "Robeson! You're on the varsity!",[2] which snaps Paul out of it. The coach makes it clear that anyone who tries to hurt Paul again will be kicked off the team, and Paul goes on to be twice named as All-American (a title given to nationally outstanding amateur athletes). It's not just football, either – Paul competes for Rutgers in basketball, baseball and track, and wins so many varsity letters (15!) that his jacket must have looked like alphabetti-spaghetti. (I presume this is how American varsity letters work – you just have to keep sewing more and more letters onto your jacket for all your different sports. Don't correct me.)

Although Paul's team comes to accept and respect him, his university career isn't all plain sailing. Especially when Rutgers plays Southern teams, opposing players kick or punch him. Crowds shout racial slurs. During a line-up, one opposing player tells Paul, "Don't you so much as touch me, you black dog, or I'll cut your heart out." Paul smashes into him, and says, "I touched you that time. How did you like it?"[3] Some teams refuse to play against Rutgers altogether, and when the team goes out to restaurants Paul has to come up with an excuse so that he doesn't suffer the embarrassment of being refused service. When he graduates in 1919, his "class prophecy" predicts that by 1940 he will be "the leader of the colored race in America"[4] and the governor of New Jersey, and he is chosen to give the commencement address, in which he looks forward to a day when "black and white shall clasp friendly hands in the consciousness of the fact that we are brethren."[5]

After getting his degree, Paul goes to law school at Columbia University, and while he's studying he makes money on the side by singing in concerts (apparently being a well-known football player was a big enough draw for music concerts back then), tutoring in Latin, and playing football at the professional level. He could easily make sports his whole career – in the first year he plays for the Akron Pros, they win the championship undefeated. He's also very popular with the ladies. In a documentary made decades later in the 1970s, a sculptor friend says, "Women really went at him from all directions – all kinds of women."[6]

One day, while recovering from a football injury, he meets his wife, Eslanda "Essie" Goode, who's working in the hospital. Essie is very ambitious for Paul, and becomes his manager and agent, finding work, negotiating rates and making connections for him. It's also while he's in law school that he is scouted into his first professional theatre role (can you imagine an untrained actor being scouted from am dram to Broadway these days?) in a play called *Taboo*, and he joins the cast of one of the first all-African-American musicals, *Shuffle Along*. The audience loves him.

And a good thing too, because the law is not working out for Paul. As Essie later says, "This was America and he was a Negro; therefore he wouldn't get far. If he put his foot on the bottom rung of the ladder of the theatre, he could climb to the top; if he started up the ladder of the law, his utmost progress would be halfway up."[7] Although he finishes law school and gets a job at a law office, his boss tells him that white clients will not want him representing them in court, and even one of the office stenographers tells him, "I never take dictation from a n*****."[8] After years studying the law, Paul gives it up after just a few months and goes into an industry where he is wanted: the theatre.

In 1924 Paul gets a part in the New York premiere of Eugene O'Neill's *All God's Chillun Got Wings*. Just being cast in such a prestigious play is enough to rocket-boost Paul's career: he is now in demand as both a singer and an actor. In *Chillun,* Paul's character is a black man married to a white woman, and he kisses her hand onstage. Her *hand!* This is enough to cause a storm in the American press, where a mixed-race couple is seen as morally outrageous. The *American* writes that the play will be the "enemy of public peace",[9] the Ku Klux Klan (KKK) sends a bomb threat, police are stationed around the theatre on opening night in case of trouble, and the opening scene, which shows black and white children playing together, is banned by the mayor. But despite the disruption, the show goes beautifully. According to the reviewer in the *American Mercury* magazine, Paul is "with relatively little experience and with no training to speak of . . . one of the most thoroughly eloquent, impressive and convincing actors that I have looked at and listened to in almost twenty years of professional theater-going."[10] He starts getting roles in movies like *Body and Soul* (1925) and *Borderline* (1930).

His side hustle – singing in concerts – becomes hugely popular, too. Unlike other singers of the period, who focus on opera and classical music, Paul sings African-American spirituals – songs made by enslaved people – like "Go Down Moses" and "Sometimes I Feel Like a Motherless Child". This is quite new. Black singers sometimes include one or two spirituals, but not a whole programme of them. Formerly enslaved people sometimes feel that such works are painful reminders of the past, and Paul himself says, "My own people . . . have felt that the old spirituals were not in keeping with the aspirations of the modern Negro."[11] Still, in April 1925, Paul performs these songs to a sell-out crowd in Greenwich Village, at a theatre so packed that people are standing in the aisles and even the wings, and still hundreds are turned away. Paul's voice is untrained, so he doesn't have the stamina, range or volume of a professional opera singer, but his natural bass baritone has enormous power. He gets minutes-long rounds of applause for just stepping onstage, and the audience calls for a whopping 16 encores.

In 1928, Paul travels to London to appear in the West End, where he first plays the role that will define his career: Joe in the musical *Show Boat*. It's a small part, but one with the most famous number – "Ol' Man River", which goes on to become Paul's signature song. It's a huge production, with 160 cast members, but Paul is mentioned by name in practically every review. After that, his next role, in 1930, is as the title character in *Othello* alongside Peggy Ashcroft and Sybil Thorndike – the second black man to play the role after Ira Aldridge (Chapter 13). The audience cheers for him so long that he does an almost unbelievable *20* curtain calls (what was it with audiences and encores back then? Did they not have homes to go to?).

At the same time, he's starting to develop his concerts, moving away from doing only African-American songs, and mixing in folk songs from the countries that he travels to. He starts learning languages so that he can sing the songs in their original tongues: not just French and German, but also Spanish, Chinese, Russian, Romanian, Yiddish, Dutch, Hungarian, Turkish, Hebrew, Swedish, Ewe, Efik and Hausa.

Paul and Essie are both very taken with how unsegregated Britain is. In the US, there are large parts of the country where Paul simply cannot tour because he's not allowed in hotel rooms or diners. But in London, the Robesons hobnob with celebrities in the fanciest Mayfair restaurants, and live in a posh house with three servants. When, on one occasion, Paul is turned away by a manager at the Savoy Hotel, the story blows up in the news.[12] Questions are asked in Parliament and the Savoy is forced to apologize. But Paul gradually starts to realize that the UK is just as segregated as the US, only along class lines instead of racial ones. As Paul has a university education and a career on the stage, he can get into places that a black dockworker cannot. When the manager of the Ritz hotel is asked whether he would let Paul dine there, he replies, "If the Negro was a gentleman, it would be unfair to refuse him."[13] In London, he can have affairs with white girlfriends, but even when he offers to leave his wife, they would never marry him. Ultimately, Paul is disappointed with the stratification in British society. He doesn't feel he's truly being treated equally until his first visit to the Soviet Union (USSR) in 1934.

Paul is really popular in the USSR, where many people are sympathetic to the cause of African-American civil rights. He and Essie are wooed by the Soviet state, being invited to parties, theatre shows, film screenings and on visits to state-run factories and hospitals. Paul notices the difference in how he is treated immediately. He says, "Here I am not a Negro but a human being . . . Here, for the first time in my life, I walk in full human dignity."[14] Paul's starting to become more openly political. And then in January 1938 he visits Republican Barcelona during the Spanish Civil War just a few months after Ethel MacDonald (Chapter 16) leaves the city. He adds flamenco songs to his repertoire for his Spanish audience and visits soldiers from the International Brigades. He is beloved everywhere he goes. One soldier said that he talked to everyone as if they were "a friend of lifelong standing."[15]

The double whammy of visiting the communist USSR and communist Barcelona within a few years is a turning point for Paul. When he comes home to the US he is a changed man. He decides to speak out against injustice more openly – not just about race inequality, but also class inequality. He says, "It is my business not only to tell the guy with the whip hand to go easy on my people . . . but also to teach my people – all the oppressed people – how to prevent that whip hand from being used against them."[16] At a fundraiser for Spain's International Brigades, he changes the words of his most famous hit, "Ol' Man River", from *I gets weary / And sick of trying / I'm tired of living / And scared of dying* to *But I keeps laughing / Instead of crying / I must keep fighting / Until I'm dying*. A song about a small, scared, oppressed man becomes a song about someone who cannot and will not give up fighting for his freedom. The audience goes wild.

Over his career, Paul raises money and shows public support for a tremendous number of disparate causes, including Indian independence, the National Unemployed Workers' Movement, US President Franklin D Roosevelt's re-election in 1944, black teachers in the Panama Canal Zone, the desegregation of baseball, war aid for China, the Civil Rights Congress, the League for the Boycott of Aggressor Nations, the Progressive Party, and a US-wide ban on lynching. He starts taking on projects that portray the struggles of the working class, like the 1938 play *Plant in the Sun*, about white and black workers joining forces, and the 1940 film *Proud Valley*, about an American man who goes to Wales to work as a miner. Paul finds time for everyone and every worthy cause. One of his co-stars in *Plant in the Sun* says, "Nobody I've ever met for intelligence, humanity and so on would ever come up to this man."[17]

By 1941, Paul's at the height of his acting and singing career. As the US debates whether to enter World War II, Paul is chosen to play the spirit of America itself in *Ballad for Americans*, a 10-minute piece broadcast on *The Pursuit of Democracy*, a patriotic radio show. It is performed to a live studio audience, which cheers for *15 minutes* after he finishes – longer than the piece itself. When Paul releases it as a record, it shoots to the top of the charts, and the radio station is swamped with positive letters and phone calls. In the following year, Paul plays Othello again, this time in America. A show where a black man makes love to a white woman and then kills her is a lot more controversial in the US than in the UK, especially with a real black man in the part rather than a white actor in dark make-up. There has never been a professional production with an actual black actor as Othello in the US before. Tickets sell out before it even opens, and its 296-performance run is a record-breaker on Broadway for a Shakespeare play. Paul is showered with awards, both from theatre critics and race equality organizations. The American Academy of Arts and Sciences award him their Gold Medal; the National Association for the Advancement of Coloured People (NAACP) give him their highest honour, the Spingarn Medal; and *Time* magazine calls him "probably the most famous living Negro."[18] The opening night audience applauds so hard that one reporter wonders that "the staid old walls didn't burst from the noise and enthusiasm"; *Variety* magazine states that no white actor "should ever dare presume" to play the part again (white actors do, in fact, so presume for decades afterwards).[19]

But at the same time, the House Committee on Un-American Activities (HCUA) starts investigating Paul as someone who might be disloyal to the US. What does "disloyal" mean to the FBI when you're talking about a person who still can't eat in the restaurants of most hotels in his own country? It means "communist" or "communist sympathizer". The FBI starts tapping his phone, bugging his hotel rooms and even trailing him in person. They do this for years. Today the FBI's file on Paul is in the public domain; it comprises more than 100 pages of phone conversation transcripts, clippings from socialist magazines, and once, bizarrely, an exchange where an FBI special agent gets hold of a notebook belonging to Paul with some sort of secret code about his illicit activities. This is immediately followed by a letter from the head of the FBI himself, J Edgar Hoover, saying, *Uh, yeah, this is just a vocab list.* Paul was learning Chinese.[20]

The fact is, Paul isn't a communist. Years of tails, bugging and mail-tampering by the FBI can't produce any proof that he is ever a member of the Communist Party, and nor can decades of historians. What he hates is not capitalism, but segregation. If you want to dismantle Jim Crow in the 1930s and 1940s, neither of the main political parties is any good – the Communist Party is the only one promising to get rid of it. The period immediately after World War II is particularly brutal for racial violence, with mass lynchings and police hostility toward black communities. Paul gives a speech at Madison Square Garden, saying, "What about it, President [Harry S] Truman? Why have you failed to speak out against this evil?"[21] He even speaks to Truman in person at the White House,[22] a disastrous meeting that ends with Truman interrupting Paul to say that *Yes, lynching is bad, but now is not the time to introduce a bill,* and telling him to leave. During a period when the KKK is openly terrorizing people, the FBI and the HCUA are instead spending their time going after Paul. The HCUA publicly says that Paul is "supporting the Communist Party", and local councils start banning him from performing in their towns. The FBI warns cinemas and theatres not to show his films or allow him to appear. In 1950, Paul sees the writing on the wall and tries to flee to London, but his passport application is denied on the grounds that it was "contrary to the best interests of the United States."[23] In 1956, Paul is summoned to appear before the HCUA, where they ask him, *If you love the Soviet Union so much, why don't you leave?* (The gall to ask this question of someone who's had his passport taken away.) Paul answers blisteringly, "Because my father was a slave, and my people died to build this country, and I am going to stay here, and have a part of it just like you. And no fascist-minded people will drive me from it. Is that clear?"[24]

After several years of being unable to perform, Paul was eventually given his passport back, and returned to Britain in triumph. He sang at the Royal Albert Hall, appeared on TV, read the Lesson at St Paul's Cathedral, played Othello again, and published his memoirs. But the time locked out of the spotlight had taken its toll, and he never again reached the heights he did in 1942. Paul packed such a huge amount of talent, skill and empathy into a very truncated career. He managed to be, within a few short decades, a professional-level athlete, a chart-topping singer, a film star, a speaker of many languages, a Shakespearean actor, and an internationally important activist with causes ranging from orphans of mining disasters to the eradication of lynchings. He was charming to everyone who met him, and good-looking to boot. He was a true Renaissance man, 400 years after the Renaissance.

REFERENCES

Introduction

1   *The Gentleman's Magazine*, "List of Births, Marriages and Deaths", 47, 1777, page 195

2   Fortey, R, *Dry Storeroom No 1: The Secret Life of the Natural History Museum*, Vintage Books, New York, 2009 ed, page 85

Chapter 1: Thomas Blood

1   Historic Royal Palaces, Tower of London Factsheet: The Crown Jewels in Numbers, 5 February 2016, web.archive.org/web/20170828190653/https://hrpprodsa.blob.core.windows.net/hrp-prod-container/11154/crown–jewels–factsheet–2–2.pdf

2   This kind of execution is only done on men. Women get burned alive instead – much more ladylike!

3   Anon, *A New and Compleat Survey of London*, Vol 1, J Ilive, Aldersgate, 1742, page 225

4   Ibid

5   Anon, *Remarks on the Life and Death of the Fam'd Mr Blood*, Richard Janeway, Paternoster Row, 1680, page 11

6   Hutchinson, R, *The Audacious Crimes of Colonel Blood*, Pegasus Books, New York, 2016, page 141

7   Hutchinson, R, page 142

8   Hanrahan, D C, *Colonel Blood: The Man Who Stole the Crown Jewels*, Sutton Publishing, Stroud, 2003, page 122

9   Hutchinson, R, page 147

Chapter 2: Lady Mary Wortley Montagu

1 Voltaire, *Selected Writings*, Thacker, C, ed, J M Dent & Co, London, 1995, page 39

2 Barnes, D, "The Public Life of a Woman of Wit and Quality: Lady Mary Wortley Montagu and the Vogue for Smallpox Inoculation" in *Feminist Studies* 38(2), summer 2012, page 336

3 Calder-Marshall, A, *The Grand Century of the Lady*, Gordon and Cremonesi, London, 1976, page 114

4 Grundy, I, *Lady Mary Wortley Montagu*, Clarendon Press, Oxford, 1999, page 46

5 Montagu, M, *Letters from Lady Mary Wortley Montagu*, Rhys, E, ed, J M Dent & Co, London, 1906, page 105

6 Ibid., page 175

7 Ibid

8 Wagstaffe, W, *A Letter to Dr. Freind; Shewing the Danger and Uncertainty of Inoculating the Small Pox*, Samuel Butler, London, 1722, page 5

Chapter 3: William and Ellen Craft

1 Craft, W & Craft, E, *Running a Thousand Miles for Freedom*, Cambridge University Press, Cambridge, 2013, page 83

2 Ibid., pages 2–3

3 Ibid., page 6

4 Ibid., pages 62–3

5 Ibid., page 31

6 Ibid., page 47

7 Ibid., page 64

8 Ibid., page 69

9 Ibid., page 73

10 Ibid., page 77

Chapter 4: Noor Inayat Khan

1 Basu, S, *Spy Princess: The Life of Noor Inayat Khan*, Omega Publications, USA, 2007, page 34

2 Overton Fuller, J, *Noor-un-nisa Inayat Khan (Madeleine), George Cross, M.B.E., Croix de Guerre with Gold Star*, East-West Publications Fonds NV, Rotterdam, 1971 ed, page 111

3   Ibid., page 127

4   Basu, S, page 94

5   Magida, A J, *Codename Madeleine: A Sufi Spy in Nazi-Occupied Paris*, WW Norton & Company, New York, 2020, page 104

6   Overton Fuller, J, page 246

7   Basu, S, pages 178–80

8   Overton Fuller, J, page 257

Chapter 5: Mary Frith

1   Anon, *The Life & Death of Mrs. Mary Frith, Commonly Called Mal Cutpurse*, Printed for W. Gilbertson and the Bible in Giltspur-Street without Newgate, London, 1662, page 6

2   Ibid., page 20

3   Ibid., page 37

4   Ibid., page 39

5   Kyte, H, *Roaring Girls*, HQ, London, 2019, page 31

6   Percy, T, *Reliques of Ancient English Poetry*, Vol 2, James Nichol, Edinburgh, 1858, page 174

7   Cressy, D, *Agnes Bowker's Cat: Travesties and Transgressions in Tudor and Stuart England*, Oxford University Press, Oxford, 2000, page 111

8   Van Heertum, F W, *A Critical Edition of Joseph Swetnam's "The Araignment of Lewd, Idle, Froward, and Unconstant Women" (1615)*, Cicero Press, Nijmegen, 1989, page 100

9   Higginbotham, J, *The Girlhood of Shakespeare's Sisters: Gender, Transgression, Adolescence*, Edinburgh University Press, Edinburgh, 2013, page 93

10   Stavreva, K, *Words Like Daggers: Violent Female Speech in Early Modern England*, University of Nebraska Press, Lincoln, 2017, page 60

11   Anon, page 70

12   Ibid., page 72

13   Kyte, H, page 46

14   Anon, pages 76–7

Chapter 6: Lady Hester Stanhope

1   Bruce, I, ed, *The Nun of Lebanon: The Love Affair of Lady Hester Stanhope and Michael Bruce*, Collins, London, 1951, page 172

2   Said, E W, *Orientalism*, Vintage Books, New York, 1979, page 246

3   Gibb, L, *Lady Hester: Queen of the East*, Faber, London, 2005, page 172

4   Said, E W, pages 178–9
5   Meryon, C L, *Travels of Lady Hester Stanhope*, Vol 2, Henry Colburn, Great Marlborough Street, 1846, page 29
6   Gibb, L, page 90
7   Bruce, I, page 117
8   Gibb, L, page 123
9   Ibid., pages 82–5
10   Meryon, C L, vol 1, page 109
11   Meryon, C L, vol 2, page 259
12   Bruce, I, page 195
13   Gibb, L, page 150
14   Ibid., page 169
15   Meryon, C L, *Vol 1*, page 106
16   Gibb, L, page 233
17   Ibid., page 186
18   Meryon, C L, *Travels of Lady Hester Stanhope*, Vol 3, Henry Colburn, Great Marlborough Street, 1846, page 251
19   Ibid., pages 286–7

Chapter 7: William Buckland

1   This chapter first appeared as "Eating The Heart of A King" on YouTube
2   Hare, A J C, *The Story of My Life*, Vol 5, George Allen, London, 1900, page 358
3   Short, R V, *The Introduction of New Species of Animals for the Purpose of Domestication, in The Zoological Society of London: 1826–1876 and Beyond*, Zuckerman, ed, Academic Press, New York, 1976, page 321

Chapter 8: Eleanor Rykener

1   Anon, 1395, trans. Halsall, P, in Internet Medieval Sourcebook, www.sourcebooks.fordham.edu/source/1395rykener.asp
2   De Bracton, H, *On the Laws and Customs of England*, trans, Thorne, S E, Belknap Press, Massachusetts, 1977, page 31
3   Kuefler, M S, "Male Friendship and the Suspicion of Sodomy in Twelfth-Century France", in *Gender and Difference in the Middle Ages*, Farmer, S & Braun Pasternack, C, eds, University of Minnesota Press, Minneapolis, 2003, page 163

4   Cook, M, ed, *A Gay History of Britain*, Greenwood World Publishing, Oxford, 2007, page 1

5   Cook, M, page 7

6   Trumbach, R, "Modern Sodomy: The Origins of Homosexuality, 1700–1800" in *A Gay History of Britain*, Cook, M, ed, Greenwood World Publishing, Oxford, 2007

Chapter 9: James Chuma and Abdullah David Susi

1   Simpson, D H, *Dark Companions: The African Contribution to the European Exploration of East Africa*, Barnes & Noble, New York, 1976, page 64

2   Ibid., page 58

3   Helly, D O, *Livingstone's Legacy: Horace Waller and Victorian Mythmaking*, Ohio University Press, Athens, Ohio, 1987, page 171

4   Livingstone, D, *The last journals of David Livingstone in Central Africa, from 1865 to his death*, Waller, H, ed, Harper & Brothers, Franklin Square, 1875, page 516

5   Ibid., page 519

6   Ibid., page 518

7   Simpson, D H, page 99

8   Livingstone, D, page iii

9   Ibid., page iv

10   Ibid., page ix

11   Simpson, D H, page 143

Chapter 10: Black Agnes

1   Watson, F, "Dunbar, Patrick, eighth earl of Dunbar or of March, and earl of Moray (1285–1369), soldier and magnate", *Oxford Dictionary of National Biography*, Oxford University Press, 3 January 2008

2   Rogers, C J, ed, *The Wars of Edward III: Sources and Interpretations*, The Boydell Press, Woodbridge, 1999, page 58

3   Scott, W, *The Tales of a Grandfather*, Adam & Charles Black, Edinburgh, 1889 ed, page 132

4   McLaughlin, M, "The woman warrior: Gender, warfare and society in medieval Europe", *Women's Studies*, 17(3–4), 1990, page 203

5   Ibid

6   Breitenbach, E, et al., "Understanding Women in Scotland", *Feminist Review*, 58, 1998, page 46

Chapter 11: Margery Kempe

1   Kempe, M, *The Book of Margery Kempe*, B A Windeatt, trans, Penguin Books, London, 1994, page 42
2   Ibid., page 46
3   Ibid., page 84
4   Ibid., page 144
5   Ibid., page 46
6   Ibid., page 123
7   Ibid., page 126

Chapter 12: La Chevalière d'Éon

1   Aldrich, R, *Gay Lives*, Thames & Hudson, New York, 2012, page 70
2   Kates, G, "The Transgendered World of the Chevalier/Chevalière d'Éon", *The Journal of Modern History*, 67(3), 1995, pages 558–94
3   Kates, G, *Monsieur d'Éon is a Woman*, Johns Hopkins University Press, Baltimore, 2001, page 72
4   Kates, G, 1995, pages 576–7
5   Ibid., page 578
6   Clark, A, "The Chevalier d'Éon and Wilkes: Masculinity and Politics in the Eighteenth Century", *Eighteenth-Century Studies*, 32(1), 1998, page 31
7   Mitchell, L G, *Charles James Fox*, Oxford University Press, Oxford, 1992, page 96
8   Kates, G, 2001, page 185
9   Ibid., page 27
10   Ibid., page 256
11   Ibid., page 275
12   Kates, G, 1995, page 560

Chapter 13: Ira Aldridge

1   Anon, *Memoir and theatrical career of Ira Aldridge, the African Roscius*, Onwhyn, London, 1849, page 20
2   Waters, H, "Ira Aldridge's Fight for Equality" in *Ira Aldridge, the African Roscius*, Lindfors, B, ed, University of Rochester Press, Rochester, 2007, page 98
3   The Coburg Theatre, *The Times*, 11 October 1825

4   Lindfors, B, *Ira Aldridge, the African Roscius*, University of Rochester Press, Rochester, 2007, page 64

5   Howe, J B, *A Cosmopolitan Actor: His Adventures All Over the World*, Bedford Publishing Company, London, 1888, page 58

6   Lindfors, B, page 51

7   Waters, H, *Racism on the Victorian Stage: Representation of Slavery and the Black Character*, Cambridge University Press, New York, 2007, page 66

8   Cowhig, R M, "Ira Aldridge In Manchester" in *Ira Aldridge, the African Roscius*, Lindfors, B, ed, University of Rochester Press, Rochester, 2007, page 126

9   *The Athenaeum Journal*, 1605, 31 July 1858, page 144

10 Anon, page 16

11 *The Athenaeum Journal*, 285, 13 April 1833, page 236

12 Waters, H, "Ira Aldridge's Fight for Equality", page 107

13 Ibid., page 113

14 Anon, page 15

15 Waters, H, "Ira Aldridge's Fight for Equality", page 103

16 Marshall, H & Stock, M, *Ira Aldridge: The Negro Tragedian*, The Macmillan Company, New York, 1958, page 181

17 Ibid., page 187

18 Andrews, C B, "A Garland of Love Letters" in *Ira Aldridge, the African Roscius*, Lindfors, B, ed, University of Rochester Press, Rochester, 2007, page 86

19 Ibid., page 91

20 Ibid., page 87

21 Ibid., page 90

22 Marshall, H & Stock, M, page 198

23 *The Athenaeum Journal*, 1605, page 144

Chapter 14: The Rebecca Rioters

1   Jones, D J V, *Rebecca's Children: A Study of Rural Society, Crime and Protest*, Clarendon Press, Oxford, 1989, page 61

2   Ibid., page 217

3   *The Planet*, "The Disturbances In Wales", 6 August 1843, page 1

4   "Rebecca Prisoners", *Carmarthen Journal*, 17 March 1843, page 3

5   Jones, D J V, page 368

Chapter 15: Julius Soubise

1   Angelo, H, *Reminiscences of Henry Angelo*, Henry Colburn, London, 1828, page 447

2   Carretta, V, "Soubise, Julius [formerly Othello]", *Oxford Dictionary of National Biography*, 2008

3   Angelo, H, pages 448–9

4   Miller, M L, *Slaves to Fashion: Black Dandyism and the Styling of Black Diasporic Identity*, Duke University Press, Durham, 2009, page 63

5   Caulfield, C, *The Emperor of the United States of America and Other Magnificent British Eccentrics*, Routledge & Kegan, London, 1981, page 72

6   Robbins, A E, *A Book of Duchesses: Studies in Personality*, A Melrose, London, 1913, page 102

7   Robbins, A E, page 105–106

8   Miller, M L, page 64

9   Angelo, H, page 454

10   McNeil, P, *Pretty Gentlemen: Macaroni Men and the Eighteenth-Century Fashion World*, Yale University Press, New Haven, 2018, page 19

11   Gerzina, G, *Black London: Life Before Emancipation*, Rutgers University Press, New Brunswick, 1995, page 57

12   Sancho, I, *Letters of the Late Ignatius Sancho, An African*, Caretta, V, ed, Penguin Books, New York, 1998, page 148

13   Gerzina, G, page 60

14   Sancho, I, page 28

15   Bowyer, T H, "Middleton Nathaniel (1750–1807)", *Oxford Dictionary of National Biography*, 2006

16   Angelo, H, page 452

17   Carretta, V

Chapter 16: Ethel Macdonald

1   Macdonald, E, "Spain & Trade Unionism", *Bellshill Speaker*, 19 March 1937, page 3

2   Dolan, C, *An Anarchist's Story: The Life of Ethel Macdonald*, Birlinn, Edinburgh, 2009, page 49

3   Orwell, G, *Homage to Catalonia*, Penguin, London, 1989 ed, page 2

4   Macdonald, E, "Save Spain, Act!", *Bellshill Speaker*, 12 March 1937, page 3

5   Dolan, C, page 138
6   Ibid., page 166
7   Ibid., page 180
8   Ibid., page 207
9   Ibid., page 224

Chapter 17: The Chartists

1   Chase, M, *Chartism: A New History*, Manchester University Press, Manchester, 2007, page 12
2   Ibid., page 98
3   Richardson, R J, "The Rights of Woman, 1840", in *The Early Chartists*, Thompson, D, ed, The Macmillan Press, London, 1971, page 117
4   Lovett, W, *The People's Charter*, C M Elt, Islington, 1848, page 9
5   Chase, M, page 308

Chapter 18: Gerrard Winstanley

1   Winstanley, G, *The Works of Gerrard Winstanley*, Sabine, G H, ed, Russell & Russell, New York, 1965, page 315
2   Gurney, J, *Brave Community: The Digger Movement in The English Revolution*, Manchester University Press, Manchester, 2007, page 75
3   Winstanley, G, *The Complete Works of Gerrard Winstanley*, Vol 1, Corns, T N, Hughes, A & Loewenstein, D, ed, Oxford University Press, Oxford, 2009, page 519
4   Ibid., page 28
5   Winstanley, G, 1965, page 2
6   Gurney, J, 2007, page 70
7   Winstanley, G, *The Law of Freedom and Other Writings*, Hill, C, ed, Cambridge University Press, Cambridge, 1983, page 365
8   Winstanley, G, 2009, page 29
9   Ibid., page 30
10   Gurney, J, *Gerrard Winstanley: The Digger's Life and Legacy*, Pluto Press, London, 2013, page 68
11   Winstanley, G, 1965, page 58
12   Ibid., page 507
13   Winstanley, G, 2009, page 21
14   O'Brien, C, "Inside Surrey's most expensive streets where two Beatles once lived and beside Hollywood blockbuster filming location", Surrey

Live, 30 December 2022, www.getsurrey.co.uk/news/property-news/inside-surreys-most-expensive-streets-25833054

15   *The Guardian*, "Latter-day Diggers claim piece of an up-market golf course", 5 April 1999, www.theguardian.com/uk/1999/apr/05/4

Chapter 19: Mary Anning

1   Torrens, H, "Mary Anning (1799–1847) of Lyme; 'the greatest fossilist the world ever knew'", *The British Journal for the History of Science*, 28(3), 1995, page 269

2   Roberts, G, *The History of Lyme-Regis, Dorset, from the Earliest Periods to the Present Day*, Langdon & Harker, Sherborne, 1823, pages 127–8

3   Torrens, H, page 261

4   Hawkins, T, *The Book of the Great Sea-Dragons*, William Pickering, London, 1840, page 24

5   Pierce, P, *Jurassic Mary: Mary Anning and the Primeval Monsters*, The History Press, Stroud, 2014 ed, page 84

6   Tickell, C, "Mary Anning Fossil Hunter", in *The Great Naturalists*, Huxley, R, ed, Thames & Hudson, London, 2019, page 215

7   Pierce, P, page 76

8   Philpot, "Letter to Mary Buckland", dated 9 December 1833, Oxford Museum of Natural History Archive

9   Buckland, "On the discovery of a new species of Pterodactyle in the Lias at Lyme Regis", *Transactions of the Geological Society, London*, S2–3, 1829, page 217

10   Carus, C G, *The King of Saxony's Journey Through England and Scotland in the Year 1844*, Chapman & Hall, London, 1846, page 197

Chapter 20: Caroline Herschel

1   Brock, C, *The Comet Sweeper: Caroline Herschel's Astronomical Ambition*, Icon Books, London, 2007, page 2

2   Herschel, C, *Caroline Herschel's Autobiographies*, Michael Hoskin, ed, Science History Publications, Cambridge, 2003, page 22

3   Lemonick, M D, *The Georgian Star: How William and Caroline Herschel Revolutionized Our Understanding of the Cosmos*, W W Norton, New York, 2019, page 42

4   Herschel, C, page 29

5   Lemonick, M D, page 43

6   Herschel, C, page 53

7   Lemonick, M D, page 74

8   Ibid., page 85

9   Brock, C, pages 136–7

10   Herschel, J, *Memoir and Correspondence of Caroline Herschel*, J Murray, London, 1879, page 55

11   Ibid

12   Herschel, C, page 86

13   Herschel, J, "Letter from Miss Herschel to Dr. Bladen", 2 August 1786, *Memoir and Correspondence of Caroline Herschel*, J. Murray, London, 1879, page 65

14   Brock, C, page 165

15   Ibid., page 159

16   Herschel, J, page 76

17   Brock, C, page 157

18   I find early modern book titles extremely funny. It's like they're having a competition to cram in as many words as possible. This one scores a respectable 24.

19   Brock, C, pages 183–6

20   Ibid., pages 201–7

Chapter 21: Peter the Wild Boy

1   Worsley, L, *Courtiers: The Secret History of the Georgian Court*, Faber and Faber, London, 2010, page 32

2   Anon, *An Enquiry How the Wild Youth, Lately taken in the Woods near Hanover, (and now brought over to England) could be there left, and by what Creature he could be suckled, nursed and brought up*, H Parker, London, 1726, page 4

3   Hobbes, T, *Leviathan*, Macpherson, C B, ed, Penguin, London, 1988, page 186

4   Defoe, D, *Mere Nature Delineated*, T Warner, The Black Boy, Pater-Noster-Row, London, 1726, page 61

5   Linnaeus, C, *Systema Naturae*, Laurence Salvus, Stockholm, 1758, page 20

6   Walker, J, ed, A selection of curious articles from *The Gentleman's Magazine*, vol IV, page 583, Longman, Hurst, Rees, and Orme, London, 1811

Chapter 22: Sabrina Sidney

1   Moore, W, *How to Create the Perfect Wife*, Weidenfeld & Nicolson, London, 2013, page 42
2   Ibid., page 19
3   Edgeworth, R L & Edgeworth, M, *Memoirs of Richard Lovell Edgeworth*, Vol 1, Cambridge University Press, New York, 2011, page 224
4   Moore, W, page 38
5   Edgeworth, R L & Edgeworth, M, page 179
6   Ibid., page 216
7   Ibid., M, page 225
8   Moore, W, page 115
9   Seward, A, *Anna Seward's Life of Erasmus Darwin*, Wilson, P K, Dolan, E A & Dick, M, eds, Brewing Books, Warwickshire, 2010, page 73

Chapter 23: Radclyffe "John" Hall

1   Souhami, D, *The Trials of Radclyffe Hall*, Quercus, London, 2012, page 4
2   Ibid., pages 90–2
3   Cline, S, *Radclyffe Hall: A Woman Called John*, J Murray, London, 1998, page 165
4   Souhami, D, page 112
5   Hall, R, *The Well of Loneliness*, introduction by Esther Saxey, Wordsworth Editions Ltd, Ware, 2005, page 19
6   Ibid., page 399
7   Ibid., page 284
8   Cline, S, page 235
9   Dawson, A, "The Stunters and the Hunted", *Daily Herald*, 20 August 1928, page 4
10   Souhami, D, page 180
11   Cline, S, page 251
12   Brittain, V, *Radclyffe Hall: A Case Of Obscenity?*, A S Barnes, South Brunswick, 1969, page 123
13   Forster, C, *Filthy Material: Modernism and the Media of Obscenity*, Oxford University Press, New York, 2018, page 90

Chapter 24: Paul Robeson

1   Horne, G, *Paul Robeson: The Artist as Revolutionary*, Pluto Press,
        London, 2016, page 11
2   Robeson, P, *The Undiscovered Paul Robeson: An Artist's Journey,
        1898–1939*, J Wiley & Sons, New York, 2001, page 230
3   Duberman, M B, *Paul Robeson*, Ballantine Books, New York, 1989,
        page 23
4   Ibid., page 30
5   Ibid., page 27
6   Robeson, P, page 91
7   Ibid., page 56
8   Duberman, M B, page 55
9   Ibid., page 57
10   Ibid., page 64
11   Robeson, P, page 87
12   *London Daily Chronicle*, "Black and White Problem Im [sic] West End
        Hotel", 23 October 1929, page 3
13   Sparrow, J, *No Way But This: In Search of Paul Robeson*, Scribe
        Publications, London, 2017, page 121
14   Duberman, M B, page 190
15   Ibid., page 218
16   Ibid., page 228
17   Ibid., page 224
18   Sparrow, J, page 196
19   Duberman, M B, page 265
20   FBI file 100-12304, "Section 1: Paul Robeson Sr", archive.org/details/
        FBI-Paul-Robeson/100-HQ-12304-01/mode/2up
21   Duberman, M B, page 305
22   *Edinburgh Evening News*, 24 September 1946, page 3
23   Duberman, M B, page 218
24   Ibid., page 228

FURTHER RESOURCES

This is a list of resources I used in my research for all of the amazing people included in this book – I didn't quote from them but I definitely pulled knowledge from them. I thought it'd be handy to include in case you wanted to dive deeper into any of their extraordinary lives.

Introduction

Carter, P, "Nash, Richard [known as Beau Nash] (1674–1761)", *Oxford Dictionary of National Biography*, 24 May 2008, Oxford University Press

Howarth, M K, "The Lower Lias of Robin Hood's Bay, Yorkshire, and the Work of Leslie Bairstow", *Bulletin of the Natural History Museum*, 58(2), 2002, pages 81–152

Shindler, K, *Discovering Dorothea: The Life of the Pioneering Fossil Hunter Dorothea Bate*, Harper Perennial, Hammersmith, 2006 ed

Chapter 1: Thomas Blood

Abbott, G, *Execution: A Guide to the Ultimate Penalty*, Summersdale, Chichester, 2005

Impey, E & Parnell, G, *The Tower of London: The Official Illustrated History*, Merrell Holberton, London, 2000

Mortimer, I, *Why do we say "hanged, drawn and quartered"?*, 2010, www.ianmortimer.com/essays/drawing.pdf

Strype, J, *A Survey of the Cities of London and Westminster*, A Churchill et al., London, 1720

Chapter 2: Lady Mary Wortley Montagu

Anand, A & Dalrymple, W, "Lady Mary: Our Woman in Constantinople", *Empire*, episode 33, Goalhanger Podcasts, 2023
Maitland, C, *Mr Maitland's Account of Inoculating the Small-Pox*, J Peele, Lock's Head in Paternoster Row, London, 1722
Paston, G, *Lady Mary Wortley Montagu and Her Times*, Methuen, London, 1907
Worsley, L, *Courtiers: The Secret History of the Georgian Court*, Faber and Faber, London, 2010

Chapter 3: William and Ellen Craft

Blackett, R J M, "Fugitive Slaves in Britain: The Odyssey of William and Ellen Craft" in *Journal of American Studies*, 12(1), 1978, pages 41–62
Hunt, J, *On the Negro's Place in Nature*, Trübner, for the Anthropological Society, London, 1863

Chapter 4: Noor Inayat Khan

Inayat Khan, N, *Twenty Jataka Tales*, Inner Traditions International, Vermont, 1975
Marks, L, *Between Silk and Cyanide: A Codemaker's War*, 1941–1945, Touchstone, New York, 2000 ed

Chapter 5: Mary Frith

Chamberlain, J, *The Chamberlain Letters*, Thomson, E, ed, Putnam, New York, 1965
Firth, V, *Women & History: Voices of Early Modern England*, Coach House Press, Toronto, 1995
Hutchings, M, "Mary Frith at the Fortune", *Early Theatre*, 10(1), 2007, pages 89–108

Chapter 6: Lady Hester Stanhope

Ellis, K, *Star of the Morning: The Extraordinary Life of Lady Hester Stanhope*, HarperPress, London, 2008
Kinglake, A W, *Eothen*, JM Dent & Sons, London, 1913
Ure, J, *In Search of Nomads: An Anglo-American Obsession From Hester Stanhope to Bruce Chatwin*, Carroll & Graf Publishers, New York, 2003

Chapter 7: William Buckland

"Scientists Crack Louis XVII Mystery", *The Independent*, 19 April 2000

Annan, N, *The Dons: Mentors, Eccentrics and Geniuses*, Harper Collins, Hammersmith, 1999

Bastin, J, "The first prospectus of the Zoological Society of London: new light on the Society's origins", in *Journal of the Society for the Bibliography of Natural History*, 5(5), 1970, page 369–88

Buckland, W, *Vindiciae Geologicae*, Oxford University Press, Oxford, 1820

Buckland, W, "Notice on the Megalosaurus or Great Fossil Lizard of Stonesfield", in *Transactions of the Geological Society of London*, 2(1), 1824, pages 390–96

Buckland, W, *The Bridgewater Treatises: Treatise VI*, Vol 1, George Routledge & Co, Farringdon Street, 1858, 3rd ed

Gordon, Mrs, *Life and Correspondence of William Buckland, DD, FRS*, John Murray, Albermarle Street, 1894

Haile, N, "Buckland, William (1784–1856), geologist and dean of Westminster", *Oxford Dictionary of National Biography*, Oxford University Press, 2014

"Megalosaurus", *Encyclopaedia Britannica*, 2024

Murray, J, *John Murray III, 1808–1892: A Brief Memoir*, John Murray, Albermarle Street, 1919

Torrens, H S, "Buckland [*née* Morland], Mary (1797–1857)", *Oxford Dictionary of National Biography*, Oxford University Press, 2008

Chapter 8: Eleanor Rykener

Ackroyd, P, *Queer City*, Abrams, Cork, 2018

Bychowski, G, "Were There Transgender People in The Middle Ages?", The Public Medievalist, 2018, www.publicmedievalist.com/transgender-middle-ages

Goldberg, J, "John Rykener, Richard II and the Governance of London", *Leeds Studies in English*, 45, 2014, pages 49–70

Leyser, H, *Medieval Women: Social History of Women in England 450–1500*, Phoenix Press, London, 2002

Mazo Karras, R & Linkinen, T, "John/Eleanor Rykener Revisited", in *Founding Feminisms in Medieval Studies: Essays in Honor of E Jane Burns*, Doggett, L & O'Sullivan, D, eds, Boydell et Brewer, Suffolk, 2016

Chapter 9: James Chuma and Abdullah David Susi

Lewis, J, *Empire of Sentiment*, Cambridge University Press, Cambridge, 2018

Saari, P & Burke, D B, *Explorers and Discoverers: From Alexander the Great to Sally Ride*, Vol 2, UXL, New York, 1995

Wainwright, J, "Extract from Diary, May–June 1873", Livingstone Online, www.livingstoneonline.org/in-his-own-words/catalogue?query=liv_000074&view_pid=liv%3A000074&view_page=0

Wainwright, J, "Extract from Diary, [November 1873–February 1874]", Livingstone Online, www.livingstoneonline.org/in-his-own-words/catalogue?query=liv_000075&view_pid=liv%3A000075

Chapter 10: Black Agnes

Cooper, M L, "Just the Good Wife? Death and Legacy of Noblewomen in the Middle Ages", *The Public Medievalist*, 2018, publicmedievalist.com/death-good-wife

Macdonald, A J, "Ramsay family (per *c*1300–1513), landowners", *Oxford Dictionary of National Biography*, 23 September 2004, Oxford University Press

Phillips, C, *The Illustrated History of Knights & The Golden Age of Chivalry*, Hermes House, London, 2014

Ross, D, *A History of Scotland*, Waverley Books, New Lanark, 2009 ed

Seale, Y, "My Fair Lady? How We Think About Medieval Women", The Public Medievalist, 2018, www.publicmedievalist.com/my-fair-lady

Chapter 11: Margery Kempe

Goodman, A, *Margery Kempe & Her World*, Longman, London, 2002

Leyser, H, *Medieval Women: Social History of Women in England 450–1500*, Phoenix Press, London, 2002

Mortimer, I, *The Time Traveller's Guide to Medieval England*, Bodley Head, London, 2008

Chapter 12: La Chevalière d'Éon

Street, G S, "The Betting Book at Brooks's", *The North American Review*, 173(536), 1901, pages 44–55

Chapter 13: Ira Aldridge

Napier, J J & Winters, S B, "'African Tragedian' in Golden Prague: Some Unpublished Correspondence" in *Ira Aldridge, the African Roscius*, Lindfors, B, ed, University of Rochester Press, Rochester, 2007

Worrall, D, *Harlequin Empire: Race, Ethnicity and the Drama of the Popular Enlightenment*, Pickering & Chatto, London, 2007

Chapter 14: The Rebecca Rioters

"Rebecca Riot re-staged by villagers to mark 175 years", BBC News, 13 May 2014, www.bbc.co.uk/news/uk-wales-south-west-wales-27375757

Evans, H T E, *Rebecca and Her Daughters*, Educational Publishing Company, Cardiff, 1910

Mortimer, I, *The Time Traveller's Guide to Regency Britain*, The Bodley Head, London, 2021

Rees, L A, "Paternalism and rural protest: the Rebecca riots and the landed interest of south-west Wales", *The Agricultural History Review*, 59(1), 2011, pages 36–60

Williams, G A, *When Was Wales? A History of the Welsh*, Black Raven Press, London, 1985

Chapter 15: Julius Soubise

Collingham, L, *The Hungry Empire*, The Bodley Head, London, 2017

Fryer, P, *Staying Power: The History of Black People in Britain*, Pluto Press, London, 1992

Marshall, R, "Douglas Catherine [Kitty], duchess of Queensberry and Dover", *Oxford Dictionary of National Biography*, 2006

Scobie, E, *Black Britannia: A History of Blacks in Britain*, Johnson Publishing Company, Chicago, 1972

Chapter 16: Ethel Macdonald

Macdonald, E, "A Spanish Diary", *Bellshill Speaker*, 2 April 1937, page 3

Preston, P, *The Spanish Civil War: Reaction, Revolution, and Revenge*, Harper Perennial, Hammersmith, 2006 ed

Working Class History podcast, "The Spanish Civil War", episodes 39–40

Chapter 17: The Chartists

Adkins, R & Adkins, L, *Eavesdropping on Jane Austen's England*, Little Brown Book Group, London, 2013

Burnett, J, *The Annals of Labour: Autobiographies of British Working-Class People, 1820–1920*, Indiana University Press, Bloomington, 1974

Fryer, P, "Cuffay, William", *Oxford Dictionary of National Biography*, 2005, doi.org/10.1093/ref:odnb/71636

Mortimer, I, *The Time Traveller's Guide to Regency Britain*, Vintage, London, 2021

Pool, D, *What Jane Austen Ate and Charles Dickens Knew*, Simon & Schuster, New York, 1993

Royle, E, *Chartism*, Longman, London, 1996, 3rd ed

Thompson, D, *The Dignity of Chartism*, Verso, London, 2015

Chapter 18: Gerrard Winstanley

Clark, G & Clark, A, "Common Rights to Land in England, 1475–1839", *The Journal of Economic History*, 61(4), 2001, pages 1009–36

Dyer, C, "Conflict in the landscape: the enclosure movement in England, 1220–1349", *Landscape History*, 28(1), 2006, pages 21–33

Firth, C & Arnove, A, ed, *The People Speak: Democracy is not a Spectator Sport*, Canongate, Edinburgh, 2012

Navickas, K, "Common Land and Common Misconceptions", History of Public Space, 2018, historyofpublicspace.uk/2018/02/10/common-land-and-common-misconceptions

Yelling, J A, *Common Field and Enclosure in England 1450–1850*, Macmillan, London, 1977

Chapter 19: Mary Anning

Purcell, R W & Gould, S J, *Finders Keepers*, WW Norton & Company, New York, 1992

Tsjeng, Z, *Forgotten Women: The Scientists*, Cassell Illustrated, London, 2018

Chapter 20: Caroline Herschel

Close, F, "Vera Rubin obituary", *The Guardian*, 1 January 2017

Hoskin, M, *Caroline Herschel: Priestess of the New Heavens*, Science History Publications, Sagamore Beach, 2013

Chapter 21: Peter the Wild Boy

Bryant, C, *Entitled: A Critical History of the British Aristocracy*, Doubleday, London, 2017

Newton, M, *Savage Girls and Wild Boys*, Faber and Faber, London, 2002

Tinniswood, A, *Behind the Throne: A Domestic History of the Royal Household*, Vintage Publishing, London, 2018

Warburton, N, *A Little History of Philosophy*, Yale University Press, New Haven, 2011

Walker, J, ed, *A Selection of Curious Articles from the Gentleman's Magazine,* Vol IV, pages 581–87, Longman, Hurst, Rees, and Orme, London, 1811

Worsley, L, "How To Survive In The Georgian Court", History Extra, 2022, www.historyextra.com/period/georgian/how-to-survive-in-the-georgian-court

Chapter 22: Sabrina Sidney

Rousseau, J, *The Émile of Jean-Jacques Rousseau*, Boyd, W, trans, Teachers College Press, New York, 1967

Chapter 23: Radclyffe "John" Hall

Jennings, R, *A Lesbian History of Britain: Love and Sex between Women since 1500,* Greenwood World, Oxford, 2007

Chapter 24: Paul Robeson

Goode Robeson, E. *Paul Robeson, Negro*, V. Gollancz, London, 1930

Stewart, J C, *Paul Robeson: Artist and Citizen*, Rutgers University Press, New Brunswick, 1998

ACKNOWLEDGEMENTS

During the writing of this book, the British Library was out of commission, recovering from a huge cyber attack that basically shut down their whole IT system, so I'm really grateful to the Internet Archive for making loads of out-of-copyright texts available to me. This book would absolutely not exist without the access they provided.

Where I can't find original sources myself, I've relied on the work of modern historians – especially Bernth Lindfors, Hugh Torrens, Robert Hutchinson, Malcolm Chase, Gary Kates, Donald Herbert Simpson, Valerie Firth, Diana Souhami, Claire Brock, Anthony Goodman, Shrabani Basu, Chris Dolan, Isobel Grundy, David J V Jones, Martin Bauml Duberman, Ruth Mazo Karras, Wendy Moore, Monica L Miller, Lorna Gibb and John Gurney. I consider most of what I do to be history *communication* rather than the actual work of history itself, so I'm truly grateful to these writers and the others in my sources for doing the hard graft of poring through documentary evidence and even, in the cases of Dolan, Duberman and Gibb, interviewing surviving witnesses so that I can repackage their findings along with silly jokes.

I also want to thank Lucy Carroll, Sophie Blackman and Henry Russell for their kind and sensible editing. My good friend Morven Bruggenwirth provided incisive and thoughtful commentary on several chapters, and I'd particularly like to thank her for bringing the horrifying details of postpartum psychosis to my attention, which went into the chapter on Margery Kempe. Did you know that giving birth can give you hallucinations?! Any poor writing in the book is something I left in against their better judgements.

Finally, I'd like to thank James Knowles for his encouragement when my motivation was low, his patience listening to bad first drafts, and his unending support. James taught me the most important life lesson out of all in this book – that standing out, leading an unusual life, being a maverick, is not nearly so important as being kind. It's not the sort of thing that'll get a history book written about you four centuries on, but the very best people in the world are not those who commit wacky crimes or have great accomplishments, but those who are radically, unswervingly generous with their time, thoughtful in their speech, and are not just willing but eager to help. Four hundred years from now, I hope this book is still in the British Library so that people in the future will know: he was the very best person.

ABOUT THE AUTHOR

Jenny Draper has been telling people about history her entire adult life, and no one's made her shut up yet. She got her start in history communication in her student job at the Jorvik Centre in York, where she worked as an actual Viking (one of the top five coolest job titles ever), dressing up in wimples and winingas, waving a really big knife around, and somehow, impossibly, getting paid for it. After that, she worked at the Museum of London for eight years, doing in-house tours on medieval houses, the Great Fire of London and the 2012 Olympics, and honing her fact-to-joke ratio to a science.

In 2021, Jenny achieved her Blue Badge, the highest tour-guiding qualification in the UK (not to be confused with the kind that lets you park in the good spaces) and became a freelance tour guide, showing people all the best bits of London that you never normally stop to look at. She also makes London history videos for YouTube and TikTok @jdraperlondon, where she gets to talk about all the things she can't fit into her tours, either because it's not within walking distance of anything else interesting, or because there's nothing left to see at all. Her favourite London film is *Paddington 2.*

INDEX

Abadam, Edward 99
abolitionist movement 20–21, 22, 159
Act of Settlement 145
Africa and European exploration 63–5
African-American spirituals 170–71
African-Americans 21, 89, 167–71
    see also slavery
Agnes Countess of Dunbar 70, 71–3
Aldridge, Ira xii, 89–95, 171
Alexander III, King of Scotland 69
Ali, Pasha Muhammad 44
All God's Chillun Got Wings (O'Neill) 170
Amends for Ladies (Field) 36
American Academy of Arts and Sciences 173
American football 168–9
American magazine 170
American Mercury magazine 170
anarchism 110
anarchists: and Glasgow 111, 115
    and the Spanish Civil War 109, 111–14
Andrew of Wyntoun 71
Angelo, Domenico 104, 105
Anne, Queen 145
Anning, Joseph 132
Anning, Mary 131–6
Anning's Fossil Depot 134
apprenticeships in Georgian society 147, 154
Astronomer Royal 140, 141
astronomy 137, 139, 142
Athenaeum, The magazine 94
Atkins, Vera 31
Aycliffe, Dr aka Thomas Blood 3

Bagamoyo, Tanzania 66
Bairstow, Leslie xi–xii
Ballad for Americans 172–3
Balliol, Edward 69–70
Bankes, William 46
Bankside, London 33–5, 36
Barcelona
    and anarchism 109, 111, 112, 113;
    and Paul Robeson 172
Bashir, Emir 47
Batten, Mabel 162–3
Bedouins 45
Belemnosepia 134
Belinda (Edgeworth) 159
Bellshill Speaker magazine 112
Bengal Famine 1770 107
Bernard, Pierre 25
Bertin, Rose 86
Bicknell, John 159
Birch, Thomas 133
Black Agnes *see* Agnes Countess of Dunbar
Black Doctor, The (play) 92–3
black roles in the theatre 90–91
blackmail and sex work 59, 62
Blood, Thomas 3–4, 5–7
Bode, Johann 140
Book of Margery Kempe, The 75, 78–9
Boston Mass., black community in 21
Bracton, Henry de 60
bridewells and vagrants 148
British Communist Party 111
British Museum 135
Brothers, Richard 43, 45
Brouderer, Elizabeth 58, 59

Brown, William Wells 21
Bruce, Michael 43, 45
Buckland, William xiii, 49–55, 133–4, 135
Buckmaster, Maurice 27
Bullock, William 133
Burnett, James 150
Burney, Charles 159
Burney, Fanny 159
Butler-Bowden family and *The Book of Margery Kempe* 79

Caldwell, John Taylor 111
Camarthen Rebecca riot 100
Cameron, Lieutenant Verney Lovett 66
Carnabwth, Twm 98
Caroline of Ansbach, Princess of Wales 14, 148, 149–50
Catalogue of Stars (Caroline Herschel) 142
Caulfield, Catherine 104
Chamber, William 99
Charles I 125–6, 127
Charles II 2, 5–6
Chartists 117, 118–23
chastity and holiness 77
Chawendé's town 66
Chuma, James 63–7
Church and sex workers in medieval England 58, 59, 60
class and British society 171
Cobham, Surrey 125, 126, 129, 130
Coke, Lady Mary 104
comets 141
common land and enclosure 126
communism: in 17th century Surrey 125, 127–30
  and Paul Robeson 172–4
Communist Party 111, 173–4
communists and the Spanish Civil War 109, 111, 113
Confederación Nacional del Trabajo (CNT) 112–13
Congo 67
Constantinople 12–13, 43
Conybeare, William 133–4
Cooke, C Thomas Herbert 99
Copeland, John 71–2

coprolite 134
Craft, Ellen and William xii, 17–23
crime in 17th century London 34–5
criminal underworld and Mary Frith 34–5
Cromwell, Oliver 2
cross-dressing 82
  and Eleanor Rykener 57, 58, 60
  and La Chevalière d'Éon 85–6
  and Lady Stanhope 44
  and Mary Frith 35–6, 38
  and Radclyffe Hall 162
  and Rebecca riots 98
Crown Jewels 1–4, 6
Cuffay, William 121–2
Cuvier, Georges 134

Dachau concentration camp 31
Darwin, Charles 136
Day, John 36
Day, Thomas 154–5, 156–9, 160
De La Beche, Henry 133
De Legibus et Consuetudinibus Angliae (Bracton) 60
Defoe, Daniel 149
Dekker, Thomas 36
democracy in 19th century Britain 117, 118–19, 122–3
d'Éon, La Chevalière xii, 81–7, 104
Déricourt, Henri 28, 29
Diggers 127–9
Dimorphodon 135
Dolan, Chris 109
Douglas, James 165
dragoons 82–3
Druze 46
Dunbar Castle, siege of 69, 70, 71–2

East India Company (EIC) 107, 108
eccentrics and eccentricities xiii
ecclesiastical courts in medieval England 58, 61–2
economic improvement following Rebecca riots 101
Edgeworth, Richard Lowell 154, 156
education
  in 17th century England 9–10, 128
  and Chartists 121
  and Julius Soubise 103–4

and Rousseau 155–6
Edward I 69
Edward II 60–1
Edward III 70, 72
Edwards, Talbot 2–3, 7
Efailwen tollbooth riots 98
Elgin, Lord (Thomas Bruce 7th
    Earl) 46
Elizabeth, Empress of Russia 82
Émile (Rousseau) 155–6, 157
*Emperor of the United States, The
    and Other Magnificent British
    Eccentrics* (Caulfield) 104–5
enclosure and common land 126
England and Ellen and William
    Craft 21–2
English Civil War 2, 3, 125–6
Europe and Ira Aldridge 93–5

Fairfax, General Thomas 128–9
fan mail and Ira Aldridge 94
fascism 111
fashion in Georgian era 105–6
Faye, Léon 30
FBI 173–4
female suffrage 120–1
feminism: and anarchism 112
    and La Chevalière d'Éon 84
    and Mary Frith 38–9
Fenn, James 150
Field, Nathaniel 36
Fillmore, President Millard 21
Flamsteed, John 142
Fortune Theatre 36
fossilized human remains from
    Upper Palaeolithic 51
fossils and fossil hunting 49, 51,
    52–3, 131, 135
foster mothers 153
franchise, extension of 119
Franco, Francisco 111, 114
free quarter and Parliamentarian
    soldiers 126
French kings' hearts 53–4
French Resistance 26, 27–9
Frith, Mary 33–9
Fryer, Peter 103
Fugitive Slave Act (US 1850) 21
Fuller, Jean Overton 31

Gainsborough, Thomas 104
gambling in Georgian society 84–5
Garrick, David 103–4
Garry, Émile 28
Garry, Reneé 29
gastronomical experiment of William
    Buckland 53–5
Gaveston, Piers and Edward II 60–1
gender
    and Eleanor Rykener 57–61
    and La Chevalière d'Éon 81–2,
        86–7
    and Mary Frith 33
    and sexuality and "inverts" 161–2,
        164
Genesis, Book of and Rebecca riots
    98
Geological Society 53, 133, 135
geology 49–50, 51–2
George I 11, 145, 148
George III 140, 141
Georgian court life and etiquette
    145–6, 147
Gestapo 25, 28–30, 31
Ghosh, Abu 45
Gibb, Lorna 47
Gill, Margaret 90
Glasgow and the Great Depression
    110–11
Goode, Eslanda "Essie" 169–70
governesses 138, 142
Great Depression 1929-39 110–11
Great Seal of England 6

Hall, Radclyffe xiii, 161–6
hanged, drawn and quartered method
    of execution 4–5
Hare, Augustus 53, 54
Harries, John fined for non-payment
    of toll 99–100
Hawkins, Thomas 133
Haxter's End 150
Haye, Dame Nicola de la 72
Henley, Henry Hoste 133
Henry II 72
Henshaw, Thomas 5
Herschel, Caroline 137–9, 140–3
Herschel, Jacob 138, 139
Herschel, William 138–40, 141

high treason, penalty for 4–5
Hobbes, Thomas 149
Homo ferens 149
homosexual 61, 162
homosexuality and "gross
    indecency" 164
Hoover, J Edgar 173
House Committee on Un-American
    Activities (HCUA) 173–4
House of Lords and the Duchess of
    Queensbury 105
Howe, J B 90
Hyde, Catherine (Kitty) *see*
    Queensbury, Catherine (Kitty)
    Hyde, Duchess of
hyenas and Kirkdale Cavern 50

ichthyosaurs 132–3
illiteracy and slaves 19
India and the EIC 107, 108
Industrial Revolution 117–18, 120,
    154
ingrafting (smallpox inoculation)
    13–15
International Brigades 112, 172
"inverts," gender and sexuality
    161–2, 164
Isabel of Conches 72
Islam 25, 41, 46

James, James and the kettle fee 98
Jenner, Edward 14
Jepson, Selwyn 27
"Jim Crow" segregation laws 168,
    173–4
Joan of Arc 60
Jones, David J V 99
Jones, Walter 99
Joynson-Hicks, William 165
Judas Maccabeus (Handel) 139

Kates, Gary 84
Kempe, Margery xiii, 75–9
Khan, Noor Inayat 25–31
Khan, Vilayat Inayat 26
King, Susan 125
King's Lynn 75
kings of England and queer sexuality
    60–1

Kirkdale Cavern 50
Ku Klux Klan (KKK) 170

ladies' companions 159
Lake Tanganyika and David
    Livingstone 63, 64
Lamartine, Alphonse de 42
land ownership in 17th century
    Britain and the Diggers 129
landlords and the Rebecca riots 99
"Le Secret du Roi" 81, 83
Leicester House 148–9
lesbianism 161–2, 163–5, 166
Leviathan (Hobbes) 149
LGBTQ+ terminology, history of 61
*Life and Death of Mrs Mary Frith,
    The* 38
Lind, Jenny 93
Linnaeus, Carl 149
literacy in medieval England 76
Littlewood, Barbara 73
Livingstone, David 63–4
    death and transportation of corpse
    65–7
    survival of MSS writings 67
Locke, John 149
London Zoo 54
Louis XV, King of France 82, 83–4
Louis XVI, King of France 85, 86
Luapula River 65
Ludlow, General Edmund 6
Luftwaffe Condor Legion 111
Lyme Regis 131–2, 134

macaroni fashion in Georgian
    England 105–6
MacDonald, Ethel 109–11, 112–15
*Mad Pranks of Merry Moll of the
    Bankside, with her Walks in Man's
    Apparel, and to What Purpose*
    (Day) 36
Maitland, Dr Charles and ingrafting 14
mammoth remains 50–51
marriage
    and 18th century aristocracy 10–11
    and medieval English society 76
Mary Queen of Scots 73
Mason-Dixon line 19, 20, 167
Matilda, Empress 72

meat carving in the aristocracy 10
medieval society 58–9, 72, 76
    and gender 57–8, 60–61
Megalosaurus 49, 52–3
Members of Parliament (MPs) 119
Merchant of Venice, The 92
Mere Nature Delineated (Defoe) 149
Middle Eastern travels of Lady
    Stanhope 43–7
Middleton, Nathaniel "Memory" 108
Middleton, Thomas 36
Milnes, Esther 160
Minerva 86
misogyny 154, 157
mixed race people and slavery 18
Moll Cutpurse (Mary Frith) 35, 36
Montagu, Edward Wortley 10–11, 12
Montagu, Lady Mary Wortley (nee
    Pierrepoint) 9, 10–11, 12–15, 43
Montagu, William and the siege of
    Dunbar Castle 71–2
Morland, Mary 51–2
Mullen, Dan 113
Müller, Dorothea and Salome 18

National Association for the
    Advancement of Coloured People
    (NAACP) 173
Natural History Museum 135
nebulae 140–41, 142
Neesom, Elizabeth 121
Nicholls, Agnes 162
Nile, Livingstone's expedition to find
    the source 64–5
nonconformists 6–7
Northern Star (Chartist newspaper)
    120
*Notice on the Megalosaurus or
    Great Fossil Lizard of Stonesfield*
    (Buckland) 52

Obi and Ira Aldridge 91, 92
O'Connor, Feargus 120, 122
"Ol' Man River" 171, 172
Old Sarum, rotten borough 118
On the Origin of Species (Darwin)
    136
Order of St Louis 83, 85
Orientalism 41–2

Orlando (Woolf) 166
Orley Farm (Trollope) 159–60
Ormond, Duke of 3, 5, 6
orphanages in Georgian England
    153–5
Orwell, George 112
Othello
    and Ira Aldridge 91, 92, 93
    and Paul Robeson 168, 171, 173
Ottoman Empire 12–13, 43

Palaeolithic discoveries 51
palaeontology xii, 49, 50–53, 131,
    132–5
Palmyra 45–6
parliamentary constituencies 118–19
Patrick, Jenny 112, 113
penance of Mary Frith 37
People's Charter, The 118–19
Peter the Wild Boy xii, 146–51
Petronella of Leicester 72
Philpot, Elizabeth 134
Philpot sisters 134
pickpockets 35, 37
pilgrimage 78
Pitt, St George Lane Fox 163
Pitt, William (the Younger) 42–3
Pizan, Christine de 73
Planet newspaper and Rebecca riots
    101
Plant in the Sun (play) 172
Platt, Parson John 129
plesiosaurs 133
Poor Law amendment re child
    maintenance 101
Popjoy, Juliana xi
pregnancy and Kempe's visions 76
Princeton, New Jersey 167
Prosper (French Resistance group) 28
Protestants and the British throne 145
Proud Valley (film 1940) 172
pterosaurs 135
Pursuit of Democracy, The (radio
    show) 173

Queensbury, Catherine (Kitty) Hyde,
    Duchess of 103, 104–5, 106, 108
Queensbury, Marquess of 163
queer 60–61, 161, 164–6

racism
and Ira Aldridge 90, 91–2
and Julius Soubise 106
and Paul Robeson 167–8, 169, 170, 174
and segregation in United States 89
and slavery 18
radio operators in the SOE 25, 26–7
Ramsay, Alexander 72
rape, Julius Soubise accused of 106–7
Rebecca Rioters xii, 97, 98–101
Red Lady of Paviland 51
Rees, Thomas 98
Renaissance man 174
rents and the Rebecca riots 99
Revolt of Surinam, The (play) 90
Richardson, R J 120
riots in 19th century Wales 97–101
Ritz, London 171
Roaring Girl, The (Middleton and Dekker) 36, 38
Robeson, Paul xii, xiii, 167–74
Rohan, Charles de 103
Roman de Silence 60
rotten boroughs 118
Rousseau, Jean-Jacques 155–6
Royal Astronomical Society 137, 142–3
Royal Geographical Society 67
Rubin, Vera 142
Running a Thousand Miles for Freedom (Craft, Ellen and William) 22
Rutgers University 168–9
Rykener, Eleanor 57–60, 61–2

Said, Edward 41–2
Sancho, Ignatius 107
Sanderson, William 105
Sappho 61
Savoy Hotel, London 171
Scotland and its English wars 69–70
Scottish stereotypes 73
secret ballots 118
secular courts in medieval England 58, 61–2
Seven Years' War and La Chevalière d'Éon 82–3

Seward, Anna 157, 158
sex work in medieval England 57, 58, 59, 62
sexuality and medieval England 57–8
Shakespeare's plays and Ira Aldridge 91, 92, 93
Show Boat (Kern and Hammerstein) 171
Shuffle Along African-American musical 169
sidereal time 140
Sidney, Sabrina 153–5, 156–60
siege warfare in medieval period 70–1
sin and Margery Kempe 76–7
Skeffington, Clotworthy 11
Slave, The (play) 90, 91
slavery 17–20
and Britain 92
and David Livingstone 63
Ellen and William Craft escape from 18–20, 22–3
and Ira Aldridge 90–91, 92–3, 94
and Julius Soubise 103, 106
and Paul Robeson 167, 170, 174
and William Cuffay 121
smallpox 11–12
smallpox inoculation 13–15
Smillie, Bob 113
Society for Psychical Research 163
Society for the Manumission of Slaves 94
sodomy 58, 60, 61
Soubise, Julius xiii, 103–8
South Wales Turnpike Trust Amendment Act 1844 101
Spanish Civil War 109, 111–14, 172
Special Operations Executive (SOE) 26–7
spiritualists 162–3
Squaloraja polyspondyla 135
St George's Hill, Surrey and the Diggers 127–8, 129, 130
St Marinos 60
St Paul's Cathedral 37
Stair-Douglas, Captain 103
Stanhope, Charles (3rd Earl Stanhope) 42
Stanhope, Lady Hester 41–7
Stanley, Henry Morton 67

Starr, John 30
Stephenson, George 165
Sufism 25
Sunday Express 165
Susi, Abdullah David 63–7
Swift, Jonathan 105
Systema naturæ (Linnaeus) 149

Tanzania and Livingstone 66
telescopes 139, 140
theatrical work in 19th century
    90–91
Thomas, Henry 98–9
Time magazine 173
Titus Andronicus 93
tollbooths 97–101
Tooke, John Horne 87
Tower of London 2–4
Treaty of Paris 83
Troubridge, Una 166
Truman, President Harry S 174
Trumbach, Randolph 61
Turner, John 126
turnpike trusts 97–8, 101

Underground Railway 167
United Socialist Movement (USM)
    111, 112
Uranus, discovery of 140
USSR and Paul Robeson 171–2

vagrancy 126, 147–8
Variety magazine 173
Vauxhall Pleasure Gardens 104
violence and the Chartists 121–2
visions of Margery Kempe 75, 76,
    77–8
Vitalis, Orderic 60

Wainwright, Jacob 65
Waller, Horace 65, 67
Waltham Black Act 148
Watch and Ward (James) 159
*Watch-word to the City of London,
    A* (Winstanley) 125
Well of Loneliness, The (Hall) 164–6
Wilde, Oscar 163, 166
Winstanley (film, 1975) 130
Winstanley, Gerrard 125–6, 127–30

wireless operators in the SOE 25,
    26–7
Wollstonecraft, Mary 142
women
    and Chartists 120–21
    and cross dressing 35–6, 44, 85–6
    and Georgian misogyny 154
    and Georgian society 84
    and Ira Aldridge 94
    and medieval English society
        58–9
    and medieval warfare 72–3
    and Ottoman Empire 12, 43
    and Poor Law amendment re child
        maintenance 101
    and property 10–11
Woodville Cooperative Farm 22
Woolf, Virginia 166
Workers' Advice Bureau 111
working class and 19th century
    Britain 117–18, 121

Yamuza *see* Wainwright, Jacob

Zoffany, Johann 104

WATKINS
1893

The story of Watkins began in 1893, when scholar of esotericism John Watkins founded our bookshop, inspired by the lament of his friend and teacher Madame Blavatsky that there was nowhere in London to buy books on mysticism, occultism or metaphysics. That moment marked the birth of Watkins, soon to become the publisher of many of the leading lights of spiritual literature, including Carl Jung, Rudolf Steiner, Alice Bailey and Chögyam Trungpa.

Today, the passion at Watkins Publishing for vigorous questioning is still resolute. Our stimulating and groundbreaking list ranges from ancient traditions and complementary medicine to the latest ideas about personal development, holistic wellbeing and consciousness exploration. We remain at the cutting edge, committed to publishing books that change lives.

DISCOVER MORE AT:
www.watkinspublishing.com

Read our blog

Watch and listen to
our authors in action

Sign up to
our mailing list

We celebrate conscious, passionate, wise and happy living.
Be part of that community by visiting

 /watkinspublishing    @watkinswisdom
/watkinsbooks   @watkinswisdom